Violence
and
Power

Violence and Power

A Collection of Essays

Ken G. Irish-Bramble

To order additional copies of this book, contact:
Xlibris
1-888-795-4274
www.Xlibris.com
Orders@Xlibris.com
776010

Dedicated to:

My children (Kenia, Kenese, Aaron, Ariadne and Alexandre);

> Remember that, "The pursuit of knowledge is more valuable than its possession".
>
> Albert Einstein

My students;

> "If we value the pursuit of knowledge, we must be free to follow wherever that search may lead us. The free mind is no barking dog to be tethered on a ten-foot chain".
>
> Adlai Stevenson.

CONTENTS

PREFACE AND ACKNOWLEDGEMENTS

I often look back fondly to my graduate school days. In fact, I hold the memories of long nights in the library and engaging intellectual discourse in and out of the classroom as some of my happiest experiences. The compilation of this book is, to some degree, an attempt to immortalize that period of my life. I do so by sharing some insight into the mind of a young, enthusiastic budding academic who relished the academy and all it stood for.

Violence and Power is a collection of essays written during my graduate school years at New York University. The essays reflect works completed across a range of sub-categories of Political Science including Political Theory, Revolutionary theory, Caribbean Politics and American Politics. Each essay speaks to issues of interest to me as a young and upcoming academic. The essays are presented here in their original form. In doing so, they retain the authentic perspectives of a young mind in formation. While the essays are somewhat dated, they cover timeless topics and provide insights which I believe are still highly relevant and important for readers to consider.

The book opens with "Predicting Revolutions". This paper was the product of a seminar taken with renowned sociologist Jeff Goodwin. Through his indulgence, the paper was presented at the Social Movements and New Social Communities

Conference, hosted by the Department of Sociology. The paper has subsequently been cited by noted scholars such as John Foran (2005). The ideas put forward in this paper are integral to my next writing project, "Powder Keg".

"Political Violence in the Caribbean" was one of my first major papers. Written under the mentorship of Professor Emeritus Christopher Mitchell, it was also my first graduate paper focusing on the Caribbean. In many ways this paper propelled me towards my doctoral thesis on political and communal violence in Jamaica. It also cemented the mentoring relationship between Dr. Mitchell and myself. (*I still have a hard time calling him Chris, despite his insistence.*) Dr. Mitchell went on to lead my dissertation committee prior to his retirement. I am forever indebted to him for his excellent mentorship.

"Political Violence in the Caribbean" uses a critique of a chapter by Jorge Dominguez to examine why democracy seems to have thrived exceptionally well in the Caribbean compared to other regions in the developing world. In examining the regions democratic record, the paper also highlights the existence of significant instances of political violence and presents a theory to explain why these incidents haven't developed into more grievous levels of unrest and political instability seen elsewhere.

Participatory Democracy is also one of the earliest pieces. It was submitted as part of the requirements for a course on American Politics taught by one of my mentors Professor Emeritus Mark Roelofs. Professor Roelofs and I developed a special relationship. I remain indebted to him for his unwavering support. The essay was written in response to an open-ended question, "Is the United States of America a Democracy?" It attempts to explain how the United States can be best understood as a democracy despite a dismal record of voter and civic participation. This piece has been used in a variety of my college classes as both required and supplementary reading.

"Why a Revolution in the United States is unlikely" represents a bridge between genres for me. In this essay, I reflected upon the intersection of American Politics, Race Relations and Revolutionary Theory. It addresses the unlikelihood of a revolutionary movement emerging in the United States. The narrow focus on race relations and even the assumption that racial injustice might be the basis upon which a revolutionary movement might be built, spoke to a very personal intellectual struggle.

Healthcare reform has been a subject of much debate in the American political arena for the past three decades. As this book is being sent to print, the subject has once again been brought to the forefront of socio-political discourse. Recent efforts by the Trump administration and the Republican controlled Congress to undermine the historic Affordable Care Act, demonstrate that the fight for Universal Health Care is not over in this country.

"Why the Clinton Healthcare Reform Plan failed?", as the name implies examines the failure of the Clinton administration to successfully pass a bill assuring every American citizen the right to affordable health care. The errors of the campaign to rally support for the bill and the structural and procedural barriers to successful passage are discussed. Furthermore, the paper implies that the industrial interests embodied in the Iron Triangle derailed the efforts to enact an essential public good.

Liberty and Poverty is a piece I am particularly fond of. This piece was submitted as a final paper for a Graduate Seminar on Liberty at NYU taught by Professor Pasquale Pasquino. The course examined the philosophical foundations of the concept of liberty in political theory. Liberty and Poverty was the product of an ongoing debate between the instructor and I over whether poverty inherently represented an impediment to liberty. The paper was a tenacious attempt to win this debate with a greatly respected intellectual. Utilizing the instructor's own course material, the author sought to establish that by any accepted definition of the term, extreme poverty represented an impediment to true liberty in a modern capitalist society. As a result, the essay is inherently circular repeatedly establishing a singular point. The acknowledgement of the debate and a concession that the role of poverty as an impediment needs to be taken into consideration in his closing lecture has been valued far and above the grade awarded.

The book closes with one of the last course-related essays. "Communal Violence in South Asia: Prospects for future comparative study" is a comparative look at communal violence in Jamaica and South -East Asia. The work presented here was central to my terminal paper.

My hope is that the works presented here prove to be informative and mentally stimulating. I must acknowledge my mother, Sarah Irene Bramble. At a very early age she instilled in me a love for learning. Her mantra to "push back the frontiers of knowledge" still echoes in my heart. Second, my father, Dr. J.A. George Irish. He, more so than any other, encouraged me to follow through with the idea of publishing these essays. I have to admit; his subtle persistent nudges were the driving force which brought this project to completion.

CHAPTER 1

Predicting Revolutions

If there are revolutions
that were truly anticipated,
where is the evidence?
> **Timur Kuran**

Revolutions are dramatic, rapid and often far reaching social, political and economic transformations of societies. Although rare, their impact is of such significance that they have been a subject of great attention for academics, political analysts and leaders world-wide. A great deal of research has been done on the question of revolutions aimed at understanding their occurrence and advancing theories concerning their causal mechanism, the processes by which they develop and their consequent impact. The ultimate goal of much of this social science research is the development of models which will not only allow for an intricate understanding of this phenomenon but also allow for the reliable prediction and management[1] of such events.

However, some students of revolutions have come to question if, given the nature of these events, they are in fact predictable. It is to this question that this paper addresses itself; fundamentally whether it is possible to develop a model which will effectively and reliably predict the emergence and successful conclusion of a revolution.

Revolutions for the purposes of this are define as:

> Rapid, basic transformations of society's state and
> class structures... Social revolutions are set apart
> from other sorts of conflicts and transformative
> processes above all by the combination of two

---

[1] This may involve attempts to avoid the, often high, cost in military expenditure, human life, and damage to infrastructure; avoid their occurrence at all, or encourage their occurrence.

> coincidences: of societal structure change with class upheaval; and the coincident of political with social transformation… What is unique to social revolution is that basic changes in societal (and economic) structure and in political structure occur together in a mutually reinforcing fashion. (Skocpol, 1979: 4-5)

Furthermore, revolutions may be divided into two stages, as defined by Charles Tilly, namely **a *revolutionary situation*** and a ***revolutionary outcome***. A revolutionary situation "entails multiple sovereignty: two or more blocs make effective, incompatible claims to control the state, or to be the state" (Tilly 1978: 10). It can be further identified when three approximate causes converge:

1. The appearance of contenders, or coalitions of contenders advancing exclusive competing claims to control of the state, or some segment of it;
2. Commitment to those claims by a significant segment of the citizenry;
3. Incapacity or unwillingness of rulers to suppress the alternative coalition and/or commitment to its claims. (Tilly, 1978: 10)

His definition of the revolutionary situation is overly broad and may include similar, but non-revolutionary situations such as a Coups d'etat or civil war. Missing from his definition is the presence of a dispute between the competing parties about fundamental adjustments to the social structure. Although the nature of this change may not be evident to actors prior to the emergence of the revolutionary situation, the development of an agenda of change is nonetheless an essential element of a revolutionary situation. Without the question of fundamental social change such a crisis-situation is reduced to a simple contest of power which may or may not culminate in change. But until the threat of societal change emerges the crisis-situation is not revolutionary. Thus, the inclusion of an agenda of fundamental structural change (social, political and/or economic)[2] embodied in the challenge to the old regime[3] must be an intricate part of any definition of a revolutionary situation.

The revolutionary outcome on the other hand is defined by Tilly as having "occur(red) with transfer of state power from those who held it before the start of multiple sovereignty to a new ruling coalition" (Tilly, 1978: 14). Again, Tilly is too broad with his definition and has omitted the crucial transformative aspect of the outcome which distinguishes it from other transfers of state power. The revolutionary outcome must involve the "transformation of basic state and class structures" embedded in Skocpol's definition of revolutions.

This distinction in the definition of revolutions is useful in addressing the question at hand. For a reliable, effective model capable of predicting revolutions to be developed it must not only be able to predict the emergence of a revolutionary challenge to the state (revolutionary situation), but also a victory on the part of the challengers which results in the attempted implementation of fundamental social change.

Revolutions have occurred throughout the world in a wide variety of states with differing, socio-political structures, cultures and levels of development. Most students of revolutions agree that revolutions can only be understood in light of the social contexts out of which they emerge. The analysis of the social context of a state at any given time involves studying a complex of social political and economic domestic and international factors including economic structures and performance, class structures, the strength and alignment of the military,

---

[2]

[3] The competing bloc or coalition in power prior to or during the revolutionary situation.

political structures performance, existence and roles played by non-governmental socio-political organizations,[4] cultural peculiarities of the state and the positioning of the state relative to other states in the international system.

These factors may, prior to and at the point of emergence of the revolutionary situation, have far-reaching impact upon the nature of the contest for state power. The social context determines first, the issue of contention between the contesting blocs and subsequently the revolutionary agenda advanced by the challengers. Second, the social context and the nature of the contention strongly influence the coalitions which band together to create the competing coalitions or blocs. It may also have impact upon the timing of the emergence of the revolutionary situation by accounting for a window of opportunity created by a weakened state, and upon the relative strengths of the competing blocs or coalitions. Yet another fundamental impact of the social context is that it also determines the terms of engagement between the competing groups; i.e. It has influence upon the level and nature of interaction between the competing groups. The social structure may or may not allow for varying levels of "legitimate" challenges to the state in the form of legal protest, legally recognized mass organizations, legislative "debate"; or in the absence or inefficiency of these, the open threat and/or use of violence.

An understanding of the social context under which revolutions occur is thus central to the proper analysis of social revolution. One of the underlying assumptions of analysis proposing the predictability of revolutions is that there exists a formula(s) of necessary and sufficient structural, economic and /or political factors which lie at the root of revolutions. Many attempts have been made to put forward such generalizable

---

[4]   This may be extended to include cultural, religious and social groups which may represents potential mediums and networks for the mobilization of the masses.

models of revolutions, but although many of these models have been successful in identifying plausible casual factors and explaining the processes by which revolutionary situations and outcomes arose from these social contexts, some still question the predictive value of such theories.

One such theory has been presented by Jack Goldstone (Goldstone, 1980, Goldstone In Keddie, 1995). According to Goldstone, the failure to successfully predict revolutions lies not in the failure of theoretical models of revolutions but in the lack of familiarity with these theories on the part of area specialists (Goldstone, In Keddie, 1995). Goldstone suggest that "predictive conclusions can be made simply from knowing what the trajectory toward revolutions looks like, even without knowing exactly what causes are pushing a society down that trajectory"(Goldstone, In Keddie, 1995: 45). According to Goldstone, the trajectory to revolution is determined by the conjuncture of three social conditions:

1. The state loses effectiveness in its ability to command resources and obedience;
2. Elites are alienated from the state and in heightened conflict over the distribution of power and status; and
3. A large or strategic portion of the population can be readily mobilized for protest actions (Goldstone, In Keddie, 1995: 45).[5]

When these three conditions occur simultaneously within a state, says Goldstone, revolution is "very likely"' if any of them is weak or absent revolution is "unlikely".

Goldstone's theory itself is problematic on various levels. Primarily his theory falls shorts in its failure to distinguish between political crises which lead to potential transfers of power and revolutions which necessarily end in the transformation of

---

[5]   See also (Goldstone, April 1980) and (Goldstone, 2001)

the society of a basic level. Although the conjuncture described by Goldstone may result in the emergence of a revolutionary-situation there is no reason to believe that such a conjunction will necessarily or with high probability lead to a revolutionary outcome. Additionally, although the weakened state is a usual precursor or contributing factor to revolutions, the Iranian (1978) and East German (1989) cases pose problems. In neither case had the state lost "effectiveness in its ability to command resources and obedience." His third point concerning the presence of a strategically mobile portion of the population, although useful for explanation ex post, poses problems, which will be addressed subsequently, when injected into a predictive model.

However, if Goldstone's broader assertions are correct, even if the correct conjunction has not yet been identified, it may still remain a possibility that with further research the correct formula of necessary and sufficient factors which, when found in conjuncture with each other result in revolution. It is precisely with this question that this paper concerns itself, not with whether or not his actual model is effective and reliable, but with whether or not such a model may in fact predict the occurrence of a revolution.

This paper will discuss the difficulty involved in the development of such a model on the grounds that:

1. Generalizable predictive models of revolutions are impossible because revolutions occur out of a conjunction of necessary conditions which include unique apparently trivial conditions[6] which are not obvious (of obviously important) prior to the emergence of the revolutionary situation;

---

[6]   These unique conditions differ from case to case and it is impossible to identify them *ex ante.*

2. A revolution is not complete and has not occurred until a revolutionary outcome has been established and that the outcome of a revolutionary situation is dependent upon the strategic interaction between contending blocs.

3. The outcomes of the strategic interaction between groups is uncertain and often unpredictable because of multiple outcome possibilities and because preference falsification and the subtle differences in social context determined by 1. (above) distort assessments of the situation.

4. That at best such models can give probabilistic predictions of the occurrence of political crisis leading to a struggle for state power.

The usefulness of models such as Goldstone's however, should not be underestimated. They may in fact go a far way in highlighting states which run a high risk of falling into political crisis leading to the emergency of a revolutionary situation consequently resulting in revolutionary outcome. However, Goldstone's carefully selected use of language betrays even his conviction on the extent to which they can predict which states will in fact continue along this trajectory ending in revolution and which states will avoid it. Goldstone strongest claims of prediction is that "if a state is observed to be moving rapidly down a trajectory that leads to revolution, then one can say unless the situation gravely changes, revolution will grow more likely. Thus, given the correct conjunction revolution is very likely, i.e that the existence of the potent conjuncture significantly increases the probability of revolutions occurring." But, as Timur Kuran, amongst others, has pointed out such predictions of revolutions are made routinely in states "featuring social tensions and the vast majority of these turn out to be false." (Kuran, In Keddie,1995: 29). Kuran maintains that for such a model to be considered predictive it must demonstrate:

               Ken G. Irish-Bramble

    a. That the prevalence of the correct predictions was above the norm, and

    b. That these predictions were held in unusually high confidence. (Kuran, In Keddie,1995: 29)

Although perfect prediction is an elusive goal in social science, a predictive model must impart a high degree of certainty as to which states will fall into a state of revolution and which will not[7].

The difficulty lies in the fact that despite similarities in state structures, levels of development and culture, no two states are identical. Subsequently, to the extent that the social contexts in any two states differ, the emerging revolutionary situation will also differ even if subtly. Nikki Keddie in a chapter entitled <u>Can Revolutions be Predicted: Can their Causes be Understood?</u> (Keddie, 1995) warns against the fallacy of assuming that these subtle differences in historically based social conflict are insignificant. Keddie argues, in her analysis of the 1978-79 Iranian revolution, that:

> Many who think revolutions should usually be predictable (assume) that since the event is major and involves large numbers of people in a dramatic way, its origins must similarly be visibly massive and distinctive. Big results, it is implicitly thought must have discoverably big causes. With regard to Iran, a whole series of cause has been noted …. Unfortunately…. most of these causes existed in other countries and did not lead to revolution. They may have been necessary causes of the Iranian revolution, but they were not sufficient causes. (Keddie, 1995: 3)

---

[7]   States may experience breakdown without experiencing revolution. *See definition of revolutions above*

Keddie's assertion that "a country about to have a revolution is not necessarily, in ways that can be measured at the time, more revolutionary in appearance than countries that do not have revolutions," (Keddie, 1995: 3) is of profound importance to the question at hand. On the one hand it poses a problem identification of necessary and sufficient causal factors which accurately account on a generalizable level for the rise of revolutionary situation. But furthermore, it illuminates another intricate fact about revolutionary processes: the emergence of a revolutionary situation does not mandate a revolutionary outcome.

Keddie suggests that the determining factors which distinguish between two apparently similar states, one of which experiences a revolution, are subtle, significant and undetectable *ex ante*. Borrowing from chaos theory Keddie argues that in the evolution of a society "subtle differences in input could quickly become overwhelming differences in output-a phenomenon given the name ***sensitive dependence on initial conditions.***" (Keddie, 1995: 6)

Historical decisions taken by state actors prior to the emergence of the revolutionary situation, alter the evolutionary path of the state. Over history as these subtle deviations in the evolutionary development of apparently similar states accumulate they result in significant deviations in the social context of the states and open a wide range of possibility of "potential outcomes." These deviations may, prior to the revolutionary situation, seem trivial but in fact may be determining factors in shaping the emergence of a revolutionary situation and in distinguishing between a country which avoids a revolution outcome and one which doesn't. In her case study of Iran, Keddie suggest that three such subtle factors account for why Iran underwent a revolution while other similarly situated countries didn't.

1. The evolution of the Shi'ite clergy in Iran, which made a powerful Khomeini and his network;
2. The particularities of the shah and the way he ruled, and;
3. The major contradiction between an increasingly autocratic, political structure and forced, inequitable, and rapid socioeconomic changes that to some degree alienated all classes in society. (Keddie, 1995: 10).

It is only in "the proper conjuncture" with these local, unique factors, Keddie argues, that the larger structural causes put forward by theorists results in revolution. Such subtle "elements turned out to be important but their importance (cannot), on the basis of past experience of human history, (be) so accurately assessed in advance as to lead to prediction of revolutions (Keddie, 1995: 19).

As Keddie illustrates, Iran at the time of its revolution resembled various other countries around the world which did not experience similar fates. "Autocracy by a widely disliked ruler was hardly unique to Iran; nor was over-reliance on oil income; large-scale rural urban migration; growing income distribution gaps; torture of political prisoner; or popular hostility to the dependence of the United States" (Keddie, 1995: 7). According to Keddie none of the larger social issues would lead the observer of Iranian politics to believe that Iran was any more at risk of revolution than a number of other states around the world. The difference hinges upon the subtle factors listed above. Yet even here, the significance and potential explosive nature of these factors was not obvious prior to the emergence of the revolutionary situation. As Keddie points out it is "not Shi'ism *per se,* that was more revolutionary than Sunnism, but rather the evolution of Shi'ite institutions in Iran that lent themselves to control by a single powerful cleric" (Keddie, 1995: 11). This development helped to make "revolutionary development (in Iran more) effective". Similar challenges to those raised by

Khomeini were also raised in other Muslim countries including Sayyid Quib in Egypt and Maududi in Pakistan, but lacked the effect structure developed in Iran necessary for an Islamic revolution.

The Shah's despotism poses yet another problem for predictability despite its obviously important role in the revolution. Despotism is by no means unusual to world politics and although the Shah's despotism stands out amongst his Muslim neighbors, it was a long-term factor and only became revolutionary in conjuncture with other elements. Furthermore, few despotic leaders have exemplified the indecisiveness of the Shah. The Shah maintained a high level of loyalty amongst the army leaders till the end of the revolution yet because of the peculiarities of the Shah's style of rule he failed to make use of the resources available to him. "If the Shah had acted repressively early in the development of the revolution.... (it) could have been stopped, at least for some years" (Keddie, 1995: 15).

Similarly, other Muslim countries experienced the rapid and unpopular socio-economic reforms undertaken in Iran including Ataturk's Turkey where "many kinds of modernization were more sudden and thorough .... family law reform was common, as were basic change in education, modernization of the economy with socio-economic dislocation, and even land reform" (Keddie, 1995: 18-9). Therefore, there was no reason for the observer to believe before-hand that the occurrence of any of these factors would lead to a revolution. Yet, in conjuncture with each other, revolution successfully occurred in Iran and not in any of the other apparently similar cases. The salient point is that many such significant factors cannot be observed beforehand and furthermore even when they are observable their potential for facilitating revolution is not obvious beforehand.

Her point is potent, not only does it suggest that the prediction of a revolutionary situation is difficult but more importantly that the prediction of a revolutionary outcome is doubly so. In moments of crisis and social strain, such as revolutions represent, subtle cultural and historical factors can become of immensely importance; a history of prior revolutions makes the notion of revolutionary action against the state more palatable to both leaders and the masses; the existence of religious or secular ideology which may be easily adapted to justify mass action against the state may provide a basis for challenges to the state; the existence of organizational networks (formal and informal) may facilitate the mobilization of masses to action. These are all important, yet subtle and particular, factors of a state's social condition, the importance of which cannot be measured prior to the emergence of the revolutionary situation.

Additionally, in moments of crisis the level and frequency of interactions and decision making and time constraints on these are increased. Outcomes of such crisis-situations are dependent upon the complex interactions of players during this period. A number of problem arise out of this for the effective and reliable prediction of the end result. First as Keddie implies because "during a revolution as many politically crucial decisions may be made in a month as are normally made in a decade and each decision may alter the overall complexion of events, "(Keddie, 1995: 20) causing the outcomes to become uncertainly obscure.

Further considerations may be added to the problem of attempting to model this interaction. Cognitive and psychological factors cannot easily be injected into generalizable models. The ability of leaders to function under crisis-situations and the nature of their approaches to the problem may be fundamental in determining the outcome of the revolutionary situations. Goldstone skims and dismisses this concern. In his discussion of the collapse of the Berlin Wall in October, 1989, he suggested that "the intervention of a single influential individual (Gorbachev), who could have acted differently, pushed the situation over the precipice of revolution before it would have otherwise reached that point." (Goldstone, In Keddie,1995: 41) For Goldstone, such factors impact only upon the timing and not the inevitability of revolutions given the conjuncture of necessary social conditions.

This dismissal is premature. First because the ability to predict a reasonable window of time in which revolutions may occur is essential if the model is to be effective, reliable and falsifiable. A model which predicts the likelihood of revolution in a state but grants no reasonable time-frame is of little use to policy makers. States suspected of being on a path to revolution must remain indefinitely on the "revolution watch" with no notion as to when it is more eminent than not. An effective and reliable model of prediction must demonstrate when states are, at least, in highest probability of revolution and a reasonable time-frame in which such may occur. Granted, exact prediction of the date and time of revolutions is beyond the capabilities of any social science model, yet a predictive model with an indefinite or vague time-frame renders the theory unfalsifiable. States, predicted to experience revolutions, yet remaining in long period of social tension without revolution, simply haven't become "ripe" yet. One can always predict ailment and misfortune in another's future, but the relevant question is when? Without this window, the prediction is of little, since it can offer no-one an opportunity to avoid it, enhance it or truly understand it.

If a potent conjuncture of factors lies at the root of revolution then a model which has effectively identified and tracked the various factors should be able to predict within a reasonable time frame when these conditions are or will be best synchronized to facilitate revolution and thus when revolution is most likely to occur. If this window is dependent upon the actions of key individuals, such as Gorbachev in the East German case, then the effective and reliable model must include their potential actions as factors.

Second, these factors of individual choices and abilities have much more far reaching impact than simply upon the timing. They may in fact be instrumental in determining whether the revolutionary situation arises in the first place and the final resolution of the revolutionary crises.

Tactical moves made by either bloc, tactical assessments each make of the other, levels of revolutionary zeal amongst the masses, charisma and the personality of the leaders involved all impact upon the interaction between the groups and the final outcome of it. Ruthless state leaders may quickly repress revolutionary movements; or poorly organized revolutionary opposition may blunder the opportunity to seize power; Revolutionary zealots may continue seemingly hopeless struggles for extended periods eventually wearing the state leaders down to a point of "compromised revolution". In effective, indecisive or overly compromising state leaders may inadvertently increase or create the windows of opportunity for revolutionary victories. Such factors have played significant roles in revolutions around the world including China, Iran, Ethiopia, El Salvador, Cuba and South Africa. We cannot predict infallibly how actors will perform under crisis-situations. The nature of the interaction is seldom obvious prior to the emergence of he revolutionary situations, if only because the key players and their alliances are unknown prior to the emergence of the situation.

These predictive problems arising out of "sensitive dependence on initial conditions[8] may be labeled **_multiple-outcome revolutionary situations_**. Keddie suggests that innumerous possible outcome may rise out of this multiple-outcome revolutionary situation. In fact, they can be more simply categorized. Five possible outcomes may arise from a potential revolutionary situation based upon their divergent evolutionary paths to their contemporary social context:

1. **The revolutionary situation is never consolidated**. Given certain social conditions potential revolutionary situation may be avoided in times of crisis even before

---

[8]   See page 8

they truly form. Countries with a long history of stable democracy and a tradition of social reform through legitimate channels may for example be likely to forgo revolution.

2. **The revolutionary may be squashed and modified status quo instated**. The state regime may successful repress the revolutionary forces and maintain control of the state and state structures. The state may subsequently take steps to modify itself as precautions against future insurgence.

3. **Resolution with reform**. The contending sides may reach a compromise leading to reform and avoiding total revolution.

4. **Elongated Stalemate**. The interaction may be extended over a long period of time with neither side capable of definitively defeating the other, resulting in a stalemate.[9]

5. **Revolutionary outcome**. The revolutionary forces may be successful in overthrowing the established regime and implementing fundamental social change.

Which of these possible outcomes manifests is dependent upon both the initial conditions and the evolutionary path taken by the state in the development of its social conditions at the time of the revolutionary situation. More importantly it is dependent upon the interaction between key groups during the transition from revolutionary situation to outcome. Only in the most extra-ordinary cases can this interaction be reasonably predicted prior to the emergence of the revolutionary situation. Furthermore, the relevant factors are easily quantifiable or coded.

Timur Kuran adds yet another element to the factors complicating the ability of social science to make predictions

---

[9] Such stalemate may eventually result in a negotiated treaty bringing about some changes.

of revolutions. Keddie's theory of ***preference falsification*** (Kuran, 1997 & Kuran, 1992) says that individuals simultaneously maintain a duality of preferences; a public preference, which he reveals to others and a private preference which is know only to him. Individual's public preferences are greatly influenced by cost/benefit analysis of involvement in revolutionary activity. Although the two impacts upon each other they may nonetheless differ and contradict each other. As Kuran illustrates it:

> A person who despises the prevailing regime is more likely …. to join an anti-government rally… if the likely price of joining the rally is a stinct in jail or ostracism by one peers at work, the prudent course of action may be to remain on the side lines, even to cheer the security forces. (Kuran, In Keddie, 1995: 31)

There exists in any revolutionary situation ***revolutionary thresholds*** or the circumstances under which (individuals) are prepared to switch political sides. These thresholds will vary across any society with differing private preferences and sensitivity to social pressure. These thresholds may converge so that a significant portion of the population simultaneously reach their individual revolutionary thresholds. These potential points of convergence are referred to by Kuran as ***multiple-equilibria*** or self-sustaining distribution of preferences upon which a revolution may ride to success. The problem rests on the fact that these equilibria the conjunction of individual thresholds which remain unknown or which are unreliably deceptive.[10]

This idea is closely connected with the arguments presented earlier in this paper concerning the complexity of the interaction

---

[10]   Kuran, Timur. "Why revolutions are poorly Predicted and Better Understood?" <u>Debating Revolutions</u>. pp31

between contesting blocs under normal and crisis-situations. According to Kuran's theory "once this multiple-equilibria has been reached, a small, intrinsically insignificant event will suffice to put in motion a revolutionary bandwagon. This bandwagon will catch everyone by surprise" (Kuran, In Keddie, 1995: 31) Preference falsification provides both competing forces and external observers with misleading information about the nature of the revolutionary situation and thus distorts their judgement in determining the relevant courses of action and likely outcomes. At points in time before and after the equilibria has been reached preference falsification will conceal the potentiality for revolution and at points in time after it will conceal the forces working against change.

Needless to say, this distortion of social conditions increases the difficulty of social scientist to predict the extent of public support for or against a potential revolutionary movement. But equally as important it complicates the interaction between groups adding to the likelihood of miscalculations on the part of key players. Since the equilibria are unknown and the individual threshold cannot be observed, it is often impossible to determine beforehand at what point a crisis-situation becomes a revolutionary one. It has often been noted that many states seem to endure potential disruptive social tension for prolonged period without falling into revolution. The determination of when, under what specific conditions and due to what specific triggering effect a condition under which both revolutionary situation and outcome will occur. As this paper has suggested many difficulties inhibit the ability of social scientists to accomplish this.

The challenge for social scientists is to develop a framework of conditions which conjunction with each other facilitate, with a high probability, the occurrence of a revolution. Granted the potential importance of subtle factors particular to each case, the model must be sufficiently broad as to include the possible combinations of factors which may facilitate the growth and success of revolutionary movements. Yet sufficiently narrow and specific so as not to be tautological or inclusive of non-revolutionary movements. Because of the pivotal importance of the interactions between actors during the transition from revolutionary situation and outcome, the model must also engender both structural and game theoretical approaches to the problem.

CHAPTER 2

Political Violence in the Caribbean

Introduction

In an article entitled "The Caribbean Question, why has liberal democracy surprisingly flourished?" (Dominguez, Pastor & Worrell (Eds.), 1993) Jorge I. Dominguez presents a comparative analysis of the Caribbean's democratic history since independence (1960's-present) to account for the relative success of liberal democratic institutions in the Caribbean region. In particular, Dominguez focuses on the success of the English-speaking Caribbean states and territories, such as Jamaica, Barbados in contrast to the disappointing performance of such institutions in other Developing countries in Latin America, Africa and Asia. Dominguez posits that the answers to this success lie in three major factors: 1. A strong value placed on liberty and individual rights embodied in the Caribbean's "habits of societal resistance" 2. Constraints placed on the Caribbean's development towards democracy by "international and institutional factors" 3. A colonial legacy that bequeathed to the region democratic traditions and which fostered a smooth transition to self-government. Anthony Payne (1988), in his book, <u>Politics in Jamaica</u>, adds several other factors to the equation of accounting for the Caribbean's relative stability and flourishing democracies. He asserts that the Colonialist experience in the Caribbean left the region with several advantages including the inheritance of major global languages (English, French, Spanish and Dutch).

While upholding the importance of the factors emphasized by these writers, this paper is critical of their conclusions on several positions. Although each of these factors contribute to an understanding of the democratic performance of Caribbean politics, the explanations offered are nonetheless lacking in the depth of their analysis of the causal mechanism by which each factor has helped to shape the democratic traditions they seek to explain. Furthermore, on a methodological note, both writers, but in particular Dominguez, have excluded from their analysis, consideration of the relative size of the Caribbean territories and its impact on the region's development. Because of this, Dominguez prematurely dismisses traditional explanations for democratic stability as unrevealing. Furthermore, Dominguez draws conclusions based upon comparative analyses of Caribbean territories and other, non-micro state, developing nations which are biased by the failure to take size (both physical and demographic) into account. The failure to consider size as a relevant factor, also accounts for a third criticism of Dominguez's work; his misleadingly optimistic view of the Caribbean territories democratic tradition. The Caribbean has in many ways demonstrated similar characteristics and tendencies towards the political violence and general instability which have plagued other developing countries, albeit on a smaller, more confined scale. As this paper will suggest, one major factor which may account for the difference in the manifestation of these anti-democratic tendencies are the structural constraints particular to micro-states such as the Caribbean territories, which make sustained contentious politics difficult.

This paper is therefore set up in three major sections, beginning with an outline of Dominguez's position. The second section seeks to readdress several of the causal factors rejected by Dominguez taking into consideration the impact of the relative size of these territories. The third establishes that the Caribbean region has in fact demonstrated several of the tendencies towards radical, revolutionary and subversive non-democratic activity on a scale comparable to that of other Third World (similarly underdeveloped) countries given its particular structural constraints.

The Caribbean Surprise

The "Caribbean surprise," as Dominguez calls it, lies in the fact that "no other region in what has been called the Third World has had, for so long, so many liberal democratic politics." (Dominguez, Pastor & Worrell (Eds.), 1993: 2)

> Since independence (beginning in 1962) ten of the twelve Anglo-phone Caribbean countries have consistently held fair elections and have been free from unconstitutional transfers of power. Also, since independence a majority of the ten consistently constitutionalist Anglo-phone Caribbean countries have witnessed at least one election as a result of which the governing party peacefully turned power over to the hitherto opposition party ... This achievement is far superior to that of Latin America and also to that of the countries of Africa and Asia that acquired their formal independence from European powers after the Second World War. Some have noted that former British colonies have had a better record than the former colonies of other major powers at sustaining liberal democracy. It is also noteworthy, however, that the former British colonies in the Caribbean have also had a far superior capacity to sustain liberal democratic politics than most former British colonies in Africa and Asia and have done so with much lower levels of violence. (Dominguez, Pastor & Worrell (Eds.), 1993: 3)

As Dominguez points out, many of the traditional arguments for the flourishing of democratic institutions do not account well for the differing performances of democratic institutions in the Caribbean as compared with other developing nations.

Economic arguments

Economic arguments, for example, suggest that there exists a correlation between economic performance of countries and their likelihood to develop sustained democratic institutions. According to the World Bank's 1990 report the gross national product (GNP) of every Anglophone Caribbean territory with the exception of Guyana was above $1,000[11] *see table 1.* As Dominguez points out, of these territories Guyana is the only territory in the course of the past forty years has been the site of a sustained authoritarian regime under Forbes Burnham. Similarly, as compared with the Anglophone Caribbean, Nicaragua, El Salvador, Honduras and Guatemala all had lower GNP per capita levels and substantially less stable democracies than their Caribbean counterparts. These observations are of course consistent with the notion embodied in the economic explanations. Yet, when the comparison is extended to the larger Third World the strength of the correlation between GNP and consolidated democratic institutions tends to falter. For example, Dominguez points out:

> The Dominican Republic's GNP per capita was about the same as that of Guatemala. Jamaica's GNP per capita was only slightly above that of Guatemala. Though in the late 1980's Guatemala took some important steps towards democratization, Jamaica has never experienced the grip of military power that Guatemala has, nor has the Dominican Republic since the late 1970's; nor has either experienced the thirty years

---

[11]   GNP figures are quoted in 1988 US dollars.

civil war that Guatemala has suffered. In the same vein, St. Lucia, Dominica, and Grenada differ little in their GNP per capita, yet only Granada experienced the authoritarian episodes of Eric Gairy's latter years in power and of the New Jewel Movement. Surinam is much more economically prosperous than St. Lucia, Dominica, or St. Vincent and the Grenadines, but only Suriname experienced nearly continuous military rule in the 1980's. (Dominguez, Pastor & Worrell (Eds.), 1993: 4)

The case for arguments tied to economic growth rates as opposed to mere economic performance is similar. Guyana, Haiti, the Dominican Republic, Suriname, and Trinidad and Tobago had a lower gross domestic product (GDP) per capita at the end of the 1980's than they did at the beginning. In the case of Jamaica, its GDP at the end of the 1980's was lower than it had been in the 1970's. Again, initial evidence for a correlation between this economic trend and the performance of democratic institutions can be drawn from these examples. In each of these territories, episodes of notable political instability surfaced including intense political violence in Jamaica's 1980 elections, an aborted coup involving the kidnaping of the Prime Minister of Trinidad and Tobago in 1990, and Suriname's decade of military rule. And yet, Dominguez notes, the relationship between trends in economic growth as "cause" an "democratic stability" as effect is muddled at best. In all the Anglophone Caribbean territories democratic institutions survived and maintained their integrity despite the upheavals. In 1980 the opposition's victory in Jamaica was recognized despite the high levels of political violence associated with the election. In Trinidad and Tobago the upheavals of 1990 occurred six years after the country's worst economic performance in 1983-4. Nor was Barbados, whose inflation rate spiraled out of control in 1974 at a rate comparable to that which preceded Brazil's military coup in 1964, affected by political instability. Similarly, in the non-English-speaking territories such as Suriname, the country's decade of military rule[12] actually came into place after a decade of economic success and not as a result of the decade of economic downfall which followed it. Economic indicators, by themselves therefore prove to be poor indicators.

Militarization

In Dominguez's comparison, traditional arguments concerning increased militarization also prove to be equally unsatisfactory in demonstrating a strong causal relationship to the consolidation of democratic regimes. Looking at the U.S. Arms Control and Disarmament Agency's report on militarization, measured as armed forces' personnel per one thousand people, the three Caribbean countries with rates of five soldiers per thousand, Guyana, Cuba and Suriname were also the three countries most plagued by sustained authoritarian rule. However, a closer look at the pattern of militarization throughout the region demonstrates a number of facts inconsistent with the cause and effect relationship between increased militarization and destabilized fledgling democratic regimes.

In the case of Suriname, for example, the level of militarization jumped only after the Desi Bousterse Coup and had remained steady at a rate of 2.8 per thousand prior to this. Similarly, in Guyana although the rate of militarization increased drastically from 3 in 1975 to 9 in 1977, this rise was in response to Forbes Burnham's increasing authoritarianism and designed as a means of protecting an emerging authoritarian regime and consequently cannot be seen as its cause.

---

[12]   1980-1991

Barbados, whose military unit dates back to 1979, had its rate of militarization rise rapidly to measures between three and four soldiers per thousand yet, remained one of the most stable regimes in the region. Furthermore, the Barbadian rate was also twice that of Jamaica and Trinidad and Tobago, both of which experienced higher levels of political violence. Broadening the basis of comparison, Dominguez further notes that Jamaica and Trinidad and Tobago increased their rates of militarization during the 1970's and 80's reaching levels comparable to that of Ghana and Uganda, without it resulting in the subsequent democratic failures experienced by their African counterparts.

Having eliminated these two traditional indicators as being inconsistent and unrevealing, Dominguez presents a series of alternative explanations for the Caribbean's liberal democratic success. According to Dominguez, answers to the Caribbean question can be found in the deep-seated commitment of the region's people and leadership to the basic ideals of democratic government. This commitment is, in Dominguez's opinion, a legacy of the Caribbean's colonial past and forged by two primary factors:

1. Habits of societal resistance to centralized power and
2. Institutional and leadership characteristics forged through the colonial and post-colonial period

Habits of Resistance to Centralized Power

As Dominguez points out, the Caribbean region is the only region in the world, except for Rwanda, where the descendants of ex-slaves govern sovereign nations. This fact contrasts greatly with the experience of other slave holding societies in the Americas (United States of America, Brazil, and the French, Dutch and Hispanic countries of the region) where power remained largely in the hands of the old elites. This legacy of slavery and the "pattern of resistance of Caribbean societies ... against slavery may also have contributed to a social structure more enduringly resistant to centralized rule." (Dominguez, Pastor & Worrell (Eds.), 1993: 7) In support of this claim, Dominguez points to the existence of maroon societies throughout the region where "in the densely-forested Guianas and in mountainous Jamaica, slaves escaped from their masters and formed communities that did not recognize central power." These values which are embedded in the Caribbean's collective consciousness and manifested in the use of various mediums including the historical use of folklore, music and humor to ridicule those who abuse their power were once used as a means of maintaining forbidden African cultural expression and as tools to plot against and, mock the masters who dominated their lives. In the modern Caribbean setting these tools continue to be used as powerful political tools to stimulate a grass roots discourse and consciousness about socio-economic and political issues.

As the author notes, the colonial experience in the Caribbean region saw the development, over an extended period, of other social characteristics conducive to the development and functioning of liberal democracy including an acceptance of religious and cultural pluralism and a high value placed on private ownership of property. However, ethno-communal pluralism has also proven problematic in some Caribbean territories, in particular, Guyana, Trinidad and Tobago and Suriname where ethnicity has been a defining characteristic of domestic politics.

Institutional and Leadership Characteristics

Drawing on Keynesian economic theory, Dominguez draws attention to a significant characteristic of the Caribbean's democratic structure, the emergence of the welfare state and the

Statist Bargain which allows for a mutually invested interest in democratic stability on the part of politicians, citizens and local business. The result has been an increased standard of living for the citizens as demonstrated by Dominguez's comparison of Caribbean countries with other Third World countries at "comparable" economic levels:

> Trinidad and Tobago and Gabon have comparable populations and about the same GNP per capita; both are oil producers, and neither had a good economic growth record from the mid-1960s to the mid-1980s. And yet in the mid-1980s the rate of illiteracy in Trinidad and Tobago was one tenth that of Gabon, while life expectancy of Trinidadians was fourteen years more. Jamaica's level of GNP per capita is comparable to Botswana's, another former British colony, and one of Africa's few Democratic regimes. At the end of the 1980s Jamaica's infant mortality rate was one-quarter that of Botswana. Though Colombia is a bit wealthier than Jamaica and has had a much higher economic growth rate, in the late 1980s Jamaica's infant mortality rate was also one-quarter that of Colombia's. (Dominguez, Pastor & Worrell (Eds.), 1993: 12)

Additionally, the development of the welfare system in the Caribbean, as systems of political patronage have served to benefit both the poor and local business communities through the provision of civil service jobs, the distribution of major contracts to party supporters and establishment of "structures of protection against imports and of direct subsidies to their operations." The result has been a vested interest and a high level of confidence in the political system as a means of supporting the aspirations of the average citizen.

Other institutionalized characteristics which fit into Dominguez's explanation of the region's democratic success including the Caribbean's position in the international arena. Dominguez places a great emphasis on the British response to decolonization in the period following the social upheavals which swept through the region in the 1930's and particularly in the post-World War I period.

> In the Anglophone Caribbean, British colonialism opened up the political system ... the process of decolonization was long and deliberate but also democratic in its direction. Thanks to the British empire, the Anglophone Caribbean successfully handled in much less repressive ways problems that some Central American countries have yet to settle. (Dominguez, Pastor & Worrell (Eds.), 1993: 15)

Therefore, summarizing Dominguez arguments, answers to the Caribbean apparent success in the development of viable and stable democracies lie in its peaceful and well administered transition from colonial rule to independence, the commitment of the region's people to democratic ideals developed through their patterns of resistance against centralized power in the pre-emancipation period and, the successful modification of democratic institutions to the unique circumstances of the Caribbean.

Critical Review

As stated in the beginning of this paper, the goal of this investigation is not to discredit Dominguez's discourse of democratic development in the Caribbean but rather to augment and improve upon it. Any analysis of the Caribbean's political development must begin with the realization that the Caribbean represents a unique culmination of circumstances conducive to democracy:

1. Relatively small size and insularity conducive to the development of a sense of community and subsequently civic mindedness
2. Structural constraints, related to the territories' size, which inhibit the establishment of long term, sustained political violence
3. Strategic location and close ties to European and North American countries
4. A close, peaceful and supportive relationship between regional states and a commitment to regionalism
5. A unique history of national identity formation, void of competing sub-national identities
6. The existence of socio-economic buffers to economic crisis

This culmination of characteristics, somewhat unique to the Caribbean, have allowed the region to survive some of the political downfalls which have crippled efforts at democratization elsewhere in the world. Neglect of these social characteristics creates a sense of surprise which is many ways unwarranted.

Dominguez's analysis therefore, although insightful, is lacking in a few areas. First, his analysis of various factors, in particular his management of economic indicators, is limited and lacks a contextualized treatment of distinctive characteristics of the Caribbean case study. Towards this end, we return to his arguments attempting to fill in some of the ambiguities and oversights in his argument and then proceed by adding a number of factors ignored by Dominguez which may provide us with a more comprehensive explanation for the Caribbean's democratic success. A second flaw to be addressed by this paper is the comparative conclusions implied in his chapter. This paper will assert that size matters i.e. that as micro-states, the Caribbean territories, in particular the island territories, have structural advantages and disadvantages, which inhibit the occurrence of certain forms of long-term, sustained political violence and help foster the development of better socio-economic indicators. Closely connected to this is Dominguez's use of traditional economic measures as a base of comparison which creates a false sense of similarity between nations by ignoring other socio-economic factors, including size, which impacts upon the quality of life of citizens within these states.

Towards a New Explanation

We begin first with the alternative explanations for the Caribbean's successful democratic development presented by Dominguez, as a means of providing background information essential to supporting the subsequent arguments outlined above. Dominguez's explanations are a first step towards the treatment of the Caribbean case study as a unique and distinct process of democratic development. Consequently, taking into consideration the region's unique development may prove to inform the interpretation of the effect of larger socio-economic causal factors and their impact of political stability.

As Dominguez notes, the Caribbean is the only region in the world where the descendants of ex-slaves now rule themselves independently. This fact is significant, primarily because of the unique colonial experience which produced this phenomenon in the Caribbean, but not elsewhere in the developing world. The Caribbean population is primarily composed of descendants of enslaved Africans, forcibly migrated to the region to cultivate sugar and other cash crops for the European colonial systems, and other "voluntary" migrant Asian laborers, imported during the post emancipation period.

The Caribbean region's colonial experience is however on other levels unique from the African, Asian and the North and South American models of colonialism. The most distinctive difference is that unlike other Developing states and former colonies, the societies of the Caribbean are themselves entirely colonial creations. The historical experience and collective consciousness of Caribbean people has been heavily dominated by the colonial experience. The implications of this fact are far reaching, particularly where the question of identity formation is brought forward.

Dominguez, by returning to chattel slavery for an answer to the question at hand, demonstrates great insight into uncovering one of the most central explanations for the Caribbean's democratic stability. The key however, does not simply lie in the fact that formerly enslaved people now control the political reins. Many cases can be cited throughout the world where formerly oppressed people with histories of resistance against centralized power have themselves grown into oppressors. The holocaust experience of the Second World War has not hindered Israeli domination of Palestinians in the name of national security and religious supremacy. Nor do patterns of resistance against centralized power explain the region's ready acceptance of democratic institutions which had for centuries been associated with the class of oppressors against whom they resisted.

What does provide insight into these, is the nature of chattel slavery itself and, the role it played in forging a unique colonial experience for the Caribbean region. Chattel slavery, unlike any other form of oppression, systematically rid the African slaves of any sense of identity outside of the colonial structure. As Africans were forcibly removed from the African continent and transported to the Caribbean, they began a process by which their collective consciousness was systematically stripped away. In place of previous identities, social structures and relations, the plantocracy, the dominant class of planters, imposed new colonial identities suited to the total domination and control of the slave population and its development. The plantocracy's control of the transfer of knowledge and information restricted the population's exposure to alternative structures was severely limited, as was their exposure to any source of identity outside of the colonial structure.

Therefore, unlike the colonial experiences in other parts of the world where old social structures remained in place the Caribbean represented a unique situation in which the colonial masters could, in essence, build political structures "from scratch." In Africa and Asia, for example, colonial structures and identities had to be superimposed upon pre-existing social structures and identities. As a result, democratic institutions had to be reconciled with tribal councils, monarchies, and imperial dynasties. Likewise, capitalist institutions had to be integrated in barter systems, local markets, and communal traditions. Most importantly, new identities had to be superimposed upon old traditional identities. In some cases, nation formation was orchestrated over a short period of time and imposed upon people who had not grown to accept them. As a result, societies were asked to function in two worlds, with different and sometimes contrasting ideologies, simultaneously.

The difficulty in consolidating democracy in these societies therefore lay in resolving new institutions and identities with old ones. In the Caribbean setting, because the old institutions had so effectively been done away with, the only identities left were themselves essentially colonial. In fact, the Caribbean's history of democratic development is as old as Europe's, dating back to the 17th century when local legislative bodies were first introduced into the region under the old representative system. It is not of little consequence that amongst the first lobbyist groups established in the British Parliament were representatives of Caribbean agricultural interests. Although these systems were in many instances weak and, as with most early democratic institutions, often representative of only the ruling class, they nonetheless represent the dominant political ideal in the region's history and the only model of self-government in the English speaking territories' collective memory.

In fact, prior to the 1804 Haitian Constitution and the 1959/60 Cuban Revolution no alternate national models of governance existed throughout the region at all. Furthermore, the English-speaking Caribbean has only one instance in its political history of political restructuring outside of the traditional Western European democratic tradition. Any hints towards experimentation with alternative models have been met with great resistance from both within and outside the region. e.g. Jamaica under Michael Manley (1972-1980), Grenada under Maurice Bishop (1979-1983). With no other viable political model and a long tradition of democratic ambitions, the Caribbean therefore represented a more willing colonial crucible; an open slate upon which colonial powers could more easily impose their ideals. Consequently, the Caribbean region was able to avoid many of the basic conflicts, which have plagued Asian and in particular, African countries in their democratic development.

A second, interrelated crisis faced by many fledgling democracies has been the issue of ethnic conflict. Donald Horowitz (1985) in his work on ethnic conflicts makes a distinction between two different types of ethnic conflicts; ranked and unranked systems of ethnic identity formation. Ranked systems in the lexicon of Horowitz, refer to those systems of ethnic division where ethnic origin and class division coincide with each other. On the other hand, un-ranked systems exist where

> parallel ethnic groups coexist, each group internally stratified ... although the question of group superiority is far from irrelevant in such a system, it is not settled. The groups are not definitely ranked in relation to each other, certainly not across the board. ... accordingly,

transactions can occur across group lines without necessarily implying anything about a hierarchy of ethnic groups. (Horowitz, 1985: 23)

These distinctions are important, particularly when recognizing that ethnic conflicts have played a critical role in determining the success and failure of democratic consolidation in so many regions of the world.

> The characteristics of ranked and unranked systems flow from their differing origins. In general, ranked systems are produced by conquest or capture. The ensuing domination lends itself to the establishment of upper and lower ranks, clientage relations, and an ideology of inferiority for the subordinated groups (*Rwanda, Southern Africa, Southern Philippines and slave societies of north and South America are all examples of such systems*) On the other hand unranked systems are produced by invasion resulting in less than conquest, by more or less voluntary migration, or by encapsulation within a single territorial unit of groups that formerly had little to do with each other - or some combination of these. (Nigeria, Sri Lanka and post emancipation Guyana and Trinidad and Tobago are examples of such systems) ... in many cases, colonial rule brought together unranked groups that had had no previous contact, as well as those that had met on the battle field or in mines, shops, plantations... attracting ethnically differentiated work forces. ... it seems evident that ranked subordination cannot long be sustained without a measure of spatial proximity to enforce it. Parallel (unranked) groups, however may be either intermixed or regionally discrete.

Typically, migration generates more geographical
intermixing than does incomplete conquest.
(Horowitz, 1985)

The system of chattel slavery, i.e. Africans treated as
commodities to be brought, sold, traded or inherited, was
squarely based upon ranked identity, i.e. that one's ethnic
roots determined one's class in the society's class hierarchy.
However, with the emancipation of slaves and the collapse of
the plantation system, the Caribbean class system effectively
transitioned from a ranked to an unranked system of ethnic
divisions. This transition was facilitated by many factors.

First was the development of an increasingly large and
influential class of free blacks and mulattoes who from the
18th century onwards increasingly made inroads into the local
political and economic infrastructure and gradually replaced
the ruling white plantocracy as the dominant class from the
mid-19th century onwards. As this transition of power and class
structures occurred the mutually exclusive ethnic distinctions
which previously dominated the ranked system of ethnic
identity faded, and were replaced by a less specific and less
well defined ethnic division based upon skin tone. As the white
plantocracy's interest and presence in the region declined, the
basis of identity formation throughout the region also continued
to evolve. Identity formation throughout the region evolved in
unprecedented ways forging a uniform national identity which
embraced ethnic and cultural diversity leaving only class division
with subtle undertones of racial identities defined by skin tone.

The exception to this treatment were in Trinidad and
Tobago and Guyana, where the new unranked identity
remained stagnant with continued competition between East
Indian migrant laborers and the Afro-Caribbean population
for resources, class status and power. Unlike the Asian, and,
the African cases, where following the decline of colonial rule,
people realigned themselves along old ethnic divisions, in the

Caribbean only the colonially defined national identity and class system remained. It is here that the foundation of the cultural pluralism Dominguez speaks of are formed.

The potential for conflict in ranked systems is obvious and, as the experiences of South Africa, the United States and Israel in the twentieth century have demonstrated, violence, discrimination, social instability, and democratic failure are inherent. But as Horowitz demonstrates, unranked systems also bear with them potential for political conflict and instability. An examination of some of the potential pitfalls of unranked system may be further insightful in understanding the specific advantages that were produced because of the Caribbean's unique colonial history. As Horowitz argues:

> Migration and incomplete conquest also give rise to different kinds of lingering historical grievances. A group whose conquest has been thwarted may nourish unfulfilled territorial ambitions, while a group whose land has been partly conquered may develop a domestic version of *revanche*. An indigenous group that was colonized and forced to live aside the entry of ethnic strangers for colonial economic purposes may later regard their presence as illegitimate. (Horowitz, 1985:30)

As illustration for his observation, Horowitz offers the examples of Nigeria and Sri Lanka. In Nigeria, British colonial rule interrupted the Hausa-Fulani invasion southwards. Fears of a renewal of their aggressions and domination resurfaced after independence with Southerners' fears that the departure of the British had opened the way for its continuance. Similarly, according to Horowitz, in Sri-Lanka Tamil invasions had resulted in a de facto partition of the island centuries before colonial rule. But the issue has nonetheless remained alive and resurfaced "with periodic political significance" (Horowitz, 1985).

The Caribbean's colonial history has made it immune to many of the ethnic conflicts and underlying identity issues faced by countries such as Nigeria and Sri Lanka. The colonization of the Caribbean saw the complete dissemination of local and indigenous people and cultures. Since African slaves were systematically stripped of their identities and since any claims to homeland were negated by their forced migration into the region, no basis existed for either form of conflict to be built upon. The exceptions to this for the Caribbean region are Trinidad and Tobago and Guyana where, competition between the two groups following emancipation from slavery (1834) over wage labor and access to other resources has continued to be a source of socio-political tension. In these two cases, the results have been similar, falling well into Horowitz's generalizations of unranked systems. Guyana, represents the more troubling example of these social-ethnic pressures manifesting themselves in potentially destabilizing ways. As Raymond Smith observes:

> ... for a short time in the early 1960's there was expulsion of minorities from rural communities, beatings and killings, and even proposals for dismantling the state and creating two "ethnic nations," African and East Indian. What began as a vague suggestion by some members of the Afro-Guyanese elite in the early 1960's was taken up and formalized as a proposal of the Society for Racial Equality and is still discussed by Guyanese inside and outside. (Smith, 1995: 224)

It is evident that in the isolated cases where Caribbean regions remained as unranked systems ethnic conflict produced similar results to those seen in other "less stable" developing countries. Yet despite these two cases, in which colonial driven migratory labor policies forged an ethnically divided population and promoted economic, cultural and subsequently, political competition, the Caribbean territories generally maintained relatively homogenous populations void of such pressures. It is also noteworthy that the vast majority of migrant laborers entering the region in the post- emancipation period were themselves also British colonial subjects.

The impact of size on Economic Factors

The level of economic development has a pronounced effect on political democracy, even when non-economic factors are considered...wealth eases burdens, both public and private, and facilitates social accommodation ... "of all the theories to explain the performance differences, the most powerful one is modernization". (Putnam, 1992: 84)

The impact of economic pressures on democratic development is well known and has been widely discussed. A major flaw of those who explore this relationship is their failure to pay primary attention to micro-states and to the differing impact of global economic trends on these states as compared to other developing nations. Furthermore, Dominguez's analysis of factors affecting Caribbean economic pressures is particularly limited because of its implicit comparative conclusions. The effectiveness of comparative analyses relies heavily on the existence of some control factor. i.e. in comparing the differences in responses to some causal stimuli a common basis of comparison must be established. In the case of Dominguez's comparative analysis, Dominguez make the assertion that the common factor which allows for comparison of the region with other developing states is their similar economic indicators measured in Gross National Product and Gross Domestic Product. Dominguez's over reliance on these traditional economic measures ignores several other factors which effect socio- economic realities of citizens in micro-states, even in light of economic downturns and therefore is based upon a false sense of similarity.

The Caribbean, as a region, is predominantly made up of micro states, any analysis of socio-economic and political trends and their impact on the region must take into account factors specific to micro-states. This is particularly true when comparative analyses are being presented setting the Caribbean territories against other developing countries. Impacts of size on traditional economic factors include the broader dissemination of benefits from economic upturns, the relative overall national benefit gained from foreign developmental aid, individual access to resources through closer connections to key political figures, vested interest in governmental policy and the existence of local support mechanisms which buffer the impact of economic crisis.

Dominguez relies heavily on traditional measures of Gross National Product in his comparative analysis. As he points out, Jamaica's GNP per capita was slightly higher than that of Guatemala in the late 1980's, yet "Jamaica never experienced the grip of military power that Guatemala has." Although certainly true, this fact in no manner suggests an inherently more stable characteristic for Jamaican democracy. This point is particularly clear when bearing in mind that the 1980 elections in Jamaica and the decade of politics which followed it were amongst the bloodiest periods of political violence in the Anglophone Caribbean's history. Furthermore, the fact that this period of political violence never culminated in an outright civil war or a military takeover of the island is due, in part, to the structural limits imposed by Jamaica's insularity, size and furthermore, to other socio-economic support systems which helped to buffer the effects of economic downturns in the island's economy.

The use of traditional indicators such as GNP and GDP as the basis for comparative studies looking at the impact of economic strains on the average citizen must therefore take into consideration the influence of other support systems, not picked up in official measures of the country's GDP which serve to buffer the impact of various economic strains associated with political instability[13]. Howard Green, formerly of the U.S. Federal Reserve Bank in Atlanta, has estimated that for the period 1968-76 "about two million migrants from the Caribbean Basin remitted approximately, $2.5 billion (US) back to the region" (Brana-Shute, 1982). Similarly, in 1980, the Prime Minister of St. Lucia estimated that total remittances from all totaled $20 million (E.C.).

These figures, have direct impact upon the citizens of the region by "rais(ing) the standard of living and material quality of life of those left behind by outward migration." (Rubenstein, 1982) They help to cushion the impact of struggling economies, economic downturns and overall poverty. As a 1998 World Bank report on the performance of micro-states in the Pacific region states, *the* economy is heavy dependent upon foreign aid remittances which help to sustain its relatively high social indicators in light of an otherwise weak economy" (World Bank: 1998). Additionally, unlike other forms of capital flow into the region, remittances go directly to those most in need of support and have the effect of easing the social pressure caused by periodic economic downturns. Cultural anthropologist, Hymie Rubenstein discusses in his work the impact of remittances in the rural English-speaking Caribbean:

> The sums sent home by migrants are often substantial. Remittances are the principle sources of hard currency in several small islands... in one small community in Tortola, B.V.I. external inputs accounted for 45% of the income of the average household. In 1957 the export value of cotton *then* Montserrat's main cash crop, was nearly nine times the value of remittance; by 1960, at the height of

---

[13]   I would like to acknowledge the error in this assertion. In fact, remittances have been factored into GDP calculations.

the return to England, a complete turnabout had occurred with the value of remittance almost four times that of cotton exports... an almost identical situation is reported for Nevis ... Seasonal migrants also sent back money ...estimate(d) *at* between one third and one half of their earnings...One rural community in Barbados ...reported that 25% of adults received funds from relatives overseas...in two rural districts in Montserrat 55% of household depended on cash from overseas... a sample of 100 households in rural St. Vincent, found 26 households counted on extra island cash gifts for at least 25% of their support while only 36 household received no external support. Although only 4 of the 100 households were almost wholly dependent on non-island residents ...almost two thirds of the total received some cash from overseas... moreover, nearly every village household not currently receiving extra island support has a history of remittance contributions from present or former members. (Rubenstein, 1982)

As Rubenstein notes, the impact of remittances serves to sustain many families throughout the region but, has not traditionally been a source of development. This assertion itself is questionable, particularly in light of the impact of in-kind remittances to the region as means of support for small businesses, usually individual vendors, specifically in Jamaica. But, even if accepted, the impact of remittances on relieving socio-economic strains improving living standards, and reducing dependence on local government are important to understanding local democracy. Moreover, they help to create a meaningful difference in the quality of life experienced by citizens of the region and other developing countries with seemingly similar economic indicators.

A look at traditional developmental aid to the region also demonstrates the Caribbean region's favorable position and consequent advantage over other Developing countries. The impact of foreign aid on the region itself demonstrates a unique advantage which is derived both from the Caribbean positions in the international arena as former British colonies and commonwealth states and as strategically significant neighbors of the United States of America and, as micro-states.

According to the World Bank reports:

> Net inflows of external financing to the fifteen Caribbean countries which are both members of the Caribbean Group for Cooperation in Economic Development (CGCED) and of the World Bank climbed systematically during the 1970's and until 1982. Between 1978 and 1981 alone they more than doubled, from US $721 million to US $1473... peak(ing) at US $1661 million or US $93 on a per capita basis and equivalent to 7 % of the GNP of the fifteen Caribbean countries. (World Bank, 1992: 41)

The use of the per capita measure of foreign aid and the measure of aid as a percentage of GNP, point to the relevance of this aid to Caribbean micro-states. The World Bank reports:

> The massive inflow of external resources during the initial years of the international economic crisis permitted the Caribbean countries as a whole to absorb the impact of massive external shocks with little consumption losses (OECS countries) and in a few countries was accompanied by the pursuit of growth oriented adjustment policies. (World Bank, 1992: 45)

Although development aid certainly has meaningful impact on the overall development of most countries and subsequently on the standard of living of individuals within these developing states, the national impact of development aid on a dollar-for-dollar basis is multiplied in micro-states. Development projects which in most larger developing countries may have direct impact on particular regions within the state and subsequently trickle out into the rest of the society, may in micro-states serve to benefit entire countries directly, nationally relieving economic strains and improving the general standard of living for all citizens. Again, the implication here is that these economic factors may generate significant differences in the socio-economic realities of citizens throughout the Caribbean region which influence and in effect buffer the impact of stagnant or declining GNP's and therefore generate differences in their responses to these economic pressures as implied in the World Bank report cited above.

Among some of the other socio-economic buffers are the "systems of political patronage" referred to by Dominguez, which allow for a more equitable distribution of resources to members of the population through government subsidized industries, distribution of contract and, the availability of civil service jobs. The overall result of these factors on micro-states and on the Caribbean has been the maintenance of a relatively high standard of living for these territories despite their limited resources. Furthermore, these economic factors have helped to sustain the region through various global economic downturns. Additional factors, including the region's favorable trading status with the EU, have also helped to enhance the region's economic performance in terms of its GNP per capita. The consequence for democratic development is that the citizens of the English-speaking Caribbean have never undergone the strains of true economic crisis and poverty which have been lingering legacies in some other areas of the world.

Given the failure on Dominguez's part to consider these similarities, it is difficult to accept the comparative conclusions he generates. It is not clear that his dismissal of economic causal factors as unrevealing is valid. Likewise, it is unclear that the region's democratic success is in fact an anomaly or a surprise. A more effective comparative analysis could be established by either incorporating these economic considerations into his analysis or by establishing a comparative analysis based upon states with greater socio-economic similarity. In the case of the latter, a comparative analysis between micro-states in the Caribbean and Pacific regions may prove more enlightening.

As the World Bank's 1991 report "Pacific Island Economies: Toward Higher Growth in the 1990's" establishes:

> The six world bank Pacific Island Member Countries (PMC) have achieved relatively high living standards in the face of many constraints. GNP per capita is at the upper-end of the lower to mid income range. Social indicators compare favorably with developing countries at the same or higher levels of income. One disappointing aspect, however is sluggish growth performance in the 1980's despite ... the poor economic performance for the PMC's stands in sharp contrast to the more than 5 percent GNP growth averaged by comparable countries in the Caribbean and the nearly 7 percent growth of the Indian Ocean Islands of Maldives and Mauritius. PMC growth was not as unfavorable, however, as that of many Sub Saharan African countries where dependence on primary exports is similar. (World Bank: 1991)

As this quote suggests, micro-states in the Pacific region, like their Caribbean and Indian Ocean counterparts featured relatively high standards of living during the 1980's and all experienced more favorable economic performance than their Sub Saharan African counterparts. They tend to maintain and bear out economic down turns better than larger states, maintain high standards of living and as the comparison with Sub Saharan economies suggest they fair better given similar economic handicaps.

Other similarities between micro-states can also be drawn upon to support a more effective comparison between micro-states as a means to un-covering the true cause of the Caribbean's democratic success. Like the Caribbean states, Samoa, for example, is heavy dependent upon foreign aid and remittances which help to sustain its relatively high social indicators in light of an otherwise weak economy (World Bank: 1998). Mauritius is one of the few nations in the world which shares a similar colonial history to that of the Caribbean, including ethnic demographics similar to Trinidad and Tobago and Guyana. It is also noteworthy that, like the Caribbean most of the world's micro-states have very stable democratic institutions. These nations therefore sharing more in common provide a better and more reliable universe for comparative studies seeking to answer Dominguez's Caribbean Question.

Militarization.

> *In these territories security has always been limited to passive defense, since none was large enough to project its will beyond its shores (unlike Cuba and, with respect to each other, Haiti and the Dominican Republic)* ... (Linton in Dominguez, Pastor & Worrell (Eds.), 1993: 238)

Young and Phillip (1986) in their summarization of the literature on militarization in Third World states argue that in much of the literature the military is viewed as a professional neutral force, "whose move into politics is the inevitable outcome of civilian irresponsibility or in response to a political vacuum created by political and economic instability"(Young & Phillips (Eds.), 1986) However, when the Caribbean case study is taken into account several other considerations must come into play.

Table 1. <u>Economic Indicators for Developing Countries</u>

Country	GNP Per Capita (US$) 1990*	Population ('000) 1990*	Daily per capita calorie supply as percent of requirements (1980's)**[14]
The Bahamas	11510	249	118
Barbados	6540	257	126
Antigua & Barbuda	4600	79	92
Trinidad & Tobago	3470	1283	126
St. Kitts & Nevis	3330	40	94
Suriname	3050	447	120
Grenada	2120	94	104
Belize	1970	189	114
Dominica	1940	82	100
St. Lucia	1900	150	102
St. Vincent & The Grenadines	1610	114	99

---

[14] This measure of daily per capita calorie supply is utilized here as a representative measure of poverty indicators as presented in the World Bank's "Current Economic Situation, Regional Issues and Capital Flows, 1992"

Country	GNP Per Capita (US$) 1990*	Population ('000) 1990*	Daily per capita calorie supply as percent of requirements (1980's)**[15]
Jamaica	1510	2390	116
Dominican Republic	820	7140	100
Guyana	370	798	108
Haiti	370	6488	84
Mauritius	1,810****		112***
Solomon Islands	960	386.7(1996)	n/a[16]
Federated states of Micronesia	$2,050	110,000	n/a
Republic of Palau	8,000 GDP	18.125 (1996)	n/a
Vanuatu	120	173	n/a
Marshall Islands	1,860 (1996)	58	
Comoros	440****		

---

[15] This measure of daily per capita calorie supply is utilized here as a representative measure of poverty indicators as presented in the World Bank's "Current Economic Situation, Regional Issues and Capital Flows, 1992"

[16] n/a indicates that data was not available

Country	GNP Per Capita (US$) 1990*	Population ('000) 1990*	Daily per capita calorie supply as percent of requirements (1980's)**[17]
Maldives	410****		
Sao Tome & Principe	240****		
Seychelles	3,800****		
Kiribati	870(1996)	81.6(1996)	
Tonga	800****/		
1,640 (1996)	106 (1996)		
Marshall Islands	1,860	58	
Western Samoa	580****		
Columbia*****	2,000	35,900 (1996)	
Botswana*****	2,600	1,330 (1996)	
Namibia*****	2,000	1,590 (1996)	
Burkina Faso*****	200	9,850	

*Source: Social Indicators of Development, World Bank; Demographic and Health Surveys[17]

** Source: Social Indicators of Development 1990, World Bank; UNICEF Barbados

***Source: National Development Plan, 1988-90, Ministry of Economic Planning and Development Vol 1. P.26

****Source: International Economic Department, World Bank; 1988 or most recent data

*****Source: Economic Intelligence Unit, 1996

---

[17] This measure of daily per capita calorie supply is utilized here as a representative measure of poverty indicators as presented in the World Bank's "Current Economic Situation, Regional Issues and Capital Flows, 1992"

As Neville Linton's quote suggests, despite Dominguez's comparison of militarization in the region to that of larger states such as Guatemala, the region's forces are small and even less well equipped. A major factor ignored by Dominguez in his discussion on the impact of militarization on democratic stability, is that beyond the size of the military forces, consideration must be given to the viability of military units and the overall influence of the military on the political process. These considerations account for the ability and practicality of military interventions into domestic politics.

In states where there exist credible threats to national security, military institutions develop into viable entities, characterized by size, accessibility of resources and relatively high levels of organization. As in the case of Brazil, Ethiopia and Nigeria, the military may then be viewed as a viable entity, well suited to the role of arbitrating domestic political stalemates or for serving as interim administrative organs in periods of political breakdown. (Cohen, 1994; Lefort, 1983) In other cases, military units may become politicized and through their own strength serve to undermine and /or

Table 2: Size of Various Security Forces in the Eastern Caribbean 1984[18]

Country	Defense	Reserves	Police	Police Special Service Department	Coast Guard
Antigua	6	0	350	55	19
Barbados	270	250	1,500	50	90
Dominica	0	0	375	80	25
St. Kitts	0	0	300	30	0
St. Lucia	0	0	425	80	23
St. Vincent	0	0	420	65	25

---

[18] Taken from Militarization in the Non-Hispanic Caribbean. *Original source U.S. House of Representatives, Armed Services Committee (1984)*

overthrow established governments. In 1969, for example highly politicized members of the military, some with expressed ambitions of contesting the presidency, carried out a bloody coup in Bolivia in the absence of the country's president. (Lloyd, 1971: 11)

For most of the Caribbean region, and in particular, the English-speaking Caribbean, no real and credible threat has been formulated against national security in a manner supportive of granting the military apparatus of the various nations an increase in influence, leverage, legitimacy or strength sufficient for them to pose a credible threat of military take over. In reality, the military apparatus of most Caribbean countries is to a great extent decorative and in the words of Anthony Payne (1993), "characterized more by their weakness (indeed, its nonexistence in some territories, such as Dominica and St. Kitts) than by its predatory instincts". As Phillips notes, for example, of the 3,370 police in the Eastern Caribbean only about 10 percent have any paramilitary training. (Phillips, In Young & Phillips, (Eds.) 1986: 58)

Dominguez's use of militarization statistics in Barbados, for example, demonstrates the fallacy of un- contextualized statistics. As Neville Linton discusses in his chapter in the Dominguez book, Barbados' initial establishment and consequent rise in militarization was in part inspired by a series of subversive political challenges to the region, including the attempted invasions of Barbados in 1976 and 1979 by Sidney Burnett-Alleyne and a band of 260 men, a series of insurrection attempts in Dominica and St. Vincent and a claim of a coup plot in Antigua. According to Dion Phillips, the position of Prime Minister Adams and the BLP in the September 1976 general elections was strongly opposed to the establishment of a standing army declaring that "the defense forces will be limited to such as are adequate to maintain law and order" (Phillips, In Young and Phillips (Eds.), 1986: 46). However, Phillips points out the leadership took a converse position in its 1981 election stating, "events within Barbados, the Caribbean and elsewhere, have proved the need for Barbados to have a limited defense Force with the capacity to withstand the immediate assault of potential marauders, terrorists and mercenaries".

Militarization in Barbados however, occurred in the context and partly in the shadow of two other major regional security developments. 1. The development of the US Joint Task Force and 2. The development of the Regional Security Service. Both of these developments in the Caribbean strategy for security helped to forge and temper the development of militarization in Barbados.

In October 1979 the Carter Administration established the Caribbean Joint Task Force with headquarters in Key West Florida. In the words of Joint Chief of Staff David C. Jones, "the Caribbean was becoming part of a comprehensive strategic vision that integrated regional issues within the larger global framework," (Young & Phillips (Eds.), 1986: 53) and, thus the United States increased its military presence in the region and cemented its leading role in providing for regional security against external forces. In the same year, under the leadership of Barbados' Tom Adams, the Regional Security System was established. The Regional Security System, which was formalized in 1982, under a memorandum of understanding signed by the governments of Barbados, St. Vincent/Grenadines, St. Lucia, Dominica, Antigua/Barbuda, and, later expanded to include all the English-speaking territories of the Eastern Caribbean negated the need for any singular territory to develop a full standing army. The cooperative spirit of the Regional Security System also placed Barbados military development in a supra-national context and under the regional scrutiny. "The main objective of the RSS is to coordinate the multiple security systems in the Eastern Caribbean by means of an international organization" (Phillips, In Young & Phillips (Eds.), 1986: 54), the central liaison office which solicits authorization and approval from all member governments for the deployment and use of force. Furthermore, as Adams argued, the existence of "one regional army, rather than a number of national armies would give *the region* an additional safeguard, namely, the protection of small governments against their own forces" (Phillips, In Young & Phillips (Eds.), 1986: 58). As early as 1979, the newly formed Barbadian military was engaged in supporting neighboring countries in the maintenance of stability[19]. Yet despite the rapid rise in Barbadian militarization in its earliest years pointed to by Dominguez, the country has experienced no subsequent threats to its national security and its military has, to a great extent, functioned as an extension of the local police forces, assisting with the tracking, and detaining of escaped convicts and as a regional peace keeping force assisting in putting down minor threats to the national security of other territories.

The Caribbean's position in the international arena, defined first by its continued relationship with the former European colonial nations and by its strategic positioning in the hegemonic confines of the United States of America as established in the Monroe Doctrine of 1824, provides Caribbean countries with a sense of military security against external invasion which is unparalleled anywhere else in the developing world.[20] A brief analysis of the national security threats to all the Caribbean states demonstrates the role of foreign powers in protecting the security of the region. In 1969 the black power revolt in Curacao was put down in part by the Dutch Marines, the 1970 black power revolt in Trinidad and Tobago was foiled in part by the US and Venezuelan armed forces and the Burnett Alleyne invasion was preempted by the French military. Similarly, both Guyana and Belize in their border disputes with neighboring Venezuela and Suriname and Guatemala, relied heavily on the support of neighboring countries Brazil and Mexico for both diplomatic and military support in the resolution and/or containment of

---

[19] In December 1979 Barbados' military assisted St. Vincent in the suppression of the Union Island Rebellion.

[20] This fact of course continues to raise issues of sovereignty for the Caribbean nations particularly as it relates to the United States.

these disputes. The Anlgo-Caribbean therefore has existed in a strong sense of external military security defined by its geographic location and strategic significance to the United States, its ongoing favorable relationship with European Powers and a historical sense of security in relation to one another.

This external sense of military security is reinforced by the sense of regional cooperation embodied in the region's continued commitment to CARICOM and the OECS. Walter Kennes (2000), for example, notes that "while peace is a precondition for successful integration, the success of integration itself tends to contribute to the consolidation of peace and helps to avoid renewed conflict" (Kennes, 2000: 53). The Caribbean case study seems to reinforce this notion. As Neville Linton notes:

> the government of Tom Adams in Barbados took the forefront in advocating regional cooperation (in security) by calling for joint coast guard patrols with Antigua, St. Lucia and St. Vincent ... following its agreement with other regional governments on joint coast guard patrols, Barbados sought to upgrade its military establishment, and Britain agreed to provide coast guard training and assistance... in October 1982 ... the Eastern Caribbean Regional Security System (RSS) was established by an MOU (Memorandum of Understanding) ... the member states were Antigua and Barbuda, Barbados, Dominica, St' Lucia and St. Vincent and the Grenadines. The agreement was for cooperation to provide for "mutual assistance on request" in "national emergencies, prevention of smuggling, search and rescue, immigration control, maritime policing policies .... and natural and other disasters and threats to national security. (Linton, In Dominguez, Pastor & Worrell (Eds.), 1993: 240)

The military role of the RSS has therefore from its conception been one of preserving the democratic tradition and not one of protecting the people from hostile external forces. This cooperative spirit is relevant in a number of ways. First, the Caribbean territories, with the exceptions of Guyana and Belize, discussed above, exist in a sphere of friendly, cooperative, and supportive micro-states, and as the quote at the beginning of this section suggests, no credible threat exists from neighboring states. Furthermore, the need for any single territory in the region to develop a sizeable and, therefore potential dangerous military establishment is alleviated. In the case of Dominica for example with its attempted coups in 1981, following which the military was disbanded, it is clearly demonstrated that the military's function was deemed and proven unnecessary for securing national security. Finally, and perhaps most importantly, there is the mutual reinforcement of democratic ideals and the potential for the isolation of "rogue" nations in an increasingly integrated and mutually dependent regional and global environment.

The active role of fellow CARICOM states in the military intervention of Grenada was in many ways a milestone for the region. Although their military role was limited, their support, and in fact, advocacy and invitation, of the invasion is testimony to the regions internal checks and balances which help to ensure compliance with the established democratic status quo. The culmination of the Caribbean's unique positioning within the hemispheric confines of the United States of America and its regional spirit has created an unprecedented international environment in which the prospects for the establishment of non-democratic regimes are slim.

A more credible analysis of the case for or against militarization as a contributing factor to the Caribbean's democratic tradition, must therefore take into consideration not just the size of the military, but also the role and function of the military within the state. Where military takeovers have traditionally occurred, they are usually conducted by viable military structures capable of defending themselves and their right to assume power. Thus even in incidents of civil war where dual sovereignty is established, military units must, minimally, be able to control and defend territory against other groups simultaneously claiming to be the sovereign power. In the Caribbean case-study it is clear that such military establishments are lacking.

This however does not absolve the military establishments of the region from involvement in anti-democratic activity. Several territories have demonstrated instances of anti-democratic activity on the part of the local armed forces: Dominica in 1981, Grenada, under the Gairy Administration, Guyana under Forbes Burnham[21] and Trinidad and Tobago during the Black Power Revolts. The Dominican case was short lived and consisted of two inter-related incidents. In the case of both Grenada and Guyana, the militarization of the population was directly connected to the increasing authoritarianism of the respective regimes. The Trinidadian case consisted of mutiny in the midst of major social unrest. These instances illustrate that despite its inherent advantages, the territories of the region are nonetheless susceptible to some of the same threats experienced in other developing nations. What differs is the scale on which these instances occur and the potential for such instances to develop into the socially and politically disastrous condition common in other regions of the world.

Common Forces Limited opportunities

> *The record is discouraging: is the Caribbean, but for*
> *the grace of God, not unlike Latin America and the rest*

---

[21]   In the case of Grenada and Guyana, many of the abuses were not conducted by the official military apparatus, but by secret police in the case of Grenada and smaller militia groups in the case of Guyana

of the Third World? (Dominguez. In Dominguez,
Pastor & Worrell (Eds.), 1993: 9)

The answer to Dominguez's question is both Yes and No. Yes, the Caribbean is in many way subject to some of the same forces which have plagued other developing countries. A close look at the region's history demonstrates that in fact the Caribbean has manifested many of the destabilizing characteristics of other less successful democracies around the world, albeit on a smaller and more confined scale. What is lacking in the Caribbean region is a pattern of sustained, large scale subversion capable of destabilizing the region's democratic regimes[22].

An insightful start to this discussion is the realization that the inherent weakness of the Caribbean military establishments does not necessarily imply a total absence of subversive potential. After all, given the small size of the Caribbean territories, the military requirements necessary to affect a coup, or other subversive acts, are themselves relatively small. The various military organs throughout the Caribbean region have on occasion demonstrated some of the subversive tendencies which have proven catastrophic in other parts of the World. Where there have been conscious efforts to establish viable military establishments (Trinidad and Tobago, Jamaica, Guyana, Grenada) due to credible threats to national security from both internal and external forces or as a means of supporting regimes with questionable legitimacy, the military has at times contributed to the political instability of those territories. Table 3 provides a brief listing of some of the instances in which political violence has manifested itself in Caribbean politics. The following brief summaries highlight instances in which Caribbean politics has demonstrated some of

---

[22] The exception to this is the recent increase in drug trafficking which has plagued the region and which is primarily based in the activities of large Latin American drug cartels, with financial and military resources far exceeding those of the region.

the patterns which have in other regions contributed to failure or collapse of democracy.[23]

Table 3. Political Violence in the English-Speaking Caribbean

Year	Country	Incident	Description/Comments
1934-38	Entire region except Barbados	Labor Unrest	Labor unrest sweeps through the Caribbean region as workers fight for improved working conditions, British government creates commission to investigate the unrest.
1938	Jamaica	Frome Riots	Part of the series of labor sponsored demonstration for better working conditions; required the introduction of British troops, regular police and special constabulary forces to contain violence and destruction of property.
1960	Jamaica	Henry Rebellion	Attempted coup organized by Jamaican national in Jamaica and New York. Operation was foiled by a combination of JA and US police forces
1961	Guyana	Politically motivated violence	Following the 1953, 1957 and 1961 victories of Cheddi Jagan under the PPP, the PNC with support from the US and British Governments, embarked on series of subversive activities including the use of orchestrated demonstrations, strikes, arson, intimidation and constitutional reforms aimed at blocking PPP's ability to rule. State of emergency is declared and British troops are requested to restore order.

---

[23] These summaries are not full case studies and do not cover all instances of political violence or otherwise potentially subversive activities. Key instances were chose as examples to illustrate the tendency towards such activity.

Year	Country	Incident	Description/Comments
1963	Jamaica	Coral Gardens uprising	Raid carried out on petrol station, eight people killed including two police officers. Not believed to have been politically motivated, but became a prominent issue in the political arena over several social issues including police tactics.
1963	Guyana	Operation Withdrawal	Armed groups and individuals associated with the People's Progressive Party (PPP) and GAWU (trade union base of the PPP use violent forms of intimidation to undermine the strength of rival MPCA.
1965	Jamaica	Anti-Chinese Riots	Most violent manifestation of an on-going tension between creole Jamaicans and Chinese immigrants dating back to 1911 with previous violent manifestations in the 1920's and in 1938. Hundreds of locals involved in attacks on Chinese immigrants over a period of two days, six people killed. Often believed to be a pre-cursor to gang warfare in Western Kingston area. Local politicians declared the attacks to be the work of rival political gangs.

Year	Country	Incident	Description/Comments
1966	Jamaica	Extended series of politically motivated strikes	Strikes persist from Mid-April -Mid June. Include: Kingston waterfront; major sugar estates (including Barnard Lodge, Appleton, Worthy Park, United Estates and Innswood); big hotels (including the Island Inn and Montego Beach Hotel); the *Daily Gleaner* (4 weeks); municipal cleaning workers; banana dock workers; Post office workers; Jamaica Public Service Company (electricity workers); the KSAC Fire Brigade (go-slow, not full strike); the Jamaica Teachers Association (3 day island wide strike); the Kaiser Bauxite housing project; construction workers at the national Stadium and New port West; Montego Bay bus strike. Mid May represents first recorded reports of politically defined gangs utilizing tactics of intimidation against rival groups.
1966-67	Jamaica	Political warfare	Establishment of political gangs in February/March 1966 leads to declaration of state of emergency in October 1966. Violence subsides after polling day February 1967.

Year	Country	Incident	Description/Comments
1968	Jamaica	Rodney Riots	Following the Jamaican Governments decision to refuse entry into the country of University Professor, black nationalist and black power advocate Walter Rodney into Jamaica, a series of protests organized by college students and other supporters develop into rioting throughout Kingston. Police used tear gas and riot squads to break up demonstrations. The university grounds are closed and cordoned off.
1970	Trinidad and Tobago	Black Power Revolts & Military Mutiny	Student organized march demonstrating against conviction of students in Toronto Canada, and dominance of foreign companies in local economy, transforms into violent confrontation with local forces. Increased politicization of conflict and attempts to involve the local military units leads to mutiny and military takeover of a local base. U. S. and Venezuelan troops respond with military blockade and offers for military intervention.

Year	Country	Incident	Description/Comments
1972-73	Trinidad and Tobago	NUFF Guerilla movement	Small band of guerilla fighters, (National United Freedom Fighters, NUFF) in part trained by members of the 1970 mutinous units of local military, carry out series of attacks against local officials, with declared goal of destabilizing government and fomenting national revolutionary insurrection.
1973	Grenada	Government sponsored attacks on members of the NJM (*Bloody Sunday*)	Government sponsored attacks were waged against the newly emerging NJM, including the murder of Jeremiah Richardson, shooting of Matthew Joseph, several beatings of known members. Key events include: On April 22, secret police open fire on unarmed demonstrators. November 18, secret police, under supervision of senior police officers, severely beat six members of NJM in protest against Gairy government (Bloody Sunday). January 21 in an effort to break up anti-government strikes and demonstrations armed police attack demonstrators and kill one demonstrator linked to NJM, whose store is subsequently looted by police.

Year	Country	Incident	Description/Comments
1978	Grenada	**Public posting of union leaders' names at government sponsored rally calls for aggressive and violent tactics to uproot Union leaders**	This incident occurred in the midst of a major union dispute with the government and followed the murder of a government minister Innocent Belmar. Gairy is quoted as saying "this is the last strike these union leaders will ever organize"
1979	Grenada	**Grenadian Revolution Begins**	Gairy's government is overthrown in an armed seizure of power.
1979	Jamaica	**Gas Price Protests**	Protest organized by the National Patriotic Movement, an offshoot of the JLP, force government to relinquish new tax to be added to gasoline prices
1979	St. Vincent	**Union Island Uprising**	Barbados sends troops to quell the unrest.
1979	Grenada	**Grenadian Revolution**	Leftist revolutionaries overthrow government and establish the People's Revolutionary Government.
1980	Grenada	**Attempted assassination of PRG top leadership**	June 19, 1980, a bomb exploded under a platform where almost the entire top leadership of the People's Revolutionary Government was assembled. Three young women were killed and almost one hundred (100) people injured

Year	Country	Incident	Description/Comments
1980	Grenada	**Bombing and Assassination**	Following the Budhlall Gang incident (3 weeks later), A bomb was detonated n Queen's Park. Stran Phillips, conspirator in the Budhlall rebellion, is shot nineteen times by PRG army troops.
1980	Grenada	**Budhlall Gang**	PRG launches a series of arrests on former members who sought to establish a separate agricultural collective. The act was in fact an attempt to push PRG towards more favorable policies. In response, brother of an arrested member and Army Commander of one of the PRG's units, plans an armed rebellion against PRG. The rebellion is foiled and the leader arrested. Other members of the gang however remained at large for several months launching a series of guerilla attacks and bombings on army troops
1981	Dominica	**Attempted coup**	Members of the local defense force, loyal to the opposition party make two separate attempts to overthrow the established government. Both plots were foiled and the defense force disbanded.
1983	Grenada	**Assassination/ Massacre**	Maurice Bishop is brutally killed by defecting members of his own PRG.

Year	Country	Incident	Description/Comments
1985	Jamaica	Riots	Two days of demonstrations in which roads were blocked with piles of debris and cars and property burned amidst several confrontations between protestors and the security forces. Seven people killed and fifteen wounded. PNP grants unofficial support to 'spontaneous demonstrations" against JLP economic policies
1990	Trinidad and Tobago	Jamaat Al Muslimeen Insurrection/ coup	Members of a local mosque raid the parliamentary building holding members of parliament hostage including the prime minister of Trinidad and Tobago, who is shot and wounded during the incident

As the Table 3 suggests, the post-independence Caribbean has in fact had its share of political violence and social unrest with instances ranging in intensity from riots to attempted coups and revolutions.

The Role of Citizen Driven Social Unrest in the Caribbean's Democratic Tradition

It is apparent that despite Dominguez's claims of an overwhelming commitment to democratic ideals, and patterns of resistance against centralized power, members of the Caribbean citizenry were willing to engage in activities with the conscious goal of undermining stability and subverting the democratic process.

Dominguez's assertion that historical patterns of societal resistance against centralized power have meaningful bearing on the development of the Caribbean's democratic character is a significant step towards understanding the pattern and role of citizen driven political violence in the region. In addition to the patterns of societal resistance personified by the Maroon societies of Jamaica and Guyana and the common use of music and folklore as political tools to spawn debates and consequently influence democratic processes, another pattern of societal resistance involving the use controlled political violence in a democratic context can be identified as emerging in the post emancipation period. Post emancipation Caribbean history demonstrates a pattern of resistance which has traditionally involved the utilization of traditional mechanisms for the redress of grievance, coupled and supported by the threat and/or use of violent resistance dating back to the Morant Bay Rebellion of 1865 for the English-speaking Caribbean and the Haitian Revolution of 1797-1804 for the larger region.

The Morant Bay Rebellion (1865), the first major uprising in the post-emancipation English- speaking Caribbean, represented a landmark in the history of Caribbean democratic development. Beyond its impact on the Caribbean's old representative system, which was dismantled and replaced with Crown Colony, or direct colonial rule, in the immediate aftermath, the events of 1865 represent a blueprint for social movements, demands for fundamental rights and the redress of grievances in the region. As Putnam suggests, "The key characteristic of a democracy is the continuing responsiveness of the government to the preferences of its citizens," (Putnam, 1993) and in the Caribbean region the preferences of the people have, beginning with the Morant Bay Rebellion[24], been expressed in democratic terms with the implicit and actual threat of violence.

One of the most interesting features of the Morant Bay Rebellion was the overwhelming confidence displayed by its leadership in the ability of the society to reform itself through established channels or democratic means. Paul Bogle, a local Baptist preacher and George William Gordon, a wealthy landowner of mixed ancestry and member of the local parliament, took up the banner of land reform in Jamaica, seeking the release of crown land to landless peasants. The local legislature had passed a series of laws from the 1830's onwards limiting the access of the recently freed slaves to land by raising the prices of land to astronomical levels and by limiting the amount of land which could be purchased by people of color. Despite the obvious bias of the local legislature and the British Crown against granting access to land to former slaves, whose labor was required to maintain the faltering sugar industry, both leaders worked collaboratively to petition the local legislative body, the local representative of the Crown (Governor Eyre) and the Crown itself for land reform policies.

Having failed to gain a favorable response, and in face of a series of attacks launched by Governor Eyre against those proponents of such reform, landless peasants engaged in an organized demonstration against the governor and local Magistrates overseeing the case of several dissidents. Under orders from the Magistrate local militia attempted to break up the demonstration forcibly and as a result a struggle ensued between the demonstrators and the court guards. In the process of this clash, the court house was set afire and nineteen whites including the chief magistrate were killed. In retaliation for this the Governor declared martial law, activated the local militia and requested military support from British troops. In the hunt

---

[24]   Arguably this may be extended to the Haitian Revolution

for participants and supporters for the rebellion approximately 1500 former slaves were killed and hundreds of homes burnt to the ground. In the following year the British Crown, fearing repeats of the incident and, particularly fearing, an increased influence in the local legislature of sympathetic representatives such as William Gordon in the local legislature, abolished the Old Representative System and instituted Crown Colony rule.

Analysis of events of political violence in the Caribbean reveal a similar pattern of resistance from leaders of mass movements from the Labor Riots of the 1930's to the riots and demonstrations which rocked Jamaica in the 1990's. The evidence suggests that the voice of the Caribbean's citizens has often held violent undertones and that at key points in the region's history have helped forge the formation of a responsive democracy. What is also revealing about the pattern of political violence is that in most cases political unrest has not been aimed at the general overthrow of governments or the revolutionary restructuring of the political system[25]. Rather a distinctive characteristic of Caribbean political violence is that it has traditionally been aimed at specific grievances to which the people, en masse, demand redress. As a result, political regimes have learned that, to be good democracies, by which we mean to be responsive to the demands of the people, allows for the continuation of rule, while failure on this level may be political suicide.

In his analysis of the assault on the Trinidadian government in 1990, for example, Selwyn Ryan notes that:

> Some deny that Bakr[26] in fact had any blueprint
> at all as to the kind of society he wished to

---

[25] The exceptions here are the Grenada Revolution and the Black Power Revolt in Trinidad and Tobago. *See Table 2*

[26] Leader of the Muslim revolt and armed attack on the House of Parliament.

> put in place of the old if he had succeeded in
> seizing power, and argue instead that his sole
> aim was to stop the NAR from demolishing the
> Mosque and other structures which housed his
> commune at No. 1 Mucurapo which he had built
> without authorization between 1983 and 1990. ...
> whatever the underlying economic and social
> factors and circumstances which prompted Abu
> Bakr to intervene militarily in Trinidad's politics,
> and whatever long term plans he might have
> entertained ... there is little doubt that it was the
> bitterness engendered by the prolonged dispute
> which he had with the municipal and state
> authorities over that piece of state land which
> triggered the crisis. (Ryan, 1991: 14)

The land in dispute was offered to the Islamic Missionary Guild in 1969 for the purpose of constructing an Islamic Cultural Center for the propagation of Islam. A lack of internal cohesion within the guild prevented the formal transfer of the land and in the 1970's Abu Bakr and group of African Muslims began to utilize the land for the established purpose, without formal title to the property.

Beginning in 1984, Abu Bakr's Jamaat al Muslimeen organization began construction of a mosque, school and other community oriented facilities on the property. In December of that year a formal challenge was raised seeking an injunction forbidding the Jamaat al Muslimeen from continuing construction. The court's ruling not only forbade the continued construction, but also ordered the demolition of the existing structures. In 1985, the court found Abu Bakr to be in contempt of court for his continued construction on the property despite the court's previous ruling. To avoid arrest Abu Bakr organized a demonstration including Islamic youth and women against his arrest. The police, seeking to avoid conflict, retreated without carrying out the arrest.

> The land issue remained more or less in abeyance until 1987 when the NAR sought to resolve the issue. In its Manifesto, the NAR had promised that "all squatters on State and State enterprises land will be given a moratorium period in which not a single house will be demolished." One is not certain whether this amnesty applied to the Jamaat, but Bakr assumed it did. After some initial hesitating, the Prime Minister agreed that the Jamaat's tenure should be regularized and the Ministry of Local Government and Community Development was advised to do so (Ryan, 1991: 21)

Despite the apparent agreement between the Jamaat al Muslimeen and the government, the organization continued to be a victim of continued police investigation. Charges of subversive action were levied against the group and its leadership with particular interest in extended visits to Libya for military training and for other purposes which were not innocuous. Police searched the facility on November 16th and December 2nd, 1988 finding no evidence of illegal or subversive activity. In April 1990, during the month of Ramadan, the Minister of Justice and National Security, Mr. Selwyn Richardson, order the installation of over 100 army and police officers on the land and announced his attention to demolish the property on the grounds of the 1985 injunction. The Jamaat al Muslimeen launched a legal battle to halt the demolition on the ground that:

7. It was unlawful for the government to demolish such structures without getting an order from the court under the Public Health Act and the Town and Country Planning Act

8. The Jamaat al Muslimeen had spent in excess of TT $3 million filling and preparing the land, and constructing the structures

9. A legitimate expectation of it being granted the land had been created.

With legal proceeding still pending the Jamaat al Muslimeen was given seven days to evacuate the premises, a period ending one day prior to the court appointment. In light of previous demolition of other property belonging to the organization:

> Attacks on the IMF and the NAR were also leveled by Bakr at the Labor Day Rally in Fyzabd on July 19, a rally that was said to be one of the largest seen for some time. Bakr was lustily applauded and one trade unionist over heard one of Bakr's lieutenants remarking that "we must take out these guys (i.e. the NAR soon." (Ryan, 1991: 25-26)

On July 27, Abu Bakr and a small band of armed men raided the parliamentary building holding the Prime Minister and several members of parliament hostage. The 1990 armed insurrection is often treated as an anomaly, an extreme and frightening case, but as John La Guerre concludes, "the Jamaat al Muslimeen was a social movement operating very much like the NJAC (National Joint Action Committee) did during the period 1970-72" (Laguerre, 1991: 53), the NJM leading up to the Grenadian Revolution and other social movements dating back to the Morant Bay Rebellion. Although lacking the level of mass support which accompanied the Morant Bay Rebellion, the civil unrest at the turn of the century for improved social conditions, the Labor Riots of the 1930's, Rodney riots or the Black Power Revolt of 1970, the case of the Jamaat al Muslimeen insurrection demonstrates the pattern of democratic and judicial appeal, with the implicit threat and use of civil unrest. The Jamaat al Muslimeen resistance of the arrest of Abu Bakr, and the eventual "coup" of 1990 therefore represents the most modern manifestation of the Caribbean's inherent use of political violence in a democratic context.

The Caribbean's overall democratic development was gradual, and it took place in transitional stages. It is enlightening to note that at each stage of its development it has been pushed forward by the will of the people often expressed through political violence. Key points in this development include the Haitian Revolution (abolition of the slave trade), Baptist Day Revolt (emancipation proclamation), the Morant Bay Rebellion (end of Representative government and the beginning of dialogue on the development of the Black population), the unrest of the early twentieth century (various commissions advocating social reform in education, housing, health service), the labor riots of the 1930's (Workers' rights and recognition of unions and the struggle for universal adult suffrage). This distinctive pattern of political behavior has not undergone systematic study by most scholars and rather the instances are treated simply as isolated instances of social unrest. However, a closer study of this pattern as a legitimate and integral aspect of the democratic character of the region's democratic tradition may in many ways serve to explain the short - term nature of the political violence in the region. The pattern seems to suggest that unrest in the region tends to be geared at specific grievances, towards specific goals, and that upon official response to these grievances the societies are quick to return to the status quo. Because of this characteristic of citizen driven social unrest, and in particular because it disallows the development of broadly expressed grievances which are more prone to produce more radical aims of overthrowing governments, the long-term effects on the continuity of democratic tradition are limited. Furthermore, the sense of legitimacy associated with these periodic outbursts as part of a pattern of development and a legitimate means of seeking responsive government allows for short healing periods amongst the region citizens.

Towards a Clearer Understanding of Caribbean Democracy.

A common mistake made by those who study the region is their treatment of the Caribbean territories individually. The result is that as compared to larger states, each individual territory in the region appears to have only a few isolated incidents of political violence. The consequence of this is that, as with Dominguez, one is driven to believe that there is in fact a Caribbean surprise and that the region is inherently peaceful. However, when the region is looked at as a whole, as in Table 3 *above*, a new picture of the Caribbean emerges demonstrating that the in fact the Caribbean's history of political violence and social unrest is comparable to that of many of the larger developing nations often labeled as unstable.

The micro- states of the Caribbean have been traditionally viewed as stable and peaceful democracies and when compared to their African, and South and Central American counterparts, they individually do indeed appear to be remarkably stable. Governments change hands between opposition parties on a regular basis. Elections are conducted fairly and regularly. Opposition leaders are usually allowed to play their roles in the legislative bodies. Coups, military juntas, revolutions and civil wars are infrequent. Yet, viewed as a single unit, the Caribbean's record of political violence and civil unrest is in some ways as disturbing as that of any of its larger counterparts of comparable size. The Caribbean has clearly displayed many of the potentially dangerous tendencies towards political violence that other Third World countries wrestle with, albeit it on a "micro- scale". What seems to differ between Caribbean states and other developing countries is the nonexistence of sustained large scale political violence. This difference must therefore provide the basis for the development of a new Caribbean question; why is the region less prone to these forms of political violence?

This paper's treatment of democratic development provides some insight into the answers to this question. Despite the emergence of critical moments in the region's history where the potential for political crisis, violence and possibly democratic collapse have emerged, this potential for growth into long-term sustained resistance is limited by several inherent characteristics of the region.

The Caribbean's development provided it with several preconditioned advantages to successful democracy. The establishment of a near homogenous colonial identity and the elimination of all other competing identities created an environment conducive to nation building. As a part of this process the Caribbean over the process of three hundred years was integrated into the European driven development of western democratic ideals. The growth and development of the free black population also allowed for the emergence in the pre- and post-emancipation period of a colored elite, well-educated and integrated in the European colonial value system, many of whom following the collapse of the sugar industry became the dominant local elite. No other developing nations, with the exception of Mauritius and some of the pacific micro-states, share a similar colonial history of development. This history of development inclined Caribbean nations towards western democratic models and allowed them to avoid many of the pains of nation building experienced by emerging nations in the twentieth century.

On another level, the region also possesses other inherent advantages which hinder broad based social grievances associated with high levels of political instability. Economic buffers help to shelter members of the population from the pains of economic crisis and have allowed the region's territories to experience standards of living higher than most other developing nations around the world. As Dominguez and Payne suggest connections into the political establishment through patronage, are an important source of support and have the consequence of making average citizens feel connected to the political establishment. It is however noteworthy that this particular system patronage, which allows for the distribution of income and resources and the subsidizing of various industries, is harshly criticized by international funding agencies such as the World Bank and the International Monetary Fund and that in their various agreements with these agencies Caribbean nations are under great pressure to reduce this practice.

From the 19th century onwards the English-speaking Caribbean has been without major instances of war and exist in peaceful co-existence with their neighbors. In fact beyond this Caribbean nations have over the past fifty years made considerable strides towards regionalism and integration. An important consequence of this is that despite Dominguez's misleading claims of high rates of militarization the Caribbean territories remain for most part de-militarized in any meaningful way. This military weakness makes the potential for successful military takeovers slim. Additionally, various regional and international checks and balances exist to enhance the region's sense of security considering their military weakness and to encourage the pursuit of democratic ideals.

Also, although personalistic, family dominated politics, with decades of rule by single parties and individual heads of state, continues to be a trade mark of Caribbean democracy, the authoritarian style of Gairy and Burnham appear to have been isolated extremes of this pattern. Inter-party violence has traditionally been isolated to only a handful of territories (Jamaica, Guyana, Grenada) and over the past decade each have made steps towards drastically reducing these practices. Citizen driven social unrest in its traditional pattern, although disruptive, does not seem to pose a major threat to the overall democratic process although as the events in Trinidad and Tobago in 1990 seem to suggest the potential engendered in it.

Towards a better Social Science Approach

The argument for the treatment of Caribbean nations as a single unit for the sake of such comparisons is that 1. Their socio-economic and political structures are remarkably similar, 2. Given their historical tendency towards federation and other forms of regional cooperation (CARICOM and OECS), the notion of a united Caribbean region is neither foreign nor unrealistic and in fact is an expressed goal for the region[27] 3. In many arenas the region already operates as an integrated unit, particularly in the delivery of specialized services, the removal of trade tariffs, the free movement of labor and often in their interaction with the larger with the international community.

Alternatively, studies which aim at inter-regional studies must take into consideration the particularities of the different regions and their development. Likewise, the assumption that micro-states experience similar phenomenon in the same manner as large states is misleadingly false. Special consideration must be given to the specific experiences of micro-states and there is a specific need for comparative studies across micro-states world-wide.

---

[27]   West Indian Commission

CHAPTER 3

"Is the United States of America a Participatory Democracy?"

For centuries man has debated the ordering of society, the distribution of power and systems of governance as a necessary part of understanding the very nature of our being and to the end of living the "good life". Throughout history, different systematic structures of governance have been advocated as superior and most desirable for the protection of the rights and interests of the members of the society. This paper concentrates on Democracy as one such structure of order and governance.

Democracy, once labeled by some of history's great thinkers, including Plato, as the worst form of government possible, has come today, to be viewed as the most desirable means of governmental representation. Leading the charge in this democratization of the world, is the United States. This paper will examine the actualization of democracy in the United States of America to ascertain the degree to which the democratic ideal has been realized, and, in doing so, attempt to answer the question, "is the United States of America a participatory democracy?" This paper will argue that despite its numerous shortcomings the United States is in fact a participatory democracy and furthermore, that its true democratic strengths are better understood by other standards of the democratic ideal.

Democracy, as an ideal, may be best defined in the adage, "government of the People, by the People, for the People." A clearer distinction can be taken from Aristotle in saying that "democracy exists wherever the free born are sovereign, and that oligarchy exists wherever the rich are sovereign." Democracy expresses the ideal of the people having a direct and/or indirect say in determining the decisions of the state, and thus themselves, both domestically and in their relations with other states. It allows the people the opportunity to ensure that their views and interests are being taken into consideration in the policy making process and also gives the people the power of review. The people impact decision making through periodic elections in which they may, in the case of direct democracy, vote upon particular policy surrounding an issue, or elect representatives to vote on their behalf, empowering them (elected officials) with the right and authority to make decisions on behalf of their masses. Citizens can further impact upon the decision-making process by directly lobbying these representatives to pass legislation favorable to their individual or group interests.

As a safeguard against the abuse of the authority granted to representatives, citizens are granted the right of review. The right of review allows citizens the opportunity to ensure that their interests are in fact being properly represented. The people conduct this review in two primary ways. First, through public debate where opposing views may be presented to or by legislators and the public at large allowing the people the opportunity to consider issues of interest to them and to express their concerns, desires, approval or disapproval. This debate over issues, necessarily involves an examination of the efforts by current and perspective representatives to address these public concerns. The debate in the United States democratic system is supported by several features, including the freedom of the press, freedom of speech, town house meetings and open hearings and, through the increasing transparency of government as a result of new developments in media coverage[28]. The second manner in which the people exercise the right of review is through their vote. Citizens hold as their most fundamental weapon or tool the power to re-elect or replace representatives. This is a particularly powerful tool in societies such as the United States where many representatives have made politics a career. Additionally, the referendum system also allows individuals the

---

[28] CSPAN coverage of legislative debates and hearings, the increased use of live television coverage, satellite televisions which allow for direct feed from the field all lead to increased exposure of the details of modern government.

opportunity to directly take ownership of the policy making process and decide public issues themselves.

If one were to ask the average person or, some students of political science for that matter, what it was that made a particular government a democracy, the response would likely center around a discussion of frequency of elections, the number of active political parties, human rights policies and individual freedoms, governmental structure and, the distribution of power. Whereas each of these may give some superficial indication of the readiness and ability of a government to effectively implement democracy, they do not actually speak to the root of the democratic ideal[29]. The fundamental right and duty of people to participate in the political process lies at the very base of any democratic regime, and any real analysis of the level of actualization of this coveted system of governance lies in the degree to which the people actually have the ability to directly influence their government.

On the surface, the passive observer may clearly notice these symbols of democracy in American society. Elections take place on a regular basis, candidates and parties respect the outcomes of these election without great protestation. Similarly, individuals freely express their political views with relatively little fear of government repression and may freely organize themselves into groups or organizations reflective of their shared beliefs or values. As a constitutional republic, the law is supreme and recognizes individual rights. As a nation, the United States has grown to respect and honor this constitution and, through strife and compromise, come to recognize these rights as being "universal".

However, a slightly closer analysis reveals several troubling characteristics of the American democratic structure. Voter participation is extremely low. The public, for the most

---

[29]   The issue of individual freedom is an exception as it is central to the concept of liberal democracy.

part, is apathetic and ignorant of democratic proceedings. Discrimination abounds and some centers of power fail to reflect the ethnic, cultural and ideological diversity of the general population. The senate, for example, remains a near exclusive club of male WASPs.

The question at hand specifically asks, "is the United States of America a participatory democracy?" Participatory democracy is seemingly the easiest form of democracy to identify. Unlike liberal democracy or representative democracy which are defined by more abstract concepts, participatory democracy can be measured. For the purposes of this paper we will define political participation in three interrelated ways:

I. Voting; as a means of selecting representatives who will act on behalf of their constituents and represent their interests in the seats of power
II. Lobbying; as a means of directly influencing the decision-making process
III. Review; as the final check and balance against the abuse of power on the part of government officials.

Voting as a Measure of Participatory Democracy in the US

The question of voting is central to all forms of democracy. However, the significance of selecting representatives lies not only in the legitimization of representatives or the collective expression of local and national interests and preferences. The representative aspect of the democratic structure also has practical benefits for the effective management of the nation. Direct democracy is obviously a slow and inefficient way of governing any large political group. Allowing each member of a community to vote on every issue of importance poses a number of problems. It requires, first, that the public be educated on every issue of importance; and second, the tedious process of having citizens debate and vote on each and every major issue. The dilemma faced by American politics is that while too much participation may reduce the everyday business of the government to a state of gridlock and place an enormous burden on conscientious citizens, too little participation negates the true representative nature of the democratic structure.

Voter participation is the most obvious and observable feature of participatory democracy. Elections are the time when the city, state or nation speaks with one voice and says, clearly, this is our choice. The problem in the United States is that typically only half of the people exercise this duty. In the 1988 presidential election 52% of the voting population went to the polls and in 1992 only 54%. Similarly, less than half of the population turns out for non-presidential elections with approximately 38% turning out in 1990. The problem is further compounded by the differing levels of participation of the various social classes. Consequently, if half of the electorate fail to participate and, if the level of participation is biased in favor of specific classes of people, then elected officials are not necessarily reflective of the general population.

The representative aspect of the American democratic establishment is designed to allow each member of the community the right and the ability to impact upon the making and implementation of policy of their State through the selection process. Two assumptions are made in such a system. First, that the elected official is elected by a majority of votes and that he therefore represents the majority of people and preferences in his constituency. The second assumption is that elected officials are therefore obliged to represent the interest of their constituents. In order for this system to function the people must therefore have the ear of their representatives.

Whether the average citizen recognizes it or not, each member of the society has interests in the function of their government. Of course, by choosing not to participate, these non-voting citizens have in fact consciously acted and deferred their will to the judgement of others. In any treatment of the political environment, they should therefore not be seen as inconsequential or "empirically invisible" in the lexicon of Downs. The consequences of the apathy of the general population to politics is profound. Primarily, the negative consequences of this public distance from politics is the inability of the citizenry to form and express, through their vote, meaningful preferences.

As Zaller (1992) suggests, the population is largely ignorant of, not only the working of the government, but of the major issues which their representatives are being asked to represent them on. Furthermore, because of their low levels of political awareness, they are unable to meaningfully process their limited information into well founded, stable preferences. As a result, the voters make uninformed decisions in their selection of candidates and representatives. The consequence for democracy is that representatives elected by such a population do not realistically represent their true preferences on the main issues; except to the extent that the population has none. Furthermore, if elected officials assume that their election to particular posts is reflective of constituent agreement with their ideological policy positions, then they may be likely to feel empowered and obligated to pursue such policies.

The notion that voting practices are limited in their ability to reflect the representative preferences of the population at large, does not necessarily negate the representative nature of American politics. First, non-voters, by abstaining from the electoral process defer their choice of a representative to other, more interested, and presumably, more informed citizens. Therefore, in their apathy, they have in effect delegated the responsibility for choosing to others and agreed to differ to their judgement. Therefore, any elected official is representative of the preferences of the majority of participating citizens, with the indifferent consent of the abstainers. Second, electoral representation may be understood in a variety of ways which do not necessarily require selection by the full body politic.

For example, it should also be noted, in defense of the elected officials, that although the preferences of the constituency are not meaningfully expressed, elected officials may nonetheless be able to understand and represent the interests of the population.

As Weisberg, Herbrig and Camboli (1999) explain although representatives are chosen to represent their constituents on the issues and to "act for" them as their substitute they may be understood to do this is two distinctly different ways. On the one hand they may be expected to act as their constituents want and to do their bidding (i.e. to act as a delegate) and on the other hand, they may be expected to act somewhat independently, but in the interest of their constituents (i.e. to act as a trustee). According to Weisberg, Herbrig and Camboli's (1999) survey of the literature, it seems apparent that representatives perform both functions across varying policy issues. Looking at Miller and Stokes' study of representative voting behavior across three different policy areas, social welfare, civil rights and foreign policy in 1958 they note:

> Miller and Stokes found different representation styles for three different issue areas. Social welfare was an area in which party dominated. Liberal districts tended to elect Democrats, while conservative districts tended to elect Republicans. Democrats in congress tended to vote liberal on these issues while republicans tended to vote conservative. By contrast, civil rights was an area in which the delegate model held. The majority division on civil rights was regional. Members from the South knew their districts opposed civil rights and they voted against it; members from the north knew their districts were more favorable and they voted more favorably. Finally, neither model held for foreign affairs. Instead,

> this area seemed to be an area of executive
> dominance. Trustees were prepared to recognize
> the president's greater expertise in this area and
> were often prepared to defer to his expertise.
> (Weisberg, Herbrig and Camboli, 1999: 71)

As is further explained, legislators use their role as delegate to:

> earn constituents' trust so that the member is
> permitted to exercise her or his judgement
> in some areas. Stokes and Miller (1962) also
> found that the public knew little about what
> the representative was doing, and they argued
> that gave members considerable flexibility - they
> could act as trustee because they knew no one
> was watching. (Weisberg, Herbrig and Camboli,
> 1999: 71)

Another consideration in understanding the role of elected officials is that, given the diversity of their constituents, it is difficult for elected officials to effectively act as delegates on many issues with which they are faced. Particularly, on more "abstract" national questions around which there is no clear majority opinion. For example, to whom does an elected official owe his loyalty and whose perspective is he expected to represent? Related to this question, Weisberg, Herbrig and Camboli (1999) highlight the tendency to over simplify the definitions of who make up a representative's constituency.

> If the geographical constituency is defined legally,
> other constituencies are defined politically -
> based on the types of constituents who support
> the member of congress. The "reelection
> constituency" consists of the constituents whom
> the member of congress believes vote for him or

her. The "primary constituency" is the loyalists who support the member of congress with intensity, and regardless of the quality of the challenger. The primary constituency provides many of the volunteers and contributors to the candidate's campaign. Finally, the "personal constituency" is the "intimates," the member's closest friends in the district. These are the old pals whom the member sees on most every visit back home, and members would have a hard time explaining to these pals a vote that goes against his or her usual pattern. (Weisberg, Herbrig and Camboli, 1999)

Of course, two other constituencies have been eliminated from this typology: members of the geographic constituency who opposed the candidate, "opposition constituency" and those who have abstained from the political process, the "inactive constituency". All these groups of individuals compose the general constituency of any elected official and all should reasonably expect him to act meaningfully on their behalf. But certainly his ability to do so as a "delegate" is inherently limited. If "the legislator's view of his or her constituency [is] thus viewed as a set of concentric circles, with the geographic constituency as the outside circle and the personal constituency as the inner circle, closest to the representative" (Weisberg, Herbrig and Camboli, 1999: 72), then even his attempts to understand what is desired of him on various issues will be heavily biased to the preferences of his inner (personal and primary) circles. However, as a capable trustee, cognizant of local problems, interests and issues, elected officials may in the exercise of their good judgement, act on behalf of all members of their constituency.

The trustee model seems to imply that voter preferences and the constituent/representative relationship is of little importance in American politics. Erickson Mackuen, and

Stimson in their book Macro Polity provide some evidence of the continued importance of voters in determining political outcomes. As they suggest, career politicians are cognizant of the importance of maintaining a meaningful connection to the voting public. Utilizing their macro approach and focusing on the American democratic system as a whole as compared to the traditional micro-level analyses of voting behavior they provide a somewhat different perspective on democratic performance. Their analysis of American voting habits suggests that a number of socio-economic factors affect the voting behavior of citizens as a whole. As with their micro-focused counterparts they highlight the importance of economic performance in determining electoral outcomes. Suggesting that voters may use the polls as a means of "rewarding or punishing" incumbents for their terms' performance.

They however go further in suggesting that politicians are sensitive and responsive to changing trends in electoral moods. For the purposes of our brief discussion here we can understand moods to represent changes in the general attitudes of members of the public caused by the "acquisition of new considerations" (Zaller, 1992: 118). Changes in public moods may be caused by recent events or information which "may increase the salience of preexisting liberal or conservative considerations thereby bringing about changes in people attitudes" towards a particular subject. Similarly, people may be "exposed to persuasive communications and accept them as considerations, thereby altering the balance of liberal and conservative considerations in their minds" (Zaller, 1992: 119). These changes are of course heavily influenced by changing elite perspectives which provide the stimuli and directional cues for shifting public perspectives (Zaller, 1992 & Hetherington, 2001).

"Evidence suggests that political variables - partisanship and ideological proximity - are the most proximate causes of the vote. The economy is present as a cause, but the economy does its work on the vote in large part via influencing political variables." (Erickson, Mackuen, and Stimson 2002: 275). If the results of this are taken at face value, the implication for our discussion are that citizens in formulating and expressing collective opinions do have meaningful and direct impact on the policy positions of elected officials. It suggests that political candidates and parties in courting their constituents for votes must present themselves as being in tuned to the ideological leanings of their constituents.

If this notion is further accepted, the influence of public moods on the actions of elected officials is not limited to members of the actively participating public. Since these moods may be diffused throughout the society and shared with both voters and free riders. If political entrepreneurs are unable to effectively distinguish between the specific moods of the active voters and freeloaders *prema facie* then the collective mood must be taken into consideration. This concept is consistent with the traditional framing of collective action problems and also lends itself to supporting the tradition of non-participation by members of the voting public. That is to say, if individual citizens perceive their particular preferences to be part of a growing trend actively expressed and pursued by others, then the need to individually express these views or take actions to secure these policies (voting for a particular candidate for example) is diminished.

Erickson concludes that one effect of politicians' perceptions of public moods is that it creates a tendency towards moderate positioning.

> Is the party closer in issue space to the median voter thereby advantaged in election outcomes? ... Yes ... For each party, a single point of movement toward the political center, again controlling for Macropartisianship, is worth .45 percentage point of presidential vote. And, of course, a move toward ideological purity similarly costs .45 of the vote (Erickson, Mackuen, and Stimson 2002: 266).

The impact of this on the overall political system is a grouping tendency towards moderate ideological stances for the two major competing parties. This phenomenon makes citizens, both active and inactive, passive participants in the framing of political platforms as political entrepreneurs make projections about the "mood" of the electorate. That is to say, that in an attempt to avoid alienating key segments of the potential voting public (those not so strongly tied to party loyalties as to be taken for granted) both parties dilute their ideological stances and take more moderate positions. As Erickson notes however, since party image is based both on current claims and on past performance, "the parties are able to use the platforms as a vehicle for altering the image of where they stand, [but] they can alter that image only slowly over time" at the risk of alienating their own "extreme" ideological base" (Erickson, Mackuen and Stimson 2002: 258).

The relationship between constituent and representative goes beyond this tendency toward party moderation. "Generally, members of congress seek to convince their constituents that they represent them regardless of the extent to which they agree on specific issues ... by attempting to convey a sense of qualification, identification and empathy" (Weisberg, Herbrig and Camboli, 1999). In other words, representatives present themselves as being connected to their constituents, sharing their values and interests and being qualified to address them on their behalf in the halls of government. Thus, in the performance of their duties these representatives often "attempt to secure committee and subcommittee assignments that will allow them to serve their constituents" (Weisberg, Herbrig and Camboli, 1999). Similarly, although "few members participate in developing most legislation ... members are more active when their district is affected by the legislation" (Weisberg, Herbrig and Camboli, 1999). Constituent interests also impact upon the nature of legislation being proposed. Weisberg, Herbrig and Camboli, 1999 cite several studies which suggest that 'constituents are the most prominent source of inspiration for legislation in agriculture and related domains. Members of congress are more likely to get their ideas for legislation from constituents rather than interest groups, bureaucrats or other "experts"' (Weisberg, Herbrig and Camboli, 1999: 73).

Representative activity is not limited to the passage of legislation. A significant portion of elected officials' time is dedicated to the provision of services to their constituents. These services encompass a wide range of activities ranging from helping to resolve personal difficulties individual constituents experience in relation to government bureaucracy to the allocation of government resources in the form of grants, projects, and programs which in turn provide jobs and help to relieve socio-economic difficulties.

> There may be several motives for engaging in service activities, including the feeling of duty or the desire to be helpful, but few would argue that legislators do not also expect an electoral payoff. Constituents who have been helped by their representative, or who know of others who have been helped, are thought to support their benefactor loyally in the voting booth. (Weisberg, Herbrig and Camboli, 1999: 75)

These activities have the effect of making the representative more visible. While most people cannot relate directly to much of national politics, these activities provide outcomes which are evident and personal and lack the abstract characteristics of many national programs. The results are therefore more easily interpreted by even the most uninformed and unsophisticated observers and place the incumbent in a positive light. Whether this activity is seen as mere pandering to potential voters or as genuine efforts to improve the lot of their constituents, the result is a tendency for representatives to dedicate much of their time to the delivery of concrete benefits to their constituents and in so doing to cater to their interests and maintain an open relationship between representative and constituents.

Lobbying as a Measure of Political Participation

Despite the key role of voting as a means of selecting representatives, there are several other measures of political participation which are of equal import. Voting for any key political position takes place periodically in time frames ranging from 2-6 years. Between these key moments several other forms of political participation must be invoked in order to support the public discourse and to ensure responsive government. A wide range of strategies may be utilized by citizens to communicate their policy preferences to elected officials, political institutions and other members of the citizenry. For the purpose of this paper we will categorize these strategies as falling under one all-encompassing term, lobbying. The range of strategies available to citizens include the staging of protests, letter writing and petition campaigns, position papers and financial contributions. Each of these widely-used strategies allow members of the public to express their views individually and collectively and influence the functioning of their government.

In order to ensure that citizens have a voice, beyond the vote, the Constitution of the United States of America grants certain fundamental rights expressed in the First Amendment.

> Congress shall make no law respecting an establishment of religion, or prohibiting the free exercise thereof, or abridging the freedom of speech, or of the press, or the right of people to peacefully assemble, and to petition the government for a redress of grievances (Constitution of the United States of America)

These rights to freedom of speech, freedom of the press and the right to petition the government help to facilitate the free exchange of ideas, allow citizens to have their interests heard by the government and allow for review of elected officials. Two important players must be featured in our discussion of lobbying as a measure of participatory democracy: professional lobbyists and the media.

In order to most effectively petition their government and maximize impact on legislation and policy making, members of the community pool themselves and their power into special interest groups and lobby their local, state and federal legislative and executive offices directly. These special interest bodies carry with them the weight of potential votes and financial assistance, and because of these assets they often win the ear of elected officials. The function of the lobbyist is to influence policy making and implementation in favor of the constituents which they represent. Despite the fact that these organizations are often manned by professional lobbyists their actions are nonetheless an important element of understanding citizen participation. These organizations operate as surrogates of the electorate vocalizing their varied perspectives on issues, attempting to influence legislation and acting as political watchdogs.

In his book <u>Mobilizing Interest Groups in America</u>, Jack Walker discusses the pervasiveness and diversity of interest groups operating in the United States. Lobbyist organization vary in size, areas of interest, origins, character (grass roots, corporate, non-for profit, trade unions, etc.). Likewise, they also differ in the repertoire of strategies they utilize to pursue their individual agendas[30]. For the purposes of this paper, the strategies utilized with be broadly groups into two categories. On the one hand are strategies which aim to influence voters and their behavior at the polls as a means of pressuring career

---

[30] For a detailed typology, see Walker, Jack (1991)

elected officials into taking a favorable stance on a given issue. The activities undertaken in this strategy include the distribution of information on the issue, staging of protests and demonstrations, letter writing campaigns and other activities intended to suggest to the targeted official the will of the constituents and with the underlying implication that their actions on that particular issue will result in a gain or loss of potential votes.

On the other hand, some interest groups, most often those affiliate with corporate interests utilize strategies which aim to empower elected officials with the increased ability to influence voters directly through their election campaigns. This of course is achieved through the provision of campaign contributions. The strategies utilized by these interest groups are also diverse. Their repertoire may include the presentation of position papers and research, the hosting and sponsorship of key events and the development of personal relationships with key bureaucratic and political figures.

However, the tools utilized by lobbyists for different, and often opposing, interests are not necessarily equal. Pointedly, it is often the poorer more numerous groups who are underrepresented. This fact speaks strongly against the balance of power in American democracy. The problem lies in the nature of the strategies used to influence law makers and in the relationships between lawmakers and their constituents.

The financial weight of interest groups often outweighs their voting potential, simply because people tend not to vote in blocks and only a very small number of groups are truly capable of shifting block votes significantly enough to alter electoral outcomes. The reasons for this are that it requires a very strong sense of collective interest and a closely-knit network to hold such voting coalitions together. Secondly, the idea of block voting implies that citizens base their voting decisions on issues. Given the relative ignorance of citizens about candidate positions on any given issue and the tendency to vote along party lines, such large-scale voting behavior is unlikely. Among the few groups capable of using their threat of block votes effectively are the Jewish population in New York City, the Cuban population in Florida and, on some key issues, trade unions[31].

Block voting, is a theoretically powerful tool for poorer citizens who have collective interests and who can muster enough support for their cause. Three problems associated with block voting will be briefly highlighted here. First, the coalitions represented by most "grass roots" or "civic minded" interest groups are loosely connected by membership. As Verba, Schlozman and Brady (1995) and Putnam (1995) show, most people who claim affiliations with these interest groups are only loosely affiliated with the organization, its work and its cause. For the vast majority of these members, their contribution to the organizations effort begins and ends with their financial patronage. Few participate in regular meetings, few review the organization's literature and few base their electoral decisions primarily on the recommendations of the organization. This is further compounded by the fact that regardless of the influence of the organization, vast numbers of the people associated with various "grass roots" interest groups are as apolitical towards the general elections as they are to the organization's functioning. Consequently, interest groups who rely heavily on the appeal of their collective votes, relay a transparently exaggerated message about their power and influence.

These issues are further compounded by the increasingly popular "mailing list" organizations such as the American Association of Retired Persons and the Sierra Club who although representing potentially powerful groups of people, are inherently loose coalitions based upon vaguely defined common interests. The disconnectedness of the membership of

---

[31] As Walker notes trade unions are the most flexible organizations in the system when it comes to the selection of tactics to influence policy. *See Walker p 11.*

such organizations make them little more than clearing houses for political dialogue between members and politicians. That is to say, that they serve the function of distributing information between these actors without exercising much control over either.

Second, if Zaller (1992) is correct, and public opinion is as unstable as he suggests. Then politicians may just as easily utilize various spin techniques to manipulate public opinion.

> Although most American are ... rationally ignorant about politics, they differ greatly in the degree of their ignorance. There is a small, but important minority of the public that pays great attention to politics and is well informed about it. Members of this minority can recognize important US Senators on sight, accurately recount each day's leading news stories, and keep track of the major events in Washington and other world capitals. ... At the other end of the attentiveness spectrum is a larger group of people who possess almost no current information about politics. In late 1986, for example, when George Bush was halfway into his second term as vice-president of the United States, 24 percent of the general public either failed to recognize his name or could not say what office he held. ... most citizens of course fall between these extremes. (Zaller, 1992: 16)

According to Zaller, these citizens respond differently to information in the formation of opinions concerning politics. Those who are least or marginally informed tend to vacillate in reaction to elite dominated cues. On the other hand, the more highly informed citizens, tend to be more stable in their opinion, which are themselves dictated by strong ideological and partisan loyalties. "If many citizens are largely uncritical in their response to political communications as carried in the mass media, and if most of the rest respond mechanically on the basis of partisan cues, how can one deny the existence of a substantial degree of elite domination?" (Zaller, 1992: 311) In a political atmosphere such as this, the notion of interest group influence over their voters may seem quite plausible. The problem lies of course in the abundance of competing political messages which are disseminated to a public which is ill equipped to effectively process it.

The third inter-related problem is, the way an uninformed public makes decisions at the polls. A number of factors have been suggested as being influential in determining voter decision making, including partisanship and candidate character/appeal. Zaller, however, illustrates perhaps one of the most whimsical approaches to voter decision making. As he notes:

> One of the most heavily researched problems in the congressional elections literature in recent years has been the advantage enjoyed by incumbents in the House of Representatives in their reelection bids ... house members have been able ... to build a "personal vote" that is loyal to them regardless of partisan considerations. Thus, it sometimes happens that a seat will be safe for a particular incumbent for a decade or more ... this development has given house members an independent standing that is almost unique in western democracies and that seems to have vitally affected the performance of the American Congress. The reason for the rise of the personal vote, however remains somewhat unclear. Less than half of the eligible electorate can recall the name of their congressional representative, and this figure has not changed in the period in which

> incumbents have become safer. But although most
> people cannot recall their incumbent's name,
> about 80% can recognize it. (Zaller, 1992: 19)

In summary, the notion of block voting as an effective tool for influencing legislator assumes a more sophisticated electorate than the current American system embodies.

By contrast, the second group of lobbyists who offer the benefits of financial support have several advantages over their grass roots counterparts. These groups, often representing large industries, have, of course, the advantage of economic guarantees over the promise of voter turnout. But of even greater significance, quite often these lobbyists are professional lobbyists who make a living representing the interests of industry before legislators. They often come from similar backgrounds and in many cases, these lobbyists are themselves former legislators or bureaucrats familiar with the inner workings of the government. They therefore come to the table with an extensive network of contacts which allow them higher levels of access to key players in the legislature. In addition to the increased access, familiarity has the advantage of making legislators more receptive to the messages relayed by these lobbyists.

The relationships between professional lobbyist and representative and, between legislators and various industries are important factors which must be given some consideration in the analysis of the working of democracy in this country. Vincente Navarro (1993) discusses the impact that strong industrial lobbyists have on the maintenance of managed care as the dominant system of health care service delivery in the US.

One of his central points is that a large percentage of legislators transition between positions in the corporate world and key positions in the public sector. Navarro argues that this relationship fosters a more sympathetic position towards their interests often at the expense of the public's interest. According to Navarro, in the early years of his presidency, all seven of

Clinton's cabinet members earned over \$1 million annually prior to joining the cabinet. Furthermore:

> 102 congressmen held stock and well-paying executive positions in banks or other financial institutions, 81% received regular income from law firms that generally represented big business, 63% received stock from top defense contractors, 45% from oil and gas industry, 22% from radio and television companies (Navarro, 1993: 44)

This issue has been emphasized because the class bias of the government has significant impact upon the actualization of democracy in the United States. The strong ties between the dominant class and government legislators and the subsequent alienation of the working class deserves real consideration in any discourse on democracy and the protection of the rights of the population of which the working class is the most numerous.

It is important to bear in mind that industry interests do not always coincide with the interests of most citizens. In fact, beyond questions of employment, they seldom do. Similarly, there may be divisions on issues, outside of management/labor issues, across class lines. Several such issues have been the subject of on-going debate throughout the history of this country among them are taxes, environmental issues, and healthcare management. Under the democratic ideal, it would seem likely that the most populous group should have their way. The interest and will of the majority should be given preference and dominance over the minority. In reality though, the strength of the industry lobbying and class biases have often overshadowed the voice of the people, to the extent that they speak.

Despite the implications for the relative weight of the competing voices of certain interest groups, the above arguments do not necessarily impact negatively on the notion of participatory democracy. The fact remains that citizens do attempt to influence government through their support of these institutions. To better understand political participation, we must therefore take into account micro level analysis of citizen participation in these institutions.

As Robert Putnam (1995) suggests, the nature of citizen support is indicative of not just apathy but a general decline in social capital and civic engagement in the voting public. Putnam suggests that over the past two or three decades participation in various forms of civic engagement have been steadily declining.

> Membership records of such diverse organizations as the PTA, the Elks club, The league of women voters, the Red Cross, labor unions ... show that participation in many conventional voluntary associations has declined by roughly 25-50% over the past decades ... while Americans' interest in politics has been stable or even growing over the last three decades, and some forms of participation that require moving a pen, such as signing petitions and writing checks, have increased significantly, many measures of collective participation have fallen sharply including attending a rally or speech (off 36% between 1973 and 1993), attending a meeting on town or school affairs (off 39%) or working for a political party (off 56%).(Putnam, 1995: 666)

Despite this general decrease in civic engagement, "few deny that the last several decades have witnessed explosive growth in interest groups represented in Washington" (Putnam, 1995: 666). These citizens groups therefore represent a key element of political participation. But while the number of interest groups and their relative visibility may have grown this does not necessarily imply an increase in individual participation on the part of the American citizenry. In the book Voice and Equality,

Verba, Schlozman and Brady (1995) suggest that 79 % of the citizenry are involved with an organization and 41% report having multiple affiliations with four or more organizations. Of these participating citizens, only 65% reported actually attending a meeting and 42% considered themselves to be active members. (Verba, Schlozman and Brady, 1995: 63) These statistics appear to be relatively consistent with the idea that citizens are only marginally involved in any civic activity. The statistics for political participation are equally as troublesome. "Seventeen percent of the public does nothing at all in politics, and another 18 percent does nothing beyond voting. Thus, just over one-third of respondents do nothing in politics other than, possibly, going to the polls. Another 9 % engage in a single activity, and the remaining 57% undertake more than one political act beyond voting" (Verba, Schlozman and Brady, 1995: 66).

Of this 66% of the population who indicate some form of political participation, they also note that, 69% limited their participation to the contribution of funds, while only 12% contributed time and 19% gave both. This tendency towards checkbook participation is again indicative of the aloofness of the American voter, and consequently, the very character of the American democratic tradition. Looking at changes over time, they further note that "the frequency of two activities has changed substantially, but in opposite directions: there has been an increase in the proportion reporting having contributed to a political campaign and a decrease in the share mentioning membership in a political club" (Verba, Schlozman and Brady, 1995: 71-72).

In their work on political participation Verba, Schlozman and Brady[32] (1995) also highlight interesting disparities in the level of political involvement of citizens across socio-economic classes. Looking at a wide range of forms of political participation, they note that "the well-heeled are much more likely than the poor to report having been asked to take part" (Verba, Schlozman and Brady, 1995: 149). More specifically, they claim that "compared to the poor, the affluent are more than four times as likely to be asked for financial contributions [and] one and a half times as likely to be asked to protest" (Verba, Schlozman and Brady, 1995: 149). Similarly:

> Anglo-whites are more likely than blacks or, especially Latinos to be asked to get involved in politics. Fifty-six percent of the Anglo-whites, as opposed to 40 percent of the African-Americans and 25 percent of the Latinos, reported receiving at least one request for political participation. ... The gender differences are less pronounced: men are slightly more likely than women to be asked to get involved politically –55 percent of the men as opposed to 50 percent of the women. (Verba, Schlozman and Brady, 1995: 151)

This data is suggestive of a socio-economic bias in recruitment of participants. This bias is naturally carried over into the demographic representation of actual participants.

> For each kind of participation, affluence and activity go together. Of the various acts, voting is perhaps the most egalitarian. Turnout is much

---

[32] It should be noted that Verba, Schlozman and Brady disagree with Putnam's conclusions that civic engagement is on a steady decline and in fact suggest that Americans still engage in a significant amount of civic volunteerism.

> higher among the wealthy than the poor, but
> voting is the only act for which the affluent are
> not at least twice as likely to be active. Those with
> the lowest family income are less well represented
> among those who take a more active role in
> political campaigns. The poor are one-quarter
> as likely as the affluent to do campaign work
> and about one tenth as likely to give a campaign
> contribution. (Verba, Schlozman and Brady,
> 1995: 189)

Along ethnic lines, differences in the levels of participation are less pronounced and less consistent in direction. African Americans were less likely to vote, yet more likely to contribute to campaign activities. Latinos however, lagged behind their counterparts on all levels.

The conclusion of these findings is that the actively participating public, which attempts to influence the policy making processes of their government are skewed along various socio-economic lines. This may therefore suggest that the opinions expressed by this population are not necessarily representative of the larger public's perspectives or interests. For organized citizen groups, the legitimacy of their positions consequently lies, to varying degrees, on whether or not the input of their active members is also reflective of that of the inactive and un-represented members of the public.

This question will be dealt with more succinctly in a later section of this paper, but, a brief summary of Verba, Schlozman and Brady's treatment of the question is appropriate here. As they accurately note, since all societies are divided in complex ways along multiple axis of cleavage, descriptive representation on all relevant demographic dimensions probably cannot be realized within the confines of a legislature of manageable size (Verba, Schlozman and Brady, 1995: 165). Additionally, demographic differences between varying groups do not imply corresponding policy differences for these groups. Quoting the work of Raymond Wolfinger and Steven Rosenstone (1980) they suggest that "differences between the public and the voters on such issues as government welfare policy, health care and abortion are negligible. Furthermore, small differences between voters and non-voters in attitudes on these policy issues are not systematically skewed in a liberal or conservative direction" (Verba, Schlozman and Brady, 1995: 166-168).

The open nature of political participation also allows for two possible checks and balances against an overly biased expression of public preferences. First, as issues gain and lose salience in the public's political discourse, varying members of the population are likely to become active and increasingly vocal. As a result, "if enough people get involved, representation on a variety of dimensions ... becomes feasible for the population of activists." (Verba, Schlozman and Brady, 1995) But more importantly, although not prominent in their treatment of the subject, is the idea that the number and diversity of active organizations and individuals expressing interests and policy preferences in the political arena, necessarily produce a heterogeneous expression of political points of view likely to encompass the views of those inactive members of the public.

Electoral Review: as a means of Political Participation

Other concerns also arise from this examination of voter participation. Another consequence of the apathy of the American electorate is its impact upon the accountability of representatives to their constituencies' interests and preferences, as poorly expressed as they may be. As implied in the preceding argument, if the majority of the population is apathetic and consequently ignorant of the issues, representatives' positions on these issues, policy options and the consequences of such options, the population is therefore ill equipped to exercise its review of the government. Representatives may therefore be free to betray the public interest and are limited only by the potential damage to reputation should their betrayal be exposed by competitors or the other politically active agents such as the media.

> Far from looking over the shoulder of their congressman at the legislative game, most Americans are almost totally uninformed about the legislative issues in Washington. At best the average citizen may be said to have some general ideas about how the country should be run, which he is able to use in responding to particular questions about what the government ought to do. (Miller and Stokes, In Weisberg, Herbrig and Camboli, 1999)

The preceding quote taken from Miller and Stokes' chapter, Constituency Influence in Congress, is a damning condemnation of the ability of the American public to effectively carry out the third measure of political participation addressed in this paper. If the statement is accurate, then it is reasonable to conclude that there can be little accountability for the actions of elected officials in their duties are representatives of their constituents. The power of electoral review as a guarantor of responsible government is manifested in two related ways. The first and significantly more rare form is through the power of recall. This power, granted to voters in constitutions of various states, allows members of the electorate to demand the resignation and replacement of elected officials, before their term is complete on the basis of some grave misconduct or incompetence/lack of confidence[33]. Although rare, this power, invested in the people, is the most powerful and resounding form of electoral review available. As seen in recent events, it embodies an overwhelming expression of dissatisfaction and results in the "immediate" call of elections and the selection of new candidates.

The more common form of electoral review is embodied in the re-election campaign of incumbent representatives. Therefore, in attempting to understand the effective use of this tool, three assumptions are key. First, that citizens are mindful of the actions of their elected officials. Second, that knowledge of representative actions play a key role in the voting decisions of the electorate. Finally, that representatives are aware of this and consequently tailor they legislative and other representative activities towards meeting the expectations of their constituents. To some extent all of these have been addressed. However, where review is concerned all hinge on the notion of a watchful public. Here the function of the media as a tool for facilitating the review process is central.

The Media as the Surrogate Agent of electoral review

The media has come to play an important role in the American democratic experience. In its function as a window into the activities of the government, and a distributor of information about developments in the society at large, the media supports participatory democracy by providing the interested citizen with "credible" information concerning various aspects of political activity. In addition, the media has grown to represent the watch dog of government, seeking out issues of "public interest" and assessing, reporting, debating and often criticizing on behalf

---

[33]   This form of electoral review is more common in parliamentary democracies where it may be initiated by members of the ruling or opposition parties and is often utilized as a political tool for rearranging alliances or coalitions.

of the public. In this vein, the media has adopted or has been designated some key roles which in a participatory democracy should lie in the hands of the citizens.

Timothy Cook (1998) argues along similar lines that the Media itself may be seen as a political institution in its own rights. As an institution, the media's primary function is that of communication. As Cook describes it, the media performs this function on two levels, in the transfer of information "from the elite to the public, as well as within the public as a whole" (Cook, 1998: 82) "The latter point is straightforward enough: as the population grew and face to face communication became less viable, newspapers changed from their early task during the American colonial era as historical repositories of what was already known to revealers of otherwise unknown information. And the public seems to see the role of the news media in similar ways." (Cook, 1998: 82). Similarly Cook argues, government officials have found the media to be an increasingly effective means of distributing information to the public and to other relevant actors by taking advantage of their already established lines of distribution. This evolving interpretation of freedom of the press "gives the news media not only greater protection from governmental interference but also a greater responsibility in political life." (Cook, 1998: 83)

A majority of journalists understand and embrace this new political function and as Cook points out they endorse "one or both of two overlapping approaches - being a neutral disseminator of information to a wide audience, and interpreting policy processes and problems and, government claims" (Cook, 1998: 83)[34].

---

[34]   Th political system is marked by a high degree of voter absenteeism and a consequent ese findings are based on the work of David Weaver and Cleveland Wilhoit The American Journalist. Pp112-117

The implications of this for the question at hand is that the media has taken the primarily role in performing a crucial role in participatory democracy. In particular, its function of interpreting and analyzing public policy. The adoption of this function by the news media has made it more than a mere clearinghouse for information on the proceedings of local and national government. Furthermore, rather than being simply a tool utilized by the citizenry to observe the activities of elected officials and governmental institutions the media has become the foremost institution for carrying out the review process.

Far from being neutral, one key function which the media performs is that of the governmental watchdog. This, in itself is not necessarily problematic. The increased access provided to the media allows it greater insight into the daily activities of the government and the protection granted them under the constitution provide them with a level of security supportive of the watchdog function. However, despite these advantages the media institutions may be ill equipped to carrying out this function. As Cook points out:

> The governmental news media in the United States present a twofold problem. One is the capacity of the news media to perform the role that has devolved on it. Journalists are not well trained, nor are news organizations well equipped, to help weigh problems, set political agendas, examine alternatives, and study implementation ... to the extent that journalism organizes politics and wields power in the American political system, it directs attention : toward episodic outcroppings rather than continuing conditions; towards issues that fade quickly in public consciousness as news persons begin to assume that the public is getting as bored as they are with the same old concerns; and away from abstract complexity toward

> simple if not simplistic renderings of problems,
> policies and alternatives. [The second] is that of
> accountability... News persons will rightly contend
> that they are answerable to their audiences. But
> on what grounds? (Cook, 1998: 167).

As Cook goes on to conclude, "Contemporary news organizations are primarily oriented toward their audiences, not as citizens but as consumers. The most prominent audience for the news are advertisers" since they and not readers provide the bulk of their income.

These criticisms are indeed valid, but perhaps the greatest problem embodied in the media's adoption of the role of policy analysts is that their activities are done without effectively incorporating the most important actors in this process, the public. The delegation of this function to the media, has left the receiving public as passive recipients and non-participants in the process. Media coverage of policy debates, for example, is often characterized by the personal interpretation of media personalities such as Bill O'reilly, Rush Limbaugh, Lou Dobbs, Tucker Carlson, and Robert Novak with "informed" input by specialist in the relevant area (political analysts, military analysts, economists, etc.). However, the consequence of this is that rather than allowing members of the public to receive the raw data and interpret it in their own terms, the audience is fed varied interpretations of the problem, policy positions and alternatives in an essentially staged debate.

This, of course sits well with many members of the public who, as we have suggested, find the process of actively participating in the politics, tedious. In Zaller's (1992) words "even if they could, the public would have little desire to be kept closely informed about the vast world beyond its personal experience. It requires news presentations that are short, simple and highly thematic - in a word, stereotyped." (Zaller, 1992: 7) The consequences for participatory democracy however are that the citizenry is once again reduced to being passive recipients of political information, merely accepting the assessments made by the media. Furthermore, the tradition of political apathy means that despite the media's role as the disseminator of information, quite often they are broadcasting to non-receptive audiences. As Zaller notes:

> In the spring of 1989, the Speaker of the House of Representatives, James Wright, resigned the speakership amid allegations of scandal, the first time in American history that this had happened. The story was heavily covered in the media over a period of several months. Yet when, about three weeks after Wrights resignation, a national sample was asked about his resignation, only 45 percent could supply any reason for the resignation - even so much as a bare mention of scandal or wrongdoing. ... In the early summer of 1989, the US Supreme Court announced a major decision on women's rights to abortion. Webster v reproductive Services. Because pro and anti-abortion activists held large scale demonstrations in an attempt to lobby the Court, there was extensive news coverage of the impending decision in the weeks before it was taken, and very heavy coverage when the decision was finally announced. Yet, in a survey done just after the decision, only 50 percent of the public could say anything at all about how the court had ruled, and, as the survey continued over the next several weeks, this percentage fell gradually to about 35 percent. (Zaller, 1992: 16-7)

Conclusion:

Therefore, on all three measures of political participation the America political system appears to be wanting. It seems obvious then that American democracy is not based upon the political participation of the masses. Although this is partially true it is not wholly so. Despite the apparently excessive strength of influence concentrated in the hands of the upper-class minority, the United States remains firmly grounded in democratic ideals, practices and institutions. The failings of the democratic system to manifest participatory democracy cannot be attributed solely or primarily to the democratic institutions themselves. If campaign financing is an issue which threatens the integrity of the democratic system, the power of the vote, if exercised, still places the power to demand change squarely in the hands of the citizens of the United States. Furthermore, the representative structure of the United States' government reflects the diversity of the participants. Where it is skewed in the interest of one group or another it is reflective of the political participation of the citizenry. It is the collective voting public which holds the reins of power, unexercised as it may be.

Additionally, from its very inception the American democratic tradition has been one which is firmly rooted in the idea of representative democracy. The commitment to this notion may be heard in the famous battle cry "no taxation without representation," the mantra of the anti-colonial war of independence. Some aspects of the representative nature of American politics were deliberately put into place. The Virginia Plan and the New Jersey Plan which provided the basis for the bicameral system in the legislature were both conceived with a strong emphasis on representative government. However, the political system has developed into one in which new representative institutions have emerged and in effect become the voice of the citizens. Lobbyists, news agencies, talk show hosts, community advocates, and a host of other individuals and institutions, have become surrogates of the individual citizen in their relations with their government. The consequences for American citizens has been an increase in their spheres of personal space. Citizens are relieved of any serious obligation to the political world around them are free to pursue more personal interests. On the other hand, their neglect of politics has created a vast majority who are ignorant of this vital system, politically unsophisticated, and who take the proper function of their government and the associated liberties for granted.

Finally, we address the question of democracy. If the United states is not a participatory democracy, where then does its democratic character lie? Democracy in the United States is best defined as a liberal democracy. i.e. A system of government in which the citizens are guaranteed maximized freedom in the conduct of their lives and the pursuit of their goals. It is perhaps this liberal ideal, which most impacts upon the poor evaluations of the country as a participatory democracy. A, perhaps unintended, consequence of the strong emphasis on "civil liberties" is the growing sense of political detachment of the American public.

CHAPTER 4

Why a Revolution in the United States is Unlikely?

Revolutions represent the most dynamic of social movements. Social revolutions refer to the implementation of fundamental social change in a state most often accompanied by the forceful overthrow of an established regime. The occurrence of social revolution usually leads to the institution of new social, political and economic structures as well as relations in society. Yet, despite a national dialogue which suggests a desire to alter socio political and economic relations to reflect the ideals of liberty and equality, and despite the presence of oppression and a growing disparity in wealth, power, influence and access to services, the likelihood of a social revolution occurring with the United States of America remains low.

This paper addresses the question as to why the occurrence of social revolution in the United States of America in the Twentieth Century or the early Twenty-first Century unlikely. The question is complex, involving both structural restraints and many subtle factors which have far reaching impacts upon the psyche of the citizens. This paper will address the question from these two standpoints concentrating particularly upon how the existence of a myth of social democracy and the capitalist myth of success serve to create an environment of stability even in the face of extreme discontent. An attached supplement to this paper addresses the case study of African-Americans and why this group in particular, despite a history of racist repression, under-representation, economic exploitation and institutionally sanctioned harassment for over four hundred years, is unlikely to form a revolutionary movement aimed at radically reforming the state. The argument made for this group will be based upon the failure to develop a revolutionary ideology and will suggest that this failure is deeply rooted in the Myth of American democracy.

In order to make a reasonable assessment of the likelihood of a revolutionary movement aimed at reforming the state, it is first necessary to analyze the structure of the state, and, more importantly, the perception of the state structure in the eyes of its citizens. Roelof's analysis of the configuration of the American political structure provides some useful insight into the analysis of the consensus/cleavage paradox which characterizes American democracy. Roelof suggest the American political system is ambiguous and exists simultaneously on two levels: on the one hand a myth of social revolutionary democracy, and on the other hand an ideology of Liberal Democracy. In this odd combination of ideology and myth lies the key to American socio-political stability. The political system is free to serve the poli-garchy of interests which dominate domestic politics in the country through lobbying, elitist contacts and industrial complexes. Conversely, those people effectively excluded from significant participation in the political system are pacified with a myth of inclusion, access and possibly meaningful reform through legitimized channels of political action.

The Liberal Democratic Ideal

The United States of America is a Liberal Democratic Capitalist system. This characterization bears with it significant underlying implications for the ideology by which people live their lives, govern themselves and, most importantly, judge the world around them. A liberal democracy may be defined as a "Framework of law in which individuals are free to pursue their personal interest with maximum freedom." Three main points can be derived from this definition:

1. That the American system is one in which liberty, equality and justice, ideals dear to the heart of its citizens, are defined by law, not by social relationship.
2. That this definition points to the great emphasis placed by the American socio –political system on individualism;

3. That the framework of law is concerned specifically with the pursuit of personal interest.[35]

Starting with the last of these factors, the American obsession with the pursuit of personal interest has a significant impact upon the working of Democracy. As politics is a function of collective action concerned with the protection and promotion of collective interest, or at least the maintenance of society, a collective body, and this granted freedom to pursue personal interest with maximum freedom has become synonymous with freedom from political activity. In practical terms it translates into a withdrawal of citizens into a personal "confessional life", unconcerned with politics except when political activity infringes upon their personal lives. As a result of this retreat of the individuals into their personal lives, engrossed in their individual interest, the American political system is marked by a high degree of voter absenteeism and a consequent political weakness of the masses. This weakness is particularly striking in light of the power of industrial interests which effectively lobby government through campaign financing or through the intricate networks of industrial complexes.

Despite their retreat from active politics and their consequent weakness, individuals within the American political system maintain a strong belief in their inclusion in the system. This belief is sustained by several factors. The potential, unrealized power of the ballot remains as conciliation to citizens believing that if they need or desire to, they may impact directly upon the political process. As true as this may be, without a properly developed collective consciousness, the individual vote holds little weight. Only through collective or block voting can the ballot be an effective weapon for social change but within the American political arena such action is rare.

---

[35] Factors 2 and 3 overlap each other in significance, particularly in the analysis being undertaken in this paper.

This failure of the ethnic groups[36] within the United States to form or maintain a collective consciousness for the purpose of political action[37] can also be greatly attributed to the individualist nature of the society. Furthermore, on the few occasions when collective voting has occurred, it becomes very issue oriented; that is that people vote on the basis of a single issue such as abortion. Collective voting matters of political agenda or far reaching social programming are atypical.[38] Thus, masses are mobilized, not around questions of reform or direction of the state as a whole, but rather around the question of their individual rights to freedom, as related to their personal interests, not national interests or collective interests.

An even more relevant consequence of the individualistic nature of the society is its failure to see problems as systematic and not simply individualistic. This problem can be greatly attributed to the political ignorance of the masses. This ignorance is a direct result of the retreat of the masses from politics combined with a system of education which serves to perpetuate the illusions of the myth of American democracy.

Political Ignorance

Many people, dissatisfied with the injustices of capitalism and/or racism, focus their antagonism at corporate structures or individuals whom they perceive as having abused or violates the rights and/or exploited them unfairly. Their failure to comprehend the intricate connections between the political

---

[36] Two notable exceptions to this rule are Jewish communities in New York and the Cuban communities in Florida.

[37] Other ethnic groups have maintained collective consciousness for other social purposes. This is exemplified in the demographic layout of urban centers such as New York which are divided up into ethnic enclaves for purposes of social comfort.

[38] In fact, in the American political system such platforms are rare.

and economic system means that their aims at reconciliation or reform seldom involve reforming the state or the economic system itself except in the most superficial symbolic manner.

This micro level analysis of the social problems which plagues many citizens has far reaching impacts in determining the susceptibility of the political system to revolutionary movements. A truly revolutionary ideology must focus on the system (political and economic) and seek to find solutions by reforming it at its very core. The American framework of analysis disallows this kind this kind of scrutiny. Because of the individualist nature of the American mind, the question is always framed, "can I make it?" The question itself poses an analytical problem. Because the question is posed on an individualist level, answers are sought on an individualist level and this may be provided through the upholding of role models and success stories. Thus, "if these people have made it, then through hard work and dedication, I too can make it." This is the basis of the capitalist success myth. The shortcoming in this simplistic perspective is that it fails to analyze the system as a whole and ask the question "can we all make it?" Americans have great difficulty distinguishing the difference between these two questions. The failure of the American mind to perceive the collective interests results in a self-centered analysis of social problems and consequently a self-centered approach to solutions. Such an approach to oppression, injustice and exploitation cannot result in revolutionary ideology, because the solution becomes not to reform the system but rather to alter ones position in the system. This reality of the goal and thrust of social movement throughout the United States itself poses the greatest hindrance to revolutionary movement in the United States.

A crucial factor in the stability of the American political system and the unlikelihood of revolutionary ideology taking foot is that all citizens perceive themselves as having a personal interest in maintaining the system. Each citizen with his/her own American Dream seeking his/her share of the pie sees the system as providing him/her with, if not the best, an opportunity to rise as an individual. American individualism has therefore resulted in a poorly developed, immature concept of social justice. Justice means that I get my share. Liberty means that no one hinders me directly as an individual in the pursuit of my interests. Revolution has occurred not when oppression no longer exist but, when I am no longer oppressed.

The shortcomings of the American understanding of the ideals which it professes through its mythological social democracy can be seen by addressing the implications of Liberal Democracy as a framework of law in which citizens are free to pursue their personal interest with maximum freedom. Equality is an ideal which is well propagated in the American myth of democracy, but this myth is subverted by the bourgeoisie liberal democracy. This ideal is corrupted by the individualism of the society and by the concentration on the legal framework in which this equality must exist. Although the term equal opportunity is often used as a trigger to stir up the American notion of social justice, the term poorly expresses the meaning of equality in the American socio-political system. Rather than expressing equal opportunity, equality in America expresses equal protection from governmental persecution, an equal protection of these rights under the law, and an equal absence of formal hindrances to the pursuit of individual interests.

Equality as established in the Constitution of the United States and in the operation of the American socio-political and economic system in no way suggests equal access to resources for the attainment of one is personal interests. Nor does it guarantee a level playing ground for all players.[39] Since the economic system itself is based, both historically and in its contemporary mode

---

[39]   Affirmative action was hailed as an attempt to create a level playing ground but only on a superficial level characteristic of a society which measures such values in legal terms and thus by quantifiable analysis.

of operation, upon inequality, the promotion of a level playing ground would require radical reform or "affirmative action" aimed at rectifying the historical disadvantage of the oppressed and exploited groups in the society not on an individualistic level but rather on a collective basis.

The civil rights movement, hailed as movement for equal opportunity, although having significant impact upon the legal framework of liberal democracy failed to be truly a movement for equal opportunity or liberation, rather, the main thrust of the movement was one of inclusion. That is, the minority groups were not, in fact, fighting for equality but in effect fighting to be recognized first as persons due the rights established in the US Constitution. Although the aims and accomplishments of this movement are worthy of praise for having significant impact upon the society, they fall far short of being revolutionary because they failed to implement fundamental socio-political or economic change. While it altered the functioning of the socio-political system, it did so only in a superficial sense by granting minority groups, including blacks and women, recognition of their political and economic rights, it failed to alter significantly the realities of their status in society.

The measures taken during the civil rights movement served to grant minority groups protection under the law from discrimination, and allowed for the better navigation of the political system. Whereas this is commendable, it is not revolutionary, but rather a form of insurgence into the political system. In fact, this political insurgence served to undermine the revolutionary potential of the movement by providing it with legitimate means through which it could address its issues. Once incorporated into the political system, one which by its very structure and mode of operation is designed to "harmonize competing interests," thus nullifying them, the actions of the potential revolutionaries could more closely be controlled by the ruling class and the administration by never allowing it to pose a serious threat to the system. Furthermore, it perpetuated the myth of involvement and access, and increased the notion that these groups had a stake in the perpetuation of the system. Lastly, it allowed for the appeasement of the movement through token gains which suggested gradual progress towards the attainment of their goal, which in any event was only inclusion, not liberation.

Hence, the Civil Rights Movement never attacked the system but rather demanded that minority groups be granted an opportunity to function within the political system. It was, therefore, not revolutionary, for it sought to change nothing more than demographic distribution of minorities throughout the society. It was simply a period of vibrant minority political activity within the establishment framework of democracy. In other words, it was politics as usual. What separates the Civil Rights Movement from other periods of political action was the fact that it involved the aggressive pursuit of an interest, which is in normal politics, silent. The Civil Rights Movement for all its achievement was merely a period of minority insurgence into a political system from which they had long been withdrawn and from which they have once again withdrawn.

I present this undoubtedly unpopular interpretation of the Civil Rights Movement to illustrate a simple point. The American notion of equality is not one measured by services provided and rewards received, nor is it, except in the most mythical sense, concerned with equal opportunity. Equality, in the American psyche, means equal liberty, and liberty means the absence of officially sanctioned obstruction or discrimination.

The Myth

The significance of the myth of American democracy is obviously a powerful tool in the management of the disgruntled masses. The democratic myth is, however, not simply a question of political ignorance. The American public is well socialized into a legendary understanding of American politics through education, media and a modified sense of social-revolutionary democracy through which Americans are taught to believe not only that their system stands for liberty, equality and justice, but that they have a duty and an obligation to lead the world struggle for the promotion of such rights. These notions of the superiority of their political system, often accompanied by a great sense of patriotism and nationalism, clouds the American mind from internal analysis and makes it less open to self-criticism. This is not to say that Americans fail to engage in political debate which is often critical of the functioning of the system. Rather, in their end analysis the conclusion is often affected by the notion that the American System is the best there is, that with continued work from within, and through the proper channels, it will gradually improve. This has two results:

1. It hinders the development of a revolutionary ideology;
2. Dissatisfaction with the system that never reaches levels which are likely to result in revolutionary attacks upon the system.

Because Americans perceive themselves as being at the pinnacle of political and economic systems, they have nothing to aim for. Great effort was placed during the Cold War on discrediting the only competing ideology, Marxist-Leninist Socialism and Communism through propaganda and political and economic isolation. Thus, seeing no other model, Americans, unlike citizens of developing countries have granted themselves no other option than to maintain the systems they have.

The control of dissatisfaction comes from the notion of reform from within the established political system or from a sense of apathy growing out of the retreat of the masses from political life into their personal interests. Americans see within their history a gradual progress towards the realization of their ideals. In the words of one Republican representative, "we may fall, but we fall forwards." This control of the tensions in the society is aided by several other structural characteristics too numerous and too complex to be addressed in their totality in this paper. Amongst them are the existence of freedom of speech and the freedom to lobby government for redress of individual grievances. Here lies an ideal segue to the notion of incrementalism, the adjustment of a society in stages toward the solution of a problem.

To the conservative mind, this may seem appealing, as it appears to provide solutions without drastically altering the society and destroying the good with the bad. This was the argument put forward by Burke in his treatise of the French Revolution. Incrementalism, however poses several problems for the solution of social quandaries and helps to hold revolution in check. It gives the impression of change when, in most cases, little has changed. While a law added here, a law removed there may solve a single element of a social problem most problems are deeply rooted in the society and require a complete overhaul. The prolongation of the process of change does nothing to aid in the resolution of the underlying cause of the problem. Incrementalism in the United States adds to the illusion of change from within and legitimizes it, while in most cases allows the problem to fester. As previously suggested, this pacifies the masses into the belief that progress is being made. Even more damaging is the fact that incremental changes are often short lived and that future incremental changes are made which reverse the pseudo progress previously made. Case and point: Attacks on Affirmative Action policies.

One of the most significant factors in determining the vulnerability of a state to revolution is the question of whether or not the people feel excluded and isolated. The concept of inclusion is central to the stability of the United States and it manifests itself in many ways in the American political system. Freedom of speech allows the masses an opportunity to air their grievances. In addition to having some therapeutic benefits for the aggrieved masses, it creates an illusion that they are actually being listened to. The same can be said to be true for the right to lobby the government and it must be granted that often these individual interests are in fact addressed. Again, the problem lies in the nature of the dialogue itself and its concentration upon individual grievances and interests.

Last, but not least, in the equation of stability is the structure and function of the legislative bodies of the United States. Being a liberal, democracy concerned with the protection of individual interests, the United States Senate and House of Representatives act as filtering houses in which interests may do battle for support of their various agendas. In these bodies, competing interests cancel each other out, disallowing divisive interests from gaining foot and filtering out interests in favor of major reform. Radical or revolutionary platforms are unlikely to ever find sufficient support in such bodies or to even make their way beyond the initial stages of review. Consequently, as long as revolutionary forces continue to utilize established political channels in their pursuit of change their chances for success are remarkably low. Yet, they are given a voice which continues to perpetuate faith in the possibility of success.

The Christmas Tree pattern of legislation, which allows each interest group to ensure they have gained from it coupled with the notion of congruent majority in a Congress dominated by industrial interest groups, whose interest are directly opposed to those of potential revolutionaries nullifies the chance of the revolution through Congress industrial interest groups dominate the legislative process through their representation in its two houses. (Interestingly their representatives are elected by the people, whose interest they do not necessarily share in common.)

The American political representatives find that they must serve two masters. On the one hand the constituents that elect them and the population as a whole. On the other hand, they must also serve the interest groups who aided them in their campaign for election through campaign financing and who will support them in their re-election. The problem is that the interests of these two masters are not always synonymous; in fact they are quite often in conflict of each other. Yet, in the logic of the American political system, which is after all about the protection of political interest, the elected officials must also serve their own interest, which lies in re-election, for which they will need the financial support of the industrial interest in order to win the votes of their constituents. Under the notion of concurrent majority, all represented interest groups have a right to veto any action which threatens their interest. In order for legislation to be passed, all interest must agree. Since the interest off the industrial groups is in maintaining the system from which they benefit, any revolutionary bill is a direct threat to their interest and will be subject to their veto. In the event that it is passed, it must be so modified that it simultaneously serves their interest. When two opposing interest are harmonized in such a manner, the result is that nothing has occurred and neither has won.

Thus, on both the ideological and mythical front the American society is not susceptible to revolution. First the American mind is impeded by its individualism, legalism and the American dream from reaching the psychological and or rational level at which revolution and the radical reformation of the political system becomes a solution. As a result, the American citizen is convinced to legitimize a political system from which they have retreated and which simultaneously serves interest which are not compatible with theirs. Once mobilized they are entrenched in a system which is not conducive to rapid or drastic change and are once again convinced to legitimize it through an illusion of inclusion and incremental change. Last but not least, the American political system creates not just an illusion of inclusion but one of shared interest through the myth of success.

<u>Supplement to the Paper</u>

<u>Black Nationalism</u>

Why the Black case study? Blacks in the United States of America represent a special case study distinct from any other minority group because of the historical role they have played in the development of the society. Firstly, blacks represent the only immigrant group in this nation which was forcibly brought here. Therefore, unlike any other non-native group, they made no conscious decision to undergo experiences which have shaped their development. Secondly, unlike any other group they were systematically stripped of their identity, not only as peoples but as persons. That is, they were not only stripped of a historical knowledge of self and of their nationalist identity but of their very humanity.

Furthermore, it is upon the blood and sweat of blacks that the economic fabric of the American society was built. Plantation economies throughout the Western hemisphere were built and developed upon the forced, free labor of blacks and flourished under their skill and knowledge of agricultural artisanry. Blacks have therefore, from the very creation of this nation been central and fundamental to its economic growth. The contributions of blacks to the development of the American society surpass the realm of agriculture and include the contributions of various black intellectuals, scientists and artists all of whom have made significant, meaningful and far reaching contributions to the development of this nation to the heights it has attained. Despite their contributions to its development, blacks, as a group, have been continually exploited and excluded from sharing in the spoils of society. The extent of their contributions, which date back past the revolutionary days, to the very earliest days of nation building, should entitle blacks within the American society to a position of equality. Yet, the history of blacks in this country has been one of continued racism, oppression and segregation both overtly and through more subtle social, political and economic means.

Despite this historical suppression, Blacks in the United States have failed to develop a revolutionary ideology or platform upon which to challenge the system for the respect and rewards due to them. They have failed to develop a revolutionary ideology of liberation and justice and continue to endure police brutality, discriminatory laws, political under-representation, economic: oppression, exploitation, and suppression as well as racism. This paper will address the failings of blacks to develop a revolutionary ideology with which to rectify their historic role as fourth class citizens, the underclass and outsiders in a land which they have built.

The fundamental failing of Black revolutionary movements within the United States is the failure to develop a well-defined sense of self as a people, in the form of Black Nationalism, throughout the African Diaspora and, for the purpose of this supplement, within the United States. Consider the following scenario[40]:

> During a course discussion, concerning individualism in the United States and the nature of the realities of the American political system, a professor poses the following proposition: One fundamental difference between the manner in which black and white Americans experience the world around them is that whereas white men see themselves merely as men, Black Men must always see themselves as black men.

---

[40]   A conversation between myself and one of my graduate professors in the New York University GSAS, Department of Politics.

The two students of African ancestry sitting in the class are asked to validate the truth of this statement. One responded in the affirmative suggesting that, even if a black person were to for a moment ignore his race as a significant part of his identity and image, the experience of living in a society dominated by whites who can perceive them as nothing other than black, serves to remind them of the significance which this character plays in determining who they are. The other student responded negatively, rejecting the notion that Blacks can never see themselves as being just men and not Black men in the American context. His basis for his suggestion that he himself thought it irrelevant and that the problem of perception lay with the perceiver who was unable to see beyond his race.

The professor further supports this argument by suggesting that in his personal experience of dealing with African American colleagues, he found that they were easily able to interact with himself and other white colleagues in an interpersonal manner and that this fact suggested that they perceived themselves simply as persons void of racial categorization. Therefore, the notion of blackness was not embedded into their consciousness.

A week later the first student is invited into the professor's office to discuss his career aspirations. The student relays to the professor his interest in several fields and explains the decision that he has made based upon job placement possibilities. In concluding their discussion, the professor makes the following comment, "well, I think that you could go into any field you choose. There is such a shortage of Black academics and the demand is so high for them that I think you'll find a position, no matter what you do."

This scenario, I think, illustrates the nature of the reality of the black identity crisis as well as the short comings of those who seek solutions to it and aim to understand it. The problem with the manner in which this real-life scenario played itself out is that the question was poorly phrased from the beginning. Rather than addressing whether or not blacks always see themselves as being black, the real question is why shouldn't blacks see themselves as Blacks? Why is there or should there be any need to, or any attempt to shed them of this identity. For the black, the Diasporic African, the descendant of slaves, the African American, black is the only nationality available to them.

The experience of slavery, the forced exodus of multi-national Africans to Americans and the systematic stripping from them of identity, name, language, history and culture left the slave to create for themselves a new identity, a new sense of self building upon the remnants of their ancient culture which they were able to maintain and simultaneously adopting new ideas, cultures behaviors and beliefs relevant to the environment in which they found themselves. The only common heritage which these new Diasporic Africans share is their classification as a race and history of their struggle for recognition and self- determination.

Thus, the denial or rejection of this identity of Black nationalism limits the ability of blacks to develop the collective consciousness necessary for a revolutionary struggle for their liberation. This rejection of their identity has several significant impacts upon the black community and manifests itself in several ways;

1. The socialization of blacks in the western hemisphere to see their color, their blackness, as being synonymous with being poor, oppressed, and subhuman has resulted in a tendency of blacks to disassociate themselves from their own people. Like the gypsy, Mother Theresa, who while struggling worldwide for the rights of poor Indians and Africans neglected the suffering of her own Roma people, the Black middle class has also turned their back upon the masses of its people. Thus, it is common for black middle-class citizens at their earliest convenience relocate themselves from the ghettos into which they were born to seldom return. Their failure to contribute their skills, knowledge, influence and example to the development of the community perpetuates the continued suffering of blacks in these communities, divides blacks as a people, disallows the development of a strong sense of community and robs the community of potential advocates and political leverage.

2. This in turn encourages a continued subconscious sense of inferiority amongst blacks. Scholars such as Rex Nettleford, studying the Caribbean region, point to a crisis of self-consciousness amongst blacks by illustrating the way they themselves project racist stereotypes upon their own people. The result is an open preference of lighter skin color gradation, suggesting that the closer to white and further away from black the better. The consciousness crisis is further illustrated in the manner in which people from the region use the term blackness as an insult. In the American context, the problem is the same but manifests itself in a notably different manner. The adaptation of the term "Nigga" (Nigger) as being synonymous with black illustrates a poorly developed appreciation of "self" amongst blacks and a subconscious acceptance of the stereotypes imposed

upon them throughout their history of oppression and dehumanization in the western hemisphere.

These are but two examples of the dangers of the failure of blacks to develop a new self-perpetuated sense of Black identity. Before a people can engage in a struggle of liberation they must first develop a sense of self, of peoplehood or nationalism. The result of this failure is that the Black struggle within the American context has not become one of liberation but rather one of integration.

The danger of this approach to the black struggle is that it:

a) Leads to a cooptation of interest and a consequent loss of focus and direction within the movement;
b) It produces resistance within the group against their own liberation and legitimization and
c) It leads to the legitimatization of their collective interest not as a people but as socio-economic class.

These three factors are closely connected and intertwined. Co-optation of interest has the impact of diluting the thrust of any revolutionary movement. The movement then readjusts its approach and redirects some of its efforts to the achievement of aims which are not necessarily directed to its benefit for example; the co-optation of women and gay rights into a struggle against racial oppression. Not denying that these issues are significant and relevant, but the need to divide one's goals into a multi-ended struggle complicates the issue at hand often means that issues central to a group are moved from the fore front to a secondary or a shared primary position. Thus, the agenda at hand becomes clouded, diluted or forgotten.

This problem of co-optation has significance even within a group, such as blacks within the United States, who have not yet developed a mature collective consciousness. The disassociation of middle class blacks from their poorer brothers has resulted in a perceived difference of interests. Integration into the establishment particularly of middle class blacks perpetuates the notion that they have a stake in the establishment which they must protect. This perceived interest in the establishment means that they as leaders or simply as participants in the struggle cannot support revolutionary ideology which attacks the establishment itself. Examples in point can be seen in the reactions of Elijah Muhammad to the continued radicalization of Malcolm X's advocacy. The Nation of Islam has been and continues to be, despite its nationalistic and revolutionary dialogue, well integrated into the establishment, receiving the majority of its funding from security contracts with the Government to patrol residential projects. The same can be seen true of the NAACP and its increasingly conservative stance on the issue of Black liberation can claim no independence from the establishment and to attack it through the promotion of a revolutionary ideology is to bite the hand that feeds you.

Particularly from the Black middle class, clear resistance to revolutionary liberation can be seen. This problem is a direct result of the failure to develop a concrete sense of nationalism and collective identity and to develop the necessary socio-economic structures which would support such. For even though the Nation of Islam and several other organizations have developed a well cemented sense of identity and a black consciousness, without the economic infrastructure to support such, their very survival is dependent upon their integration into the very system which they oppose.

The thrust of integration itself undermines the development of Black Nationalism by attacking its legitimacy. As illustrated in the aforementioned scenario the question as to why this Black consciousness must be perpetuated is raised. It is important to note that in the American context, a nation of immigrants, the same question is never asked of the Jews, Irish Americans, Dominicans, Cubans, Italians, or Asians. It is taken for granted that they must maintain their nationalist identities. Yet, for

Blacks, the very mention of Black Nationalism sounds alarms of radicalism and revolution. It must be noted that although Blacks were, in effect, founding fathers of this nation by virtue of their contribution, they like their Asian counterparts, stand out as distinct by the very nature of their physical appearance and their integration can never be unnoticeable. Therefore, whereas Italian immigrants can forget their ethnic identity, if they so choose, the Black has no such option and cannot, even if he so desires, rid himself of his superficial distinctness. When the movement is fought on a platform of integration, the question becomes, if one is fighting for integration and equality regardless of race, why stress the difference? The answer lies in the word "regardless." If the true aim is for equality regardless of race, class or creed then there should be no need for any people to attempt to shed themselves of their nationalist identity. The thrust should be to express this identity and to grant it legitimacy. But, this aspiration is an illusion and a part of the American myth. An examination of the melting pots of American society, such as New York, shows vividly that in fact the melting pot does not exist; rather that the society exists in an immiscible state. Hence, the very aspiration is an illusion.

Integration within the American society reflects the nature of its political function. It is a managed system of pockets of interests and identity, where those with the strongest sense of collective identity wield the greatest political power and influence. This can be seen in the success of such nationalistic groups of Jews and Dominicans in New York and Cubans in Florida; and further illustrated in the political success of industrial lobbyist groups who develop a collective consciousness around the protection of their economic and political interest. The failure of Blacks to similarly develop such a consciousness weakens their struggle for the attainment of social, political and economic leverage within the society. Thus, their struggle dooms them to continued impotence.

The root causes of the failure of Blacks in the United States to develop this consciousness can of course be traced back to the experience of slavery. Under the conditions of chattel slavery, the creation of such an identity was strictly forbidden and deliberately discouraged and undermined. This factor has had far reaching consequences in determining the path which the black liberation struggle has undertaken. Beginning with the effects upon this experience of emancipation, this period must be granted some brief attention to properly understand the historical context in which this weakness has developed.

The emancipation of slaves in the Western hemisphere amply demonstrates the lack of legitimacy granted to blacks in the struggle for their own liberation. The emancipation of slaves gave no regard to the legitimization of the interests, desires and aspirations of former slaves. It must be noted that at no point during the process of abolishing slavery and attempting to "rectify its evils" were Blacks ever consulted to determine their desires. The blank promissory note of 40 acres and a mule represents the full extent to which any regard was given to the development of blacks within the American society. The aim of the establishment was and remains that Blacks should maintain the same socio-economic status which they have historically held and that the status quo not be disturbed.

The solution presented for the Black problem was that they should no longer be tied to their plantations by physical chains. Yet full integration on an equal basis was never seen as a solution. Therefore, the solution was and remains, no solution. Leaving aside the fact that it took a hundred years after the emancipation of slaves for Blacks to be recognized as people with rights, privileges and aspirations worthy of attention, in a word "persons"; and for any meaningful integration to have occurred, the immediate superficial integration of blacks into the American society undermined the development of a positive black consciousness at the point in history when it was most critical. The Emancipation of slaves represents the first and most crucial point in African American history when the former slaves should have begun to redefine themselves as a people. The immediate "integration" of them into society as fourth class citizens undermined the development of a positive perception of self. Rather, it continued a tradition of self-definition in contrast to the dominant class. Thus, black meant not white. It is here that the origins of the black inferiority complex begin. On the one hand, it quelled the revolutionary fire for "freedom," without granting meaningful freedom; on the other hand, it perpetuated the same social relationships which they had traditionally fought against.

This period in history should have represented the development of a new nationalistic identity, in the tradition of the exodus from Egypt of the people of Israel. Rather, through integration, the roots of nationalism were swallowed up in a nationalistic black hole. Integrated into a society from which they were excluded, rather than building a new nation, Blacks were forced to struggle for recognition and legitimization. This tradition of struggle continues, unbroken through the civil rights movement and beyond.

This corruption of the process of nation building is echoed clearly in the popularized speech by Rev. Dr. Martin Luther King Jr. professing a dream of integration. It is clearly visible in the aims and aspirations of the civil rights movement and more importantly in its outcomes. The failing of the movement to develop a Black Nationalist agenda has resulted in solutions which do not represent the interest of a people but rather which reduce the question of discrimination to the individualistic level. Thus, solutions such as Affirmative Action provide no plans for the development of a people but rather seek to correct individual cases of discrimination. Rather than provide a solution for the development of a black education system which adequately caters to the needs of black children, it sought a solution in integration without regard to whether or not their need would be adequately met in such arrangements. After all, if discrimination exists in 'Integrated" society and inequality and racism are the order of the day, how then can integrating young blacks into a school system which is a fundamental unit of socialization for the greater society and which reflects the views and beliefs of the larger society, rectify the problem? The failure to develop a Black Nationalist ideology and the attempts to become more American and less Black has meant that Blacks in their struggle for their liberation continue to turn to the establishment against which they fight for solutions to their problems. No revolutionary outcomes can come forth from such an approach. In the history of the black struggle, the notion of self – empowerment has been a missing factor.

It has been suggested, and may seem implicit in the course of this discourse, that there exists no truly revolutionary ideology in the black community and those notions of self-empowerment and self-definition are anomalies. To assume or suggest such would be false. The very mention of names such as Marcus Garvey, Stokely Carmichael, Huey P. Newton, Bobby Seale and the Black Panther Party, Rastafarian notions of Black Nationalism and repatriation, all revolutionary and nationalistic in their advocacy and doctrine, should be sufficient to dispute the notion. In fact, the problem is not that they do not exist but rather that they do not take hold in the American society, that when they do, they often do so in a superficial manner and that Black Nationalism remains stagnant in its very early stages of development.

The decades following the Civil rights movement, in part spurred on by the rise in Black Nationalist struggles of liberation throughout Africa, has vitalized the nationalist aspirations of blacks in the United States. An interesting dialogue of afro centrism and black economic empowerment has found favor with a growing population within the black community. These notions coupled with an ongoing tradition of redefinition of language and the growing legitimization of Black culture as being of worth and a source of pride have begun to lay the foundation for a redefinition of blackness and the black community. The question still remains to be answered, to what extent this new sense of identity will find root deep in the consciousness of African-Americans. After all, dashikis, afros, Dread-locks and buy black campaign may be merely superficial, a mere fad and may soon pass away. In any event, this new development of a new identity is not being accompanied by a revolutionary dialogue and the myth of inclusion in both the political and economic structures continue to be real to African-Americans. Even in light of their budding nationalism, their goal is directed to the integrated society in which there is no regard paid to race or creed. But there is hope!

CHAPTER 5

Why the Clinton Health
Care Plan Failed?

The United States is the sole remaining western Democracy to continue to allow a large "percentage of its population to go entirely without health insurance coverage." The world is left to ponder why and how the most affluent nation on the planet can continue with a health care system which is unable to contain costs and leaves forty million citizens with no health insurance and millions more with inadequate coverage. (Roche, James 2001)

The preceding quote by James Roche in his article "Health Care in America: why we need Universal Health Care and why we need it now", is a powerful introduction to any discussion on the state of health care and the disappointing failure of health care reform in the United States. It would be expected that in the world's leading democracy, a country with a historical emphasis on individual rights, that the right of access to healthcare would be readily recognized, protected and promoted. However, a brief look at the history of health care reform demonstrates a historical resistance to, or neglect of, the idea of health care as a fundamental right which should be guaranteed to citizens. In fact, in Collins v Harker Heights, the Supreme court ruled that the constitution does not guarantee certain minimum rights of treatment nor "otherwise impose an affirmative obligation on the state to ensure that life, liberty or property do not come to harm through other means." This ruling negates the right to health care and, hence any basic standard for its provision. The supreme court, therefore, established that substantive due process under the due process clause of the Fourteenth Amendment does not extend to a fundamental right to healthcare, but on the contrary, that this clause was intended to limit the State's power to act.

Beyond the constitutional question, one must nonetheless question why such an inherently important and cross cutting issue for many citizens, despite being the subject of decades of debate, has nonetheless resulted in a failure to implement a health care system capable of providing a reasonable level of coverage to the majority, if not all, its citizens. It seems that the political importance of this debate should be enough, in any responsive democracy, to force representatives to enact laws favorable to the vast majority of their constituents. However, in the United States of America, health care reform, and in particular the development of a universal health care system, remains an elusive desire of a vast segment of the citizenry. As Theda Skocpol notes:

> Six times over the course of the twentieth century in the late 1910s, during the 1930s, in the late 1940s, during the mid-1960s, during the 1970s and in the early 1990s - reform minded professionals pushed for government financing of health care for all, or large categories of Americans. Again and again comprehensive plans for rational and cost-efficient reforms were drawn up, amidst considerable or great optimism that at last "the time was ripe" for the United States to join the rest of the civilized democratic-industrial world in providing broad health care coverage for its citizens. Only once did such efforts succeed, during the mid-1960s, when Medicare and Medicaid were enacted at the height of the great society (Skocpol in Aaron, 1996: 53).

This paper investigates some of the problems surrounding recent efforts to reform the existing system of health care delivery in the United States. It focuses heavily on the failure of the Clinton Administration to successfully deliver meaningful changes to this system, despite it being a central pillar of the platform upon which he was elected. However, the central focus of this paper is not to investigate, in detail, the Clinton Health Care Plan itself, but rather to highlight some of the larger structural characteristics of the American democratic system which necessarily impede the passage of broad sweeping reform. Furthermore, this paper focuses on reform efforts in the 103rd congress (1993-94) which represented a unique window of opportunity for success. The challenges faced after the 1994 elections were significantly different and consequently should be treated separately.

The paper is divided into several basic sections. First, it highlights the extent of the social problem created by the current health care system. Second, the paper provides a brief overview of the history of health care reform in the United States and the nature of the current health care system. Next, we examine several theories which have been advanced to explain the failure of Clinton's 1993-94 health care reform package.

FRAMING THE PROBLEM:

The opening statements to this paper, provide only a superficial look at health care delivery in the United states as a social problem which desperately needs to be addressed. It is estimated that in 1995, as the Clinton health care reform package floundered:

> thirty-seven million Americans [seventeen percent of the population], had no health care coverage or had grossly inadequate coverage. Moreover, it is estimated that two million Americans lose their health insurance every month, most for short periods of time and some for considerably longer periods. Furthermore, many of the elements of the American population ... (children, adolescents, elderly, minorities and women) do not have full access to quality healthcare. (Resnick & DeLeon, 1995: 3)

Of those American citizens who have health care coverage, it is estimated that as many as "fifty million have major gaps in their benefits and the overwhelming majority do not have comprehensive coverage." (Navarro, 1993) In addition to this, the cost of healthcare is rising at alarming levels. In 1992, the cost of long-term health care was averaged at $27,243 per annum, an alarming figure given the national median per annum income of $30,000.

Furthermore, the United States currently boasts the most expensive health care system in the developed world; spending some 1.3 trillion dollars in 1998. Yet, the world's leading democracy and most developed nation ranks alarmingly low using social indicators. In 1992, the United States ranked eighteenth in the world in life expectancy among females, and twenty-third for males. In the area of infant mortality, the United States ranked twenty-first in the number of deaths of children under the age of five, and twenty-fourth in the number of babies born with adequate birth weight. (Roche, 2001: 1) These numbers on their own are astounding, but in light of the relative expense of the system as compared to other developed nations with better social indicators it is increasingly perplexing that the need for health care reform is not a pressing issue on the agenda of American lawmakers.

According to Roche (2001), 'Americans spent an average of $4,095 per person on health care in 1997, substantially more than in other industrialized countries, such as Switzerland ($2,611), Japan ($1,760) or Great Britain ($1,391); all countries having lower infant mortality rates and higher life expectancies. Furthermore, as Robert Resnick and Patrick DeLeon (1995) point out, "Our nation's health care costs continue to rise faster than any other segment of our economy - and at a rate more than double general inflation." Given this, it is evident that the current system is not only both ineffective and inefficient but that the number of citizens without proper care is likely to continue to rise without some government intervention.

By the time of the 1993-94 Clinton health care reform effort, polls across the United States reported overwhelming support for health care reform. The public strongly believed there was in fact a health care crisis and that the system needed to be fundamentally rebuilt.

THE HISTORY OF HEALTH CARE REFORM:

Efforts at health care reform have focused on a number of important considerations. First is the economic cost of the delivery of service or "cost containment". Second is the protection of patients' rights and the regulation of service delivery. Third is the guarantee of access to health care by a wider cross section of the population. And finally, the maintenance of reasonable profit margins for both health care service providers and insurance companies.

According to Rushefsky and Patel (1997), the first efforts to provide national health insurance (NHI) began with the Progressives of the early 1900's. With the election of 1912, health care reform became a central issue in the presidential race. However, candidate Theodore Roosevelt, who "strongly supported national health insurance, as well as other progressive reforms (workmen's compensation, child labor laws)" (Rushefsky & Patel, 1997: 4), was defeated at the polls by Woodrow Wilson. Wilson was less supportive of national health insurance and failed to aggressively pursue the issue. However, Progressives continued to push for reform and managed to garner support from some influential groups including the American Medical Association in 1917. With the involvement of the United States in World War I, the issue lost salience and the Progressive's efforts failed.

Under the New Deal, another effort was once again made to reform health care service. In this era, Blue Cross and Blue Shield programs ascended in popularity accompanied by the rise of private insurance companies who would eventually replace the traditional fee-for-service relationship between patients and their physicians. In developing his New Deal initiatives, Roosevelt intended to propose a national health insurance plan as part of his social security act, "but reluctantly concluded that national health insurance could not be passed, largely because of the opposition of the American Medical Association" (Rushefsky & Patel, 1997: 5-6). In addition to the opposition of powerful groups such as the American Medical Association, internal differences between Northern Democrats and the influential and conservative Southern Democrats also impeded the passage of health care reform.

> As was to be true later on, the democratic party in the 1930s was not unified behind a health care plan. Attempting to pass a package that included NHI with Social Security would doom Social Security. The Social Security Act of 1935, the fundamental piece of social welfare legislation in the history of the United States, created the social security, welfare, and unemployment compensation programs that other western industrialized nations had. But, unlike those others, health care was not a part of the program (Rushefsky & Patel, 1997: 6).

The divisions within the Democratic party similarly hampered the development of the next reform effort, under Truman in the 1940s. Truman made health care reform an integral part of his election campaign and despite attacks from the Republicans that his program was socialist, managed to win the Presidency. Although there was Democratic control of the senate, the domination of Southern Democrats again made it difficult for the President to muster support for his national health insurance plan. Despite not developing a comprehensive plan, the Eisenhower administration (1953-61), did succeed in making some incremental changes to the system. In 1960, the Kerr-Mills bill provided matching funds to states to help offset the cost of health care for poor elderly patients. The War on Poverty, campaigns of the Kennedy/Johnson administration also made significant incremental steps towards reforming health care policy. Most notably, the Medicare and Medicaid bills passed by congress in the 1960s built upon the Kerr-Mills bill and provided government sponsored medical coverage for the elderly.

In an effort to control the rising cost of health insurance, the Nixon administration supported the development of health maintenance organizations (HMOs) in 1973. These institutions, which dominate the health care service industry today, receive fixed payments for group members and provide a comprehensive set of healthcare services. Because no additional charges are made for additional services, these organizations have an "incentive ... to control costs and provide preventative services to [their] members" (Rushefsky & Patel, 1997: 8).

According to Rushefsky & Patel (1997), several attempts were again made during this period to have national health insurance plans implemented. In 1970, Senator Edward Kennedy (D-Mass) proposed the Health Security Act. This was essentially a single payer, universal national health insurance system. Prior to that, the president of the United Auto Worker (UAW), Walter Reuther, called for the enactment of such a system. The Nixon Administration responded in 1971 with the Comprehensive Health Insurance Plan (CHIP), mandating employer-provided health insurance. However, Nixon's plan would have left some 20-40 million people uninsured. Yet another proposal focused on covering only the most costly (catastrophic) medical expenses.

> None were enacted ... because of continued opposition by the AMA and other interest groups,

> conservative opposition to NHI, the economic
> distress of the period and at best lukewarm
> attitude of the administration to the new social
> program. (Rushefsky & Patel, 1997: 8)

Several other minor attempts were made in the 1970-80s to regulate health care reform with little success. So, the health care system remained fundamentally unchallenged until Clinton's historic 1993-4 attempts.

Our current system of health care service delivery is dominated by managed care programs. Managed Care Organizations (MCOs) date back to the great depression of the 1930's and were promoted as an effective means to cut the costs associated with "fee-for- service" healthcare and to ensure that only the most "appropriate" and cost effective high-quality care is provided to patients. The 1973 Health Maintenance Organization Act signed into effect by President Nixon formally presented managed care organizations as an alternative to fee-for-service operations. Today, over 170 million Americans receive their medical services through some form of managed care. (Weide, 2000: 6) The lucrative nature of their business can be seen in the fact that these managed care organization currently enjoy a 10% annual growth rate (Resnick, 1995)

Several criticisms have been raised about managed care systems. One popular criticism is that it involves third party intervention into the traditional relationship between the physician and the patient. A second related criticism is that these managed care systems place a higher priority on cost effectiveness than on the effective treatment of patients. Inherent to this system of health service delivery is the integration of medical and coverage decision making. Since any resource allocation has medical consequences, MCO cost control strategies impact on the standard of care and limit or eliminate physician autonomy.

With the victory of the Democratic candidate William Clinton in the 1992 presidential election, the Democratic party experienced for the first time in over a decade a "unified" government. In addition to their recent victory in the presidential election, the Democratic majorities in the House and Senate seemed to present a window of opportunity for unification around the issue of health care reform. It is in this environment that Clinton undertook to boldly act on an issue which the Democratic party had successfully campaigned around and, to enact new laws which might essentially change health care service in the United States.

In light of this unique opportunity, why did the Clinton efforts to enact health care reform fail? Several explanations have been offered for this failure. The true causes, perhaps lie in a combination of them. Among the arguments offered for the failure of the Clinton plan are:

a. The plan was "too big" and proposed too far sweeping an effort at reform

b. The strategy adopted by the Clinton advisors in constructing the bill excluded key political figures whose support was necessary for its passage

c. There was a lack of unity within the democratic party

d. The medical insurance lobbyist are too well entrenched and invested in the political system to be easily defeated

e. The Clinton Administration failed to maintain public interest and activism around the issue of health care reform

f. The American Political structure (especially the committee system) is structurally biased against major reforms and favors incremental change instead.

It must first be recognized that the task of uncovering the true root of the failure will inevitably be a mammoth undertaking. At this time, this paper examines some of the structural and institutional characteristics of the American political culture and highlights some of the pitfalls which may have and most likely did contribute to this particular policy failure.

THE PLAYERS & THE IRON TRIANGLE THEORY:

A good starting point for this is the examination of the various groups with expressed interests in the policy decision. Three major groups can be easily identified. First, we have the general population, which according to polls, were largely in favor of a major revamping of the health care system. According to several sources (Navarro, 1993; Heclo, 1996) leading up to the presentation of the Clinton health care bill, 82% of the general population supported efforts for government intervention in the health care system. The second group, to be considered are the various interests groups representing the major insurance companies and other associated groups in the medical industry. The third and final group is composed of health care professionals, who for various reasons oppose the current system of health care service delivery.

Of these three groups, two have vested interests in revamping the health care system, while the other is the main beneficiary of the status quo. However, it is important to realize that power and influence are not equally distributed among these competing groups. It is assumed that in a democratic system the people or, to be more precise, the voters are the source of authority for elected officials. It would therefore seem logical that in the performance of their duties, that elected officials should pander to the interests of the voters and aim at passing laws favorable to them. However, several characteristics of the American voter combine to reduce their influence on individual policy decisions.

One enduring theory often invoked to explain the lack of responsiveness of legislative institutions to the interests of their constituents is the Iron Triangle or Sub- Government theory.

This theory suggests that policy decision making is heavily dominated by the 'influence of "cozy little triangles" of private, congressional, and administrative actors more durable than any single presidential administration'(Gais, Peterson and Walker, Jr. in Walker, Jr., 1991 : 123). Under the traditional theory, policy decisions on a particular issue are made by tightly controlled and restricted groups of individuals representing these three areas. "A system of sub-governments has strong built-in barriers against all efforts at redistribution. New programs could be added as long as the established system was not disturbed" (Gais, Peterson and Walker, Jr. in Walker, Jr., 1991: 125). "The participants would remain the same through several different presidential administrations and their fortunes would not be materially affected by the shifting partisan balance in Congress" (Gais, Peterson and Walker, Jr. in Walker, Jr., 1991: 126). Through this tightly knit network, the status quo could be protected and moderate reforms could be made, but "efforts to eliminate programs or change budget shares in order to free resources could be successful only if political leaders were willing to make extremely large investments of energy and prestige" (Gais, Peterson and Walker, Jr. in Walker, Jr., 1991: 125).

In more recent decades however, several scholars have been increasingly critical of the Iron Triangle theory as a paradigm with which to understand the policy making process in contemporary American politics. Thomas L. Gais, Mark A. Peterson and Jack L. Walker, Jr., for example highlight Hugh Heclo's (1978) objection to this theory in their analysis of the Iron Triangles on the American democratic process.

> The iron triangle concept is not so much wrong as it is disastrously incomplete ... the conventional view is especially inappropriate for understanding changes in politics and administration during the recent years ... looking for closed triangles of control, we tend to miss the fairly open networks

of people that increasingly impinge upon government. (Heclo, 1978. :88 In Gais, Peterson and Walker, Jr. in Walker, Jr., 1991 : 124)

As Gais, Peterson and Walker, Jr. suggest, the proliferation of interest groups from the 1960s onwards and the shifting ideological perspective against the influence of commercial interest groups on the government produced fundamental changes in the decision making process. The re-distributive policies of the 1960s-80s saw the introduction of new opposing groups into the political bargaining process and moved the responsibility for policy decision making to a broader, more diverse arena outside of the closed committee groups which dominated the traditional sub-government system (Gais, Peterson and Walker, Jr. in Walker, Jr., 1991: 126-128). As a result, they conclude that by 1980 the old sub-government system was no-longer capable of effectively monopolizing the policy making process. "Many iron triangles remained in operation, but their influence was less pervasive than in the 1940s and 1950s, and the governmental system could no longer accurately be characterized as a loose collection of sub-governments" (Gais, Peterson and Walker, Jr. in Walker, Jr., 1991 :125).

If it is true that the sub-government system was handicapped by the emergence of new interest groups and other related developments in the political process, it does not necessarily follow that these developments effectively eliminated the existence of the Iron Triangles. While it is certain that modifications may have been made to the manner in which these groups influence policy making, their impact on the political process cannot be ignored. Even within the context of increased competition, the presence of opposition groups does not imply that these groups are equally effective in their attempts to influence the legislative process.

A closer look at the players involved in attempts to influence the healthcare debate illustrates the enduring effectiveness of the relationship between corporate interests and policy makers. The three groups identified above fit well with the classifications utilized by Gais, Peterson and Walker, Jr. in their analysis of the influence of interest groups on national politics. In this section we focus heavily on two of these groups, citizen groups (representing the various coalitions of voters) and profit or occupational[41] groups (insurance companies, HMOs). The third group consisted of a variety of health care professionals and other not for profit groups concerned mostly with issues of medical liability and doctor autonomy and may best be classified as falling into what Gais, Peterson and Walker, Jr. in Walker, Jr., refer to as their mixed category. However, the disparities in influence may be adequately illustrated by looking at the two most ideologically opposed groups who dominated the 1993-1994 debate.

The two opposing camps utilize contrasting strategies, classified by Gais, Peterson and Walker, Jr. as inside (occupational groups) and outside (citizen groups) strategies. These strategies are however not equally effective. As they point out:

> citizen groups, once they experienced conflict were twice as likely as all types of occupational groups to appeal to the public through the mass media and to engage in various forms of grass roots mobilization at the local level. Citizen organization were also much less likely to engage in lobbying administrative agencies than were all types of occupational groups, although [there were] no appreciable difference among groups

---

[41] The category of Occupational Groups encompasses both traditional industrial lobbying institutions and other employee related lobbyist groups which emerged and developed from the 1930s through 1980s.

in their willingness to lobby Congress (Gais, Peterson and Walker, Jr. in Walker, Jr 1991: 132).

The differences in the strategies employed by citizen groups is not only reflective of the nature of these groups, but also speaks to their relative ineffectiveness when opposed to large highly entrenched industrial groups. As they note, "the occupational associations ... concentrated their efforts on institutional lobbying" (Gais, Peterson and Walker, Jr. in Walker, Jr., 1991: 132). As a part of their continued efforts to maintain strong ties with law makers, "In the 1970s ... individual corporations increased the amount of representation they maintained in Washington, and corporate political action committees were established at a rate greater than committees associated with any other institutions" (Gais, Peterson and Walker, Jr. in Walker, Jr 1991:132). By the end of the 1970s 28% of the profit sector organizations had moved their offices to Washington compared to 4% of the citizen groups.

Looking first at citizen groups, a few inherent features of these groups must be considered. The American voter is for the most part apolitical. Of the eligible voting population, only a small number ever exercise their right to vote and even fewer vote on a regular basis. In addition to their absence from the electoral system, few members of the voting population give much regard to the daily working of their political system. Zaller (1992) in his works on the American voters suggests that the level of general ignorance of the population is high even around issues which seem to have potentially great impact upon their lives. The apathy and "ignorance" of the American public towards the actual policy decisions made by their representatives means that despite the increasing transparency of the political system, elected officials are less accountable to their constituencies.

A second interrelated characteristic of the voting population is the nature of voting habits. Although no definitive study has been, or perhaps can be, done on how people actually vote, one fact about the American voter is notable. For the most part, American voters in the exercise of their electoral power, act as individuals i.e. few groups in the United States vote in blocks. This is of relative importance when considering the influence of citizen groups or "grass roots" lobbyists. Although some members of the population may individually, or in organized groups, take action to influence their elected officials' positions on issues, the relative weight of their actions are small given their voting behavior. Few organizations, despite their claims to represent large numbers of voters, can reasonably claim to control the voting behavior of their members. Therefore, beyond the general public relations question, the relative weight of their endorsements is suspect.

If we take for granted that the majority of the active voting population is loyally divided along party lines and that these voters will cast their votes along similar lines, the question remains, on what basis do the remaining "undecided voters" cast their vote? It is this population that the candidate seeking election or, more importantly for our discussion, re-election, must aim to "win over." The effectiveness of lobbyists representing civic interests lies firmly in their ability to secure or to withhold votes for the candidate. Most lobbyist who fall into this camp therefore operate on the assumption that the "undecided's" vote is determined by the candidate's position on key issues. The problem for such lobbyists however is their credibility in their claims to be able to deliver their votes in significant numbers.

This factor is made even more potent when the impact of competing lobbyist groups is examined. Unlike civic interest groups, corporate interest groups rely less heavily on their ability to deliver the direct vote. Rather, these groups provide electoral support to candidates' through campaign contributions.

As Vincente Navarro points out, in the ten-year period from 1981 to 1991:

> The insurance industry's political action
> committees (PAC) contributed $60 million to
> members of congress, with much of the money
> going to the chairs and key members of health-
> related committees ... The twenty- five members
> who received the greatest amounts of medical
> industry PAC money all hold leadership positions
> in the House or are members of the Ways and
> Means or Energy and Commerce committees.
> (Navarro, 1993: 33-4)

In addition to monetary contributions made to individual representatives some industries and PACs also give generously to both dominant parties.

> In 1991, Aetna, Warner-Lambert, Chubb the
> American Dental Association's PAC and the
> Humana hospital chain each gave so-called
> "soft-money" contributions of $20,000 to the
> Republican party, Blue cross and Blue shield
> gave $29,000 to the Republican party and almost
> $17,000 to the Democrats. Upjohn gave $25,000
> to the Democrats and $23,000 to the Republicans
> and Glaxo, another drug company gave $50,000
> to the Democrats." (Navarro, 1993: 33)

By the time that President Clinton presented his health care reform package:

> ... according to a study by the Center for Public
> Integrity, health care reform would become "the
> most heavily lobbied legislative initiative in recent
> US History." During 1993 and 1994, "hundreds of
> special interests cumulatively ...[spent] in excess

of $100 million to influence the outcome of this
public policy issue." (Scokpol in Aaron, 1996: 45)

These monetary contributions bear greater practical
significance to career politicians than the promise of voter
patronage at the polls. Whereas the influence of various civic
groups on their membership may be questionable, campaign
contributions allow candidates an opportunity to reach voters
directly and to deliver their own messages via the media or
through direct campaign rallies. The relative advantage of
corporate lobbyist however is not routed simply in their ability
to finance election campaigns. Access to elected officials is also
biased in favor of corporate lobbyists.

Navarro argues that class divisions in the American society
favor the corporate interest groups by allowing them greater
access and closer bonds with influential officials as compared
to average constituents. One aspect of this close relationship is
the fluidity of career transitions between major corporation in
the private sector and the higher echelons of public service. For
example, in the 1992 elections the chief health advisors for both
competing presidential candidates were Washington lobbyists
for the insurance or pharmaceutical industries (Deborah
Steelman for the Republican Party and Bruce Field for the
Democrats). Similarly, he argues, there exists a revolving door
which moves politicians and the staff of major congressional
committees to jobs in the corporate sector. Navarro offers
several examples of this pattern as it relates to the health care
industry, including Former Presidents Ronald Reagan and
George Bush both of whom worked for major companies in
this industry. Other examples of this relationship include,
Gordon Wheeler, former Congressional Liaison to the Office of
Management and Budget and Assistant to President Bush who
later acted as Political Affairs Director for the Health Insurance
Association. John Salmon, former Aide to House Ways and
Means Committee Chair, Frank McLaughlin, former Aide to

former House Speaker Tip O'neal and Dawson Mathis, former Member of Congress are all examples of this revolving door and are all now representatives of major corporations in the health care industry. (Navarro 1993: 36)

This relationship between the corporate world and the national government illustrates an inherent advantage which corporate lobbyist hold over citizen groups. Not only are these professional lobbyists familiar with the inner workings of government but, by virtue of their previous positions they have established personal and professional working relationship with many of the key players who impact upon the policy making process. The competing forces of these two lobbyists groups therefore represent a grave mismatch.

However, to simply accept this as a explanation for the failure to implement health care reform is to suggest that the American democratic system is corrupt to its core and that in the world of American politics only the dollar counts. Furthermore, this inequality in access and influence exists throughout the American political system and as a result cannot account for those few great moments in American history in which the interests of the common man have prevailed over those of the corporate interest groups. Despite the obvious influence of the insurance groups on the electoral outcomes of the 1992 election, a serious effort was made on the part of some elected officials to pass legislation that may have adversely affected the industry. Therefore, even though the relative influence of the corporate interest groups and their lobbyist must be factored into any analysis of the question at hand, other factors must be taken into account.

HARNESSING PUBLIC SUPPORT:

One such factor was the failure of the Clinton Administration to effectively maintain the public's interest and mobilization in favor of healthcare reform. Despite the relative effectiveness of the enduring relationships associated with the Iron Triangles, the fact remains that career politicians have a vested interest in re-election. In this light, it is generally considered political suicide to ignore resounding calls for action from the constituents.

However, Heclo notes, one key component, the public demand for reform may have been overestimated. As he posits:

> at best, public opinion polls showed a vague, simple-minded disposition towards cost-free health reform. Clearly there was nothing resembling a serious reform movement ... instead ... the appearance of grass-roots mobilization was orchestrated from above after the partisan policy lines had been drawn in Washington (Heclo, In Aaron 1996: 27).

Although Heclo may be fundamentally correct, it may be argued that what he describes is not at all uncommon of American politics, even during periods of mobilization (Walker Jr., 1991, Zaller, 1992). The American public is notorious for its lack of in-depth knowledge of any policy issues, even during periods of heated political debate, and mobilization of these groups is quite often orchestrated from the top down. Furthermore, other sources do suggest that whatever the level of mobilization, there did appear to be a general demand for health care reform among the voting public.

Theda Skocpol provides another explanation for the faltering mobilization of the public around the Clinton health care plan, when she suggests that a key factor in its demise lies in the failure of policy makers to effectively harness and fuel public support in favor of reform. Clinton needed to maintain public interest and momentum around health care and failed to do so. As she states, it is:

> never realistic to expect major stakeholders in the present system to keep bargaining over changes in the rules of the game, unless they saw that the voting public continued to want such changes ... Clinton and his allies had to hold the public's interest and support ...simply to ensure that leaders in and out of congress would remain willing to bargain." (Skocpol in Aaron, 1996: 40)

Certainly, in the months leading up to the Clinton initiative, there was ample evidence of a commitment on the part of policy makers to respond to the public's demand for reform.

> Bold proposals for reforms of health care financing proliferated inside and outside of government. Two dozen reform bills were introduced during the 102d Congress. Reform proposals, many of them sweeping, also came from business groups, trade unions, insurance companies, and assorted health policy experts. Even the America Medical Association, historically the bitterest of all enemies of governmental sponsored health reforms, came up with its own plan for universally guaranteed health insurance. (Skocpol in Aaron, 1996: 36)

In this regard, the Clinton administration made several critical mistakes. First, they failed to effectively develop political rhetoric which would unite both middle class and working-class voters around a single initiative. Second, they failed to effectively communicate their plan of action to the voting public and consequently maintain the apparent momentum for reform. And finally, the Clinton administration appeared too willing to compromise on their bill and therefore created a window of opportunity which invited a flood of demands and criticisms.

Heclo suggests that one of the characteristics of a successful reform policy is an easily identifiable and unifying goal which benefits "self conscious and at least moderately powerful constituencies" (Heclo in Aaron, 1996: 26). The challenge for the Clinton administration was to develop a platform which simultaneously addressed the concerns of a diverse group of interests. This included the middle-class citizens, satisfied with their coverage, but concerned about the rising cost of their health care and the potential loss of health care during periods of un-employment, and working class and unemployed citizen many of whom had no coverage or inadequate coverage. On the other hand, for any initiative to be successful, the interest of employers, health care providers and insurance companies had to be considered. This diffuse constituency, who stood to benefit from this reform effort was, "without doubt a large number of Americans, but they were Americans who posed the classic problem of collective action by a poorly organized, non-affluent body of people"(Heclo in Aaron, 1996: 26).

Furthermore, Heclo suggests, in contrast to the successful rallying cries of 1912 and 1932, the 1993-94 reform act:

> did not enjoy the advantage of a single, easily understood objective. Far from encapsulating a single message, the reform action to be taken pointed variously towards controlling runaway health costs, and to covering the 36-37 million uninsured, and to securing uninterrupted and adequate coverage to persons already insured. (Heclo in Aaron, 1996: 25)

Of course, these goals are not mutually exclusive but rather are closely inter-related. The failure to establish a clear platform, representative of the public's interests, around which the various interested parties could unite may have contributed to wavering public support evident in the latter stages of the reform initiative. Additionally, it may be indicative of a larger failure of effective communication with the public.

As Skocpol points out, between September 1993, when Clinton publicly declared his intentions to reform the health care system and the Summer of 1994, when the bill was presented to Congress, there was little public discourse about the actual plan. Although the task force assigned to develop the bill met with dozens of advisors from all the interests concerned, no concerted effort was made to keep the public abreast of the progress of the task-force, its ideals or even its goals. Furthermore, as Daniel Yankelovich (1995, also in Aaron 1996) notes, the public served merely as confused spectators who never became knowledgeable about the specifics of the plan and its implications for their lives." Therefore, the failure of communication runs deeper than the mere development of "appealing labels and advertising slogans" but more relevantly to the absence of public explanatory discourse.

This discourse, which takes place in what Heclo describes as the gestation period of a reform policy, allows for the gradual working through and development of arguments surrounding an issue. It is through this process that participants in the political system achieve a general understanding of the issue at hand. As a result, factual claims are tested and countered, the "problem" is defined and redefined and, alternatives advanced and attacked. "The very ability to sustain the policy argument over time helps persuade people that there is a real problem that will not go away until something is done" (Heclo, in Aaron 1996: 23). By doing so, the policy position is fine tuned and rendered more acceptable to the parties concerned.

Skocpol suggests several contributing factors to this neglect. During this period the White House was faced with a number of crucial issues which had to be addressed including the crisis in Somalia and the consolidation of the NAFTA treaty. Additionally, she suggests, Clinton expected key elements of the initial plan to be modified before it was finally passed. Given the public criticism he faced for compromising during the 1993 budget debates, Clinton was unwilling to take an early stance on the bill (Skocpol in Aaron, 1996: 41). He therefore delayed marketing the bill until it was clear what provisions might be accepted or rejected. Furthermore, Skocpol also suggests that the Democratic party "no longer has a nationally widespread, locally rooted infrastructure of loyal local organizations and allied groups (such as labor unions) through which it can run grass-roots political campaigns." (Skocpol in Aaron, 1996: 41) As a result, efforts to stimulate positive public discourse about his bill faltered.

The Administration relied heavily on the mass media to provide coverage of developments in the health care plan. The media however, focused more heavily on the personalities involved in the debate than on the substance of the issues at hand (Skocpol in Aaron, 1996: 41). In the summer of 1993, this media coverage was therefore supplemented with an effort to orchestrate grass roots dialogue on the heath care package. This effort included the establishment of a non-partisan "National Health Care Campaign" and later, the "Health Care Reform Project". These initiatives failed for several reasons. Most importantly, they failed to secure endorsements of the plan as a whole from several important citizen groups including the American Association of Retired People. As a result, although these organizations, that made up the foundation of the Administration grass roots efforts, endorsed various broad ideals expressed in the plan, they "did not specifically promote or explain the President's bill" (Skocpol in Aaron, 1996: 42).

The Republican party, on the other hand, launched an effective counter-attack against the bill. According to Skocpol, beginning toward the end of 1993, the Republican party adapted a strategy of "counter-mobilization" against reform.

> During 1994 the hard-line conservative attack
> on Clinton's Health Security plan brought

together more and more allies and channeled
resources and support towards anti-government
conservatives with the Republican party. ... The
National Federation of independent Business and
other associations mobilized against the proposed
"employer mandate". Portrayals of the Clinton
plan as a bureaucratic take-over by welfare-state
liberals were regular grist for Rush Limbaugh and
other right-wing hosts of hundreds of news-talk
radio programs. ... Similarly, Christian Coalition
groups, already attacking Bill and Hilary on
cultural issues, began to devote substantial
resources to the anti-health reform crusade. On
February 15, 1994 ... [the coalition] announced
that it was beginning a $1.4 million campaign
to build grass-roots opposition to the Clinton
Plan, with tactics to include 30 million postcards
to Congress distributed to 60,000 churches ...
(Skocpol in Aaron 1996: 46).

Therefore, it can be seen that where the pro-reform alliances
failed to effectively unite around the bill, opposition forces
developed effective coalitions against it. Furthermore, the
Republican party appears to have developed a more effective
means of grass roots dissemination of information than the
Democrats had. As a result, they dominated the public debate
around health care reform and by the time the reform bill was
presented, the current of public opinion had begun to shift.

Yankelovich concludes 'the Clinton plan's loss of public
support occurred not because a majority of voters rejected the
plan on its merit but because its opponents found it easy to raise
the public's fear about reforms people did not understand"
(Yankelovich in Aaron, 1996: 74).

The fact remained, however that at its core the reform effort was directed to a politically weak constituency, who would gain, and a well-organized and financed set of interests centered in the insurance industry, who would lose (Heclo, in Aaron 1996: 27).

DIS-HARMONY IN THE DEMOCRATIC PARTY AND THE SUB COMMITTEE SYSTEM

Throughout 1993-1994, in fact, reform minded politicians and groups in and around the democratic party could not unite on even the most basic "how to" features of health reform. ... democrats treated the president's bill as grist for protracted bargaining over this or that provision and as fodder for infinitely complicated legislative maneuvering in five different House and Senate committees (Skocpol in Aaron, 1996: 42-3).

Hugh Heclo notes that the fundamental policy reform has typically been associated with the appearance of powerfully unified party majorities in Congress and the White House. However, as he notes, this notion of a unified party majority goes beyond the existence of a mere numerical majority in the legislative and executive branches. Rather it refers to "party formations unified on the heels of an election repudiating what has been portrayed as a regime of the status quo" (Heclo, In Aaron 1996: 21). According to Heclo, the 1992 elections seemed to resemble such a period in American history and "the political setting seemed generally favorable for the president's reform effort" (Heclo, In Aaron 1996: 27).

The real issue however, was "whether [the] party had a working or effective, not just a numerical, majority" (Rushefsky & Patel, 1997: 95). As most scholars (Skocpol In Aaron, 1996, Rushefsky & Patel, 1997, Weissart & Weissart, 1996) posit, the democratic party was "not, in a fundamental way, united." Ideological differences between "liberal" and "conservative" democrats disallowed the development of a party consensus on what remedies were needed and/or would be accepted. Furthermore, Robin Toner of the New York Times suggests, the Clinton approach to the development of their initial health care reform bill excluded many members of the Legislative body from the dialog, with its closed-door task force deliberations. This closed-door approach to the development of the plan alienated many potential key supporters and further fostered the sense of division within the ranks of the Democratic party.

> The 1992 elections brought in the largest first year class in the House since 1949 - sixty three democrats and forty seven Republicans- but these newcomers were not political neophytes. Many had come up through the political ranks, including state legislative stints. ... after five months of toeing the line, they began showing their independence. With eighty two more Democrats than Republicans in the House, the President's hallmark budget and tax package passed with only two votes to spare (Weissert and Weissert, 1996 : 16)

As several scholars (Heclo, Skocpol, Weissart & Weissart and Gais, Peterson and Walker, Jr.) have noted, this sense of independence and a decline in strict partisanship was not limited to the Clinton experience but rather was part of a burgeoning tradition in the United States Congress which some (Heclo, in Aaron, 1996 & Gais, Peterson and Walker, Jr. in Walker, Jr., 1991) trace back to the 1970s.[42] During this period, the influence of party whips and the traditions of apprenticeship declined and legislative politics became increasingly "personalistic" or "candidate-centered" rather than "party-centered". Additionally, reforms in the policy making processes, redistributed the responsibility for policy making to a broader cross section of the legislature. This transition saw the rise in significance of subcommittees and an increase in policy debates on the general floor open to all representatives.

As Gais, Peterson and Walker, Jr. note:

> Congressional leaders making committee assignments felt compelled to ... *accept*, as members on committees, some legislators who did not embrace the narrow preferences that had dominated in the ... past ... even the House Appropriations committee, which always valued consensus among its members, was unable to maintain its tradition against dissent in committee reports and dissidents on the Ways and Means Committee exploited rule changes to carry their tax reform proposals to the House floor or to the Democratic caucus (Gais, Peterson and Walker, Jr. in Walker, Jr., 1991: 135)

In this environment with its several tiers and committees operating in the policy making process an increasingly important question is to which committee a bill is referred. "A complex bill, such as the Clinton Health Security Act, affects so much of the economy that multiple committees can claim

---

[42] Rushefsky & Patel (1997), although citing similar changes in the political structure, provide a contradictory account of changes in partisanship. According to them, partisanship voting increased in the period 1988 - 1994. See page 98

jurisdiction"(Rushefsky & Patel, 1997: 93). Oversight for the 1993-94 health care reform efforts in congress, fell under the auspices of at least eight committees and sub committees.

1. **Senate finance committee**:
    Subcommittee on Medicaid and Health-Care for Low Income Families
    Subcommittee on Medicare, Long-term Care and Health Insurance
2. **House Ways and Means Committee Subcommittee on Health**
3. **Senate Labor and Human Resources Committee**
4. **House Commerce Committee**
    Subcommittee on Health and the Environment
5. **Senate Appropriations Committee**
    Subcommittee on Labor, HHS and Education
6. **House Appropriations Committee**
    Subcommittee on Labor, HHS and Education
7. **Senate Budget Committee**
8. **House Budget Committee**

This political structure provides numerous opportunities for political entrepreneurs, or anti-reform members of the legislature, to intervene in the passage of any bill. Furthermore, as Skocpol comments, "Key congressional Democrats ... were unlikely to join any disciplined collective endeavor, because many had health plans of their own or were committee chairs determined to have a piece of the legislative action" (Skocpol, in Aaron 1996: 50).

As Nicholas Laham notes:

'A combined total of 31 Democratic Senators and 145 Democratic house members served as cosponsors of the two national health insurance bills introduced in the 103rd Congress -Clinton's

> Health Security Act and an alternative measure introduced by Senator Paul Wellstone of Minnesota and Representative Jim McDermont of Washington on March 3, 1993, ... by contrast, only one Republican lawmaker, Senator James Jeffords of Vermont, served as a cosponsor of national health insurance legislation in the 103rd Congress[43] (Laham, 1996: 143).

However, he notes, despite their general support for national health insurance, Democrats in Washington remained deeply divided over what kind of program should be established. The Democratic party appeared to be divided into three basic camps. Liberal Democratic members of Congress supported the establishment of a single-payer plan, in which the federal government would guarantee coverage of every individual as an entitlement of American citizenship, and finance the cost of health care through tax revenues. This approach was generally seen as politically infeasible by Clinton and other moderate democrats, who instead supported building upon the current employment based insurance system. The third group, consisted of conservative democrats who opposed an overhaul of the overall healthcare system and preferred policies promoting incremental minimal change (Laham, 1996: 143).

With Clinton's expressed willingness to compromise on various aspects of his proposed bill and the substantial support of the liberal democrats for the competing bill, the democratic party became embattled over the provisions in the bill rather than united around the cause.

---

[43] Rushefsky & Patel (1997) note that three other Republican alternatives were tabled in1994. The Chafee plan, Phil Gramm's medical savings account plan and the don Nickles' plan to use tax incentives.

> Single payer health insurance commanded
> substantial support among the Democratic
> majority in the 103rd Congress. Fully five
> senators and ninety-one House members served
> as cosponsors of the single payer insurance
> bill ... given th[is] substantial support ... the
> Health Security Act stood no chance of passage
> without the solid support of virtually all ninety
> six cosponsors of the Wellstone Mcdermott bill"
> (Laham, 1996: 150).

One group, led by representative Henry Waxman of California (chairman of the Subcommittee on Health and the Environment of Energy and Commerce Committee), urged compromise, recommending that congressional supporters of single payer insurance back the president's bill as the most comprehensive health care reform plan lawmakers were likely to pass. They were opposed by another group, led by McDermott, who urged that congressional supporters of single-payer insurance reject the bill since it did not go far enough in achieving comprehensive health care reform (Laham, 1996:151).

Waxman made it clear that his appeals for cooperation were contingent upon the bill being presented in its unmodified form. He was especially concerned that Clinton would compromise on universal coverage in order to attract more conservative Democrats. Waxman, who personally preferred the single payer approach, recognized the inherent difficulty of passing such legislation. Therefore, despite his reservations that Clinton's plan was not the easiest way to accomplish their shared goals, he recognized it as the most comprehensive bill that would likely be passed.

> Waxman argued that the real choice the 103rd
> Congress faced was between passing the Clinton
> Plan and taking no action on health care reform
> at all... supporters of single payer insurance

would be wise to support the Clinton plan, since it represented a vast improvement over the current health care system and contained many positive features congressional supporters of the Wellstone-McDermott bill could back, the most important of which were universal coverage and medical cost containment (Laham, 1996: 152).

Dermott, was less compromising, insisting that Clinton's bill simply didn't go far enough in guaranteeing universal coverage for all. In order to appease McDermott and the liberal democrats, Clinton included a clause which gave each state the option of "replacing its private insurance with a government program. McDermott rejected this concession because the Health Security Act did not require the states to establish a single payer health insurance plan; rather each state was free to decide on its own whether to do so (Laham, 1996: 158). Believing that individual states would not willing utilize this option, the compromise was seen as empty.

As public opinion towards broad sweeping changes in the health care system shifted, Waxman's fears gained credence in October 1993 when Clinton agreed to modify the provisions of his original health insurance plan relating to universal coverage. As a result, Clinton isolated the liberal democrats whose support was crucial to the passage of his bill.

Despite the obvious failure of the Clinton administration to build an effective coalition among Democrats in congress and, consequently to take advantage of the numerical majority they experienced until the 1994 elections, he nonetheless was more successful than any other president in advancing the cause of health care reform.

As Laham notes, prior to Clinton's 1993-94 efforts:

national health insurance legislation had been approved by only a single congressional committee - the Senate Labor and Human Resources Committee, which passed a comprehensive health care reform bill in the 102nd Congress. By contrast, slightly modified versions of Clinton's ...plan were approved by three of the five congressional committees in the 103rd Congress exercising jurisdiction over healthcare reform. A fourth committee, the Senate Finance Committee, approved a scaled down version of the Clinton Plan. Approval of healthcare reform legislation by the labor and Human Resources and Finance Committees cleared the way for Mitchell to bring a scaled down version of the bill to the Senate floor for debate... mark[ing] the first time in American history that either house of Congress undertook a formal debate on national health insurance (Laham, 1996: 165).

The difficulties faced by Clinton in passing this initiative are also indicative of inherent institutional characteristics of the American Political system. Several institutional factors make the passage of such a bill difficult, even under the most favorable conditions. The number of committees which must approve of a bill and, which have the power to amend or veto bills provide numerous opportunities for bills to be "stone walled" on their way to becoming law. Furthermore, the diversity of interests involved in these committees ensures that bills are "watered down".

The committee system is inherently unaccommodating to large scale reform. Since each committee has the ability to "mark-up" bills as presented and to pass them with a variety of amendments, it has often been suggested that, without an overwhelming consensus on the terms, the final legislative product of any reform effort is often radically changed, and final policy changes are limited to minor incremental modifications, by the various demands, interests and objections of committee members.

As Gary Orfield (1975) suggests in his classic work Congressional Power, differences in the distribution of committee membership often create a legislative environment which is inherently opposed to the passage of large scale reform. As he notes, newly elected reformers often "seek assignment to committees dealing with education, housing, jobs, urban programs and civil rights," in an effort to advance the reform policies they are committed to introducing and supporting. "Conservatives on the other hand, enjoy disproportionate strength in the powerful committees controlling the budget, taxation, health and welfare policy, military policy, and the internal legislative process of Congress" (Orfield, 1975: 263). One result of this is "democratic liberals, working from power bases on a few key legislative committees, often see their heralded legislative accomplishments eviscerated by ... conservatives who work from power bases further along in the legislative process."

A second consideration highlighted by Orfield's work is the process of accommodation. As he argues:

> Committee action on visible issues where active floor debate may occur is often influenced by a desire to prevent embarrassing floor defeat for the committee bill. Since committee power is threatened once members learn that a committee bill can be successfully challenged on the floor, committees often try to preserve their power and prestige by making the necessary accommodation to any strong and determined majority (Orfield, 1975: 265).

Consequently, in the development of large scale reform bills, the reformatory character of the bill is undercut both by the conflicting perspectives, interests and influences of various committees and by the tendencies of those committees must strongly committed to its passage to make pre-emptive compromises in light of anticipated opposition on the floor.

Despite congressional developments since Orfield's work was penned, evidence of both inherent tendencies can be seen working against the passage of Clinton's health care reform bill. In the case of the Clinton health care plan, the disunity of the Democratic Party, the existence of competing plans and the development of a Republican strategy of interference also collaborated to produce gridlock in the 103rd Congress.

As Rushefsky & Patel (1997) point out deliberations in the various committees and subcommittees produced approval of a variety of amended bills. As early as March1994, the House Ways and Means health subcommittee approved a Medicare amendment bill proposed by its Democratic chairman, Pete Stark, while rejecting the three major bills on the table. In May 1994, the Senate Labor and Resource committee approved, an amended version of the Chafee plan. In June the Senate Labor and Education Committee approved the amended Kennedy version of the Health Security Act. Therefore, in a three month period, although various committees had committed themselves to the passage of a bill, the decentralized decision making process and the lack of consensus adversely affected progress towards a single bill that could be passed.

In June, when Senate majority leader George Mitchell declared that he wanted a bill presented to the floor for debate by July, the Republican minority formulated a two-part strategy for disrupting the process. "The first action was to have as many votes on amendments as possible. The second was to defeat any amendments that would improve the democratic bills, especially those aimed at meeting objections by small businesses" (Rushefsky & Patel, 1997: 105).

By the end of June, the House Energy and Commerce committees reported that they could not form a majority behind any bill and that they would take no action. The Senate Finance

Committee was deadlocked and the House Ways and Means Committee was reluctant to present a bill without a clear sense of their commitment. When the issue was opened up for debate in the Senate (August 9) and House (August 15) a flurry of compromises was presented in an effort to muster a majority vote. The result however, was that by this time the compromises had filtered out most of the radical reforms initially proposed by the Health Security Act. Universal coverage and employer mandates were among the most drastically affected. The final bills proposed to the 103rd congress recommended coverage of 92-95% of the population to be phased in over six to eight year periods, a radical departure from Clinton's goal. Yet, despite these compromises, proponents of health care reform were still unable to secure a majority vote.

CONCLUSION:

The elections of 1994 represented a significant change in the political environment in which health care reform was to be addressed. In 1994, Republican electoral victories produced a historical realignment of national and state politics. Not only did Democrats lose control of the Senate, but for the first time since the 1970s Republicans controlled the House and also dominated state gubernatorial elections. This return to divided government presented a new challenge for proponents of health care reform. More importantly it represented the resounding closure of a historical window of opportunity for any broad-based health care reform.

Although many of the pitfalls which befell health care reform efforts are institutional, the events of the following years of Republican majority rule also highlighted the inherent weaknesses of the Democratic party's strategy for taking advantage of their numerical majority. The presentation of a clear agenda for change in the "Contract with America" served as a clear road map for legislative action. Furthermore, the efforts of Speaker of the House Newt Gingrich to strengthen partisan action produced a series of legislative bills around which there was relative consensus. Major health care reform was however, clearly not on the agenda and any effort to raise the issue were presented in the context of incremental changes. In fact the bills proposed by the 104th Congress focused on cutting the Medicare and Medicaid budgets by $180 billion and $174 billion respectively. As Paul Starr put it:

> ... [it] is the ultimate irony that appears to be coming true year after the end of the Clinton attempt: a movement that began with liberal proposals to control cost and expand coverage has produced conservative legislation that raises costs and reduces coverage. ... The lesson for the next time in health care reform is faster, smaller. "We made the error of trying to do too much, took too long, and ended up achieving nothing" (Johnson & Broder, 1996: 609).

While the Clinton Administration deserves great credit for tackling a problem that Presidents had found reason to postpone for six decades or more, and for placing it at the center of national debate and consciousness, they cannot avoid blame for its ultimate failure (Johnson & Broder, 1996: 609).

> The very rich and the very poor had health care coverage. So did the elderly. The millions of ordinary working Americans without coverage were the people for whom the Democrats supposedly stood... The most stunning fact about this entire affair is that when the Democrats controlled both house of congress and, had in the White House ... the two most knowledgeable

and committed advocates of universal health care coverage in history, they failed over two years even to bring the measure to a vote. This failure spoke to weaknesses in both the presidency and in Congress. But it screamed to the world that the Democratic Party, the oldest and arguably the most successful political institution in the free world, had lost its core, lost its heart and lost its soul (Johnson & Broder, 1996: 622-23).

Despite its resounding defeat, it is doubtful that the question of health care reform is dead. Already, as the 2004 Presidential election develops, several Democratic candidates can be heard uttering the familiar rhetoric, calling for reformation of the inadequate system of health care provision. The resilience of the issue is not solely based on its appeal to democratic voters, but rather, the realities of health care service delivery in the United States, mandate that the issue eventually be addressed. With the failings of our current economy, the number of uninsured individuals in the United States in 2003 has risen to over 43 million. The Republican party with its traditional anti-big government philosophy is unlikely to take up the banner of sweeping reform and government sponsored programs. So, the rallying cry of universal coverage remains uniquely Democratic. The key elements to success in this area are the effective mobilization of the masses of people who are adverse affected by the current system, and the unification of a diverse core of Democratic leaders around the issue and a possible solution. Despite institutional impediments, with a clear mandate from the people and a committed core dedicated to the development of a solution, large scale reform is possible.

Chapter 6

Liberty & Poverty

"Freedom is just a metaphor, when you have nowhere to go."
Shawn Mullins

Introduction:

A near consensus exists in societies around the globe that liberty is a virtue and/or goal worthy of pursuit. Yet the meaning of the word liberty is still somewhat debatable. The following paper investigates the concept of liberty itself and in so doing brings attention to what I believe to be an often overlooked aspect of this concept. In doing so this paper will draw upon a variety of interpretations of the concept and utilize them to illuminate the shortcoming in the dominant approaches to the concept of liberty. This paper, although drawing on several theories of liberty does not propose to trace the history of the development of the concept of liberty nor shall it concentrate its critique on any one of these theories or approaches. Rather, this paper is the product of a process of deliberation over the practical understanding of liberty and in particular the connections between liberty and poverty, utilizing the writings of a variety of scholars as a base upon which to develop its argument and as illuminating support for its claims. It should be noted that although this project focuses on an investigation into the relationship between poverty in liberal societies and the practical meaning of the term liberty its implications may be expanded to any social structures which have the impact of impeding individual human development at its most fundamental level.

The question at hand is perhaps best posed in the form of the following scenario.

The story is told of a man who was arbitrarily imprisoned from childhood and held in solitary confinement having no contact with the outside world for some years. Upon his thirty fifth birthday, he is release into the world and told that he is free. He is void of social skills, economic resources, social connections or networks, and political leverage. He in essence lacks any of the necessary tools for his personal development and arguably for his very survival. Yet, he is un-impeded by law or man from the pursuit of his goals (whatsoever they may be). The only obstacles lying between him and the free pursuit of his goals or conduct of his life are his history and his lack of resources.

Four questions emerge from this scenario and I endeavor to address them in the forthcoming pages. (1) Is such a man free? Can he be said to experience a state of liberty? (2) If, as Berlin suggests, such a man is not meaningfully free then the question may be extended beyond the individual to a societal level; are those members of a society whose free conduct of their lives and pursuit of their goals are limited by social arrangements such as poverty and histories of unfreedom free? (3) Furthermore, can a society whose social, economic and political structures facilitate, perhaps necessarily so, this unfreedom be said to be a liberal/free society? (4) And finally, how does this affect our understanding of the nature of liberty itself? It is to these questions that this paper will address itself.

It is my assertion that the individual in the preceding scenario is NOT FREE despite the removal of both physical and meta-physical barriers which had previously restricted his actions. I additionally posit that, if the liberal society is to be understood as those social arrangements which maximize individual liberty, institutions which have the effect, even if not the intent, of hindering human development to its fullest potential violate individual liberty and that to the extent that they do so they produce a society lacking in liberty. Furthermore, on a somewhat more academic level, I take issue with the dominant schools of thought on this issue; and suggest that the relationship between poverty and liberty has all too often has been prematurely dismissed as a question of justice, and not necessarily intricate to the understanding of liberty itself. This assertion implies two fundamental and interconnected ideas which will be challenged by this paper. First, that a person may simultaneously exist in a state of poverty and liberty. Second, that since the question of justice only has meaning in relation to a social arrangement between two or more people, that there may simultaneously exist a liberal and unjust society.

To effectively undertake this in the manner deserved would be a voluminous task for any one sitting. This paper therefore represents the initial stages of a larger and on - going investigation into the questions at hand. This paper must therefore establish a clear and direct relationship between poverty and liberty such that it may be established that the state of poverty is inconsistent with a state of liberty. A second underlying task of this paper is therefore to suggest that, where the concept of the liberal society is concerned, the two concepts are inseparable. I begin by addressing the concept of liberty itself as it is traditionally understood in the literature. I then discuss the other key concept in this inquiry, poverty. Next, I demonstrate how these two concepts are inter-twined in the modern society and their impact upon each other.

Defining Liberty

Over the past four centuries several theories of liberty have been developed, many have been particularly concerned with the development of the "liberal society," i.e. the socio-political structures which best facilitates maximum freedom[44] for its citizens. No author on the subject has been more widely read, and quoted than Isaiah Berlin, who in his classical essay "Two Concepts of Liberty", outlines two "central concepts" of liberty which have in many ways dominated the historical discourse on liberty. This paper draws heavily upon these two concepts and therefore some time must be spent illuminating their meaning and implications. Berlin makes a clear distinction between what he terms Negative and Positive Liberty. According to Berlin:

> The negative sense is involved in the answer to the question 'what is the area within which the subject- a person or group of persons- is or should be left to do or be what he is able to do or be, without interference by other persons? The second, ... the positive sense, is involved in the answer to the question 'What or who, is the source of control or interference that can determine someone to do, or be, this rather than that? (Berlin 1969)

This distinction on the part of Berlin highlights two closely inter-related aspects of the concept of liberty. On the one hand, the absence of interference by human beings in the development of others. That is to say, a man may be said to be **unfree** to the extent that his pursuit of his goals (to do or to become something) are hindered by the actions of other men.

On the other hand, positive liberty refers to the degree of control which a man exerts over his own destiny or, the degree to which he determines what he will become or do. It is, in Berlin's own words, "derived from the wish on the part of the individual to be his own master." (Berlin: 1969)

---

[44] The terms freedom and liberty are often used inter changeably throughout this paper and are meant, in most cases, to represent the same essential concept.

> I wish my life and decisions to depend on myself,
> not on external forces of whatever kind. I wish to
> be an instrument of my own, not other men's, acts
> of will. I wish to be a subject, not an object; to be
> moved by reasons, by conscious purposes which
> are my own, not by causes which affect me, as it
> were from outside. (Berlin, 1969: 43)

Clearly, such a man may be said to be unfree to the extent that his destiny is determined by the desires, wishes and action of others than himself.

David Miller (1991) singles out three doctrines derived from Berlin's understanding of Liberty which he says may "usefully be isolated":

a) Freedom as the power or capacity to act in certain ways, as contrasted with the mere absence of interference;
b) Freedom as rational self-direction, the condition in which a person's life is governed by rational desires as opposed to desires that he just as a matter of fact has;
c) Freedom as collective self-determination, the condition where each person plays his part in controlling his social environment through democratic institutions.

The two concepts (Positive freedom and negative freedom) may be clearly seen as flip sides of the same coin as two intricate variables in an equation. The negative concept of freedom focuses its attention outwardly to the action of others, and their ability to halt one's progress and development, while the positive focuses its emphasis inward to the individual's degree of control over his/her own life and direction. Therefore, while the negative aspect focuses on obstacles to the achievement of goals the positive aspect is concerned with the driving and/or navigational force behind the individual's goals and actions.

As Maccallum clearly suggests the two concepts of liberty may be synthesized into a single, more concise definition. The two concepts, he suggests, are not in fact quite as distinct as Berlin presents them. Rather, liberty is best understood as a triadic relationship between actor/agent, goals and obstacles/hindrances; where the agent is least hindered from the achievement of his goals, he is most free.

Although Maccullum's point is potent in its demonstration of the inter-relatedness and therefore the potential for synthesis of the definitions of liberty, Berlin's distinction between negative and positive freedom is still very insightful in the analysis of the concept of liberty and its pursuit in civil society. The concept of positive freedom is too often understated in much of the discourse on liberty. Maccullum's approach, for example, although identifying the rightful place of goals in the triadic model nonetheless focuses his definition and measurement of liberty on the degree to which one is hindered from their pursuit; an essentially negative understanding of the relationship. He however, fails to grant equal import to self-determination even at the level of goal formation. Although the two concepts may be synthesized into a singular idea both aspects must be afforded at least equal attention and import in the understanding of true liberty. It may even be argued that, it is the concept of positive control and self-determinism in relation to one's destiny which must take prominence in any understanding of liberty.

Suppose for a moment that one were set on a path towards a goal. Imagine further that this path was free of all obstacles and that the goal or object lay straight ahead along this path and with some degree of exertion would be well within one's grasp. Imagine further that this path had be constructed in such a manner that insurmountable walls were constructed on either side, left and right with little space to maneuver. One is therefore unable to detour from the path; yet this path led directly, via the quickest route to the goal or object. Now add to this scenario other beings set on the same path before and after, some willingly embarking on this quest other simply placed upon it without consent. Which of these beings, can be said to be free? Clearly none. Those who willingly embarked upon it lack the freedom to change their minds, set new goals or plot their own paths. Those placed there unwillingly are but slaves to the will and ambitions of others. Although both groups of beings have unhindered paths to the defined goals, they lack any control over these goals or the path to them.

Clearly, an individual who is unhindered in the pursuit of his goals but who lacks deterministic, "positive" liberty in the conduct of his life is unfree. In his discussion on "Liberty as Non-domination" Philip Pettit, (1997) puts forward the example of the slave of a benevolent master, who although not "interfered with" is still unfree, to illustrate the point that "slavery and unfreedom are *both* consistent with non-interference[45]." (Pettit: 1997, 64) For although he is not interfered with in the conduct of his life he is unfree because he lacks the deterministic power to plot his own path of development. This lack of positive freedom, which, another thinker, Freejohn () labels "dominance", lies at the root of his enslavement and is the greatest "hindrance" to the liberty of agents. For he who lacks positive freedom can never take advantage of his negative freedom much less ever overcome any obstacles in his way. His positive freedom is key to his ability to perceive goals in his own terms and to act meaningfully towards them.

As Geuss argues in his criticism of Berlin:

> If one reflects on the intuition that lies behind
> the negative conception of freedom, one might
> come to think that ... I am freer the more possible
> courses of action stand open to me, thus any

---

[45] Pettit's notion of interference is consistent with the notions of obstacles and hindrances found in most discussions on negative liberty such as Berlin and Maccalum.

obstacle which closes off a course of action as a possibility for me is a restriction of my freedom. If this is the right way to think about freedom, then the central thing is the extent of the spectrum of possible courses of action that stand open to me at any given point in time. (This) however will depend upon on any number of factors; in many cases it will depend as much on how much power I have as on the existence or non-existence of obstacles. Obstacles lose their salience in the discussion of freedom; there is in principle no reason why an increase of my power might not lead to as great an increase in my freedom as the removal of obstacles would. (Geuss: 1995, 93)

Those who are hindered in their actions but who possess the necessary "control" (or "power") to exercise latitude in their actions and are therefore able to overcome or circumvent the obstacles placed in their path by the actions and wills of others are free. For no man is ever completely un-inhibited in the pursuit of his goals, but if he is free to take actions which will counter-act, undermine or circumvent these hindrances, he may "freely" pursue the objects of his desire. It is he who lacks positive freedom who is most unfree, for he lacks the power and lee-way to materialize his ambitions. He cannot overcome even the slightest of obstacles placed in his path by nature, law or man. Thus it is clear that the positive aspects of liberty, more so than, or at least equally to, the negative, determines the true degree of liberty possessed by an individual.

Thus, it is that when Berlin suggests that individual political liberty is not the greatest need for the poor, marginalized and destitute, what he is actually suggesting is that before one can exercise or make use of these aspects of liberty one must first possess some positive, deterministic, internal liberty which may facilitate self-directed personal development, the conceptualization of goals/objects of desire and the conscious plotting of a path to their attainment.

Hindrances

It is the ambitious goal of this paper to suggest that by either definition of liberty, states of dire poverty and destitution are, by their nature, states of unfreedom. Given the centrality of the notion of hindrances to the negative understanding of liberty, an intricate understanding rests upon a clear understanding of the notion of hindrances themselves.

One of the immediate questions raised by the negative approaches to liberty is, since man is never completely uninhibited in his abilities, what constitutes an obstacle or hindrance where liberty is concerned? Some obstacles are clearly beyond the control of man and such constraints although placing limits upon the achievable goals of the individual agent are not and should not be classifiable as obstacles to his freedom. Man, for example, has little or no control over the laws of nature or over the limits of his individual abilities. These claims are a source of little controversy. They have been supported in various ways by some of the most notable scholars on the subject and require little more exposition. The constraints of nature and personal ability in essence form the framework in which an individual agent's freedom is to be understood. Thus, when we speak of liberty we refer to the degree of freedom which an individual possesses within the realm of these uncontrollable constraints of ability and nature to pursue his goals. Obstacles therefore are reserved to those constraints and hindrances which are not inherent to natural environment or personal attributes and which may be attributed to the conscious and subconscious actions and wills of other men.

This notion however lends itself to the belief that the "state of nature", in which man is totally uninhibited by socially constructed constraints, is the truest form of liberty in which man may exist. Philosophers for centuries have correctly argued that this state of nature, however, is to the contrary a state of unfreedom. They have collectively, and with varying degrees of effectiveness argued essentially the same argument; in the state of nature the individual is unfree because the unconstrained freedom of his neighbors, who necessarily have conflicting interests, impinges upon his own freedom. The state of nature is, as Hobbes describes it, "the war of every man against every man." In such a state of nature, overlapping, unregulated freedoms are themselves a hindrance to all individual agents. In short men (inclusive of women) are hindered by the freedom of their neighbors.

That the natural state of man is not a state of freedom is absolutely correct. But not merely because one man's freedom is restricted by the freedom of other men. For he is free to preempt their actions and "do them in" as surely as they are free to "do him in." He has every incentive to do his brother in first and he is perfectly unrestricted, within the limits of his individual ability, from doing so as is his neighbor. He is free (in the negative sense) but insecure.

It is this insecurity which most causes him to be unfree. He is restricted from the pursuit of his goals or "rational self-direction" by a necessary pre-occupation with the mere preservation of his life; his most basic instinct. He is unfree because in such a society all of his attention, energy and resources must be spent in preserving his life and eliminating his enemies, who are many. He is thus unfree to pursue his true/higher interests. He is unfree to pursue his other desires. For man is not by nature brutal, although he may be selfish. He does not truly desire to do his brother in, but wishes only to exercise his liberty in pursuit of the happiness defined by his goals; a liberty which may be deprived of him by his neighbors' freedom.

In any society where men are preoccupied with the preservation of life and not with the pursuit of their higher goals/ambitions (to the extent that they possess such goals) such men are unfree. They exist in much the same state as man in the state of nature. They are slaves to their fears, forever warding off their fellow men who wish to do them harm to deprive them of their opportunities to pursue their higher goals; men who in pursuit of their own goals suppress their ability to achieve. Such suppressive men and the institutions they employ are obstacles to the freedom of not only their victims but also themselves since their potential productive energies are wasted on secondary goals of suppression and not on their truer goals. Though they may be the majority, though they may be faceless, though they may be semi-conscious of their action nonetheless they are an impediment to the achievement of the victims (which includes themselves) goals, happiness and freedom.

Social Institutions as Hindrances to Liberty

It must therefore be painfully obvious that for the collective existence of men some socially constructed restraints must be put in place in order to protect the liberty of individuals in the society from each other[46]. This protection is provided in modern societies in the form of the law. Where the law is not arbitrary, even handed in its regulation of all men, predictable and "unchanging", the law becomes an element of the framework, or realm, in which an individual's freedom is to be understood. The law itself therefore, becomes a part of the environment/ infrastructure and as with the law of nature, "civil law" cannot be separated from the physical infrastructure, for a city without the law is, by definition, no longer a city, inasmuch as, a river without the law of gravity is no longer a river. Furthermore, the law, being negative and concerned with extremes, establishes

---

[46]   Included in those from whom individual agents seek protection are non-human persons (corporations) and the government.

the limits within which one is free to pursue one's goals to one's fullest potential.

Through its neutrality, the law provides the same degree of freedom as associated with the state of nature, while removing the sense of insecurity and the preoccupation with self preservation which inhibits man from the pursuit of goals. As a result, freedom is not diminished by the transition from the state of nature to modern society but rather, where the law meets the necessary criteria, freedom is augmented. It is therefore necessary to establish that civil law is as even handed as the laws of nature to whatever degree that is humanly possible.

This emphasis on the even-handed character of the law may at first glance seem to be an issue of equality and thus justice. However, since some hindrance is a given (laws of nature, civil laws) by virtue of the environment, and, since civil law's neutrality is a necessary condition of its exclusion from the category of hindrances to freedom, it is necessary to account for and test for qualification under the given criteria established above. The role of civil law in the provision and facilitation of liberty is therefore contingent upon its "just"[47] character and therefore its character cannot be separated from its function. It is this necessary characteristic of civil law which constitutes the un-ignorable overlap and connection between liberty and justice.

If the law is applied equally to all citizens it provides the same degree of freedom to all individuals and in no way limits their freedom. Where however, the law is unequal and discriminates against individuals the law is no longer exempt from being understood as a hindrance, for the law is no longer a neutral element of the environment/infrastructure, but rather becomes

---

[47]   The term justice is given a very narrow meaning here referring only to the non-arbitrary, even handed, predictable and unchanging character of the law, with no appeal to ethical or moral standards which may vary from society to society.

a tool working in favor of selected segments of the population, whether or not they consciously utilize it.

Having excluded individual potentials and aptitudes, laws of nature, and qualified civil law from the class of obstacles or hindrances to liberty, adherents to the negative concept of liberty often conclude that the only elements which count as hindrances to liberty are obstacles created by other humans with the intent and/or effect of hindering the development of other humans may be considered as hindrances to liberty. The difficulty in protecting individual liberty therefore lies in assessing where the boundaries of social interference should be drawn and how broad the minimum area of individual liberty should be. Various formulae have been developed to suggest what areas of individual life should be left out of the control or direct influence of other beings and the government. Perhaps most sensitive and consequently problematic of them has always been the question of property.

The image of the savage man gathering his acorns in the forest, claiming them as his for as long as he can gather and protect them, and entering into a social contract with other like beings for the protection of their property and lives lies at the foundation of many modern liberal democratic societies. The dominant perspective on this issue however, is tainted by an over-emphasis on the negative aspect of liberty. Whereas it is easily recognized that the right of the savage to gather and claim his acorns should never be impeded, implicit in the Lockean notion of the savage's right to protect his acorns is the right of all savages to collect them. i.e. The very right of the savage to protect his acorns is based upon his right to gather in the first place, and likewise his right to gather is based upon the right of all to gather. This right is also an intricate component of liberty and must be equally protected.

Having developed a fair understanding of the concept of liberty itself we turn our attention to identifying two other critical terms in this discussion, Poverty and Liberal Society.

Poverty

It is important to establish that where in the course of this paper we refer to poverty that we understand it in its "absolute" and not its relative sense. That is to say, we are not concerned simply with the unequal distribution of resources, for this paper is not a discourse on justice, morality or equality. We are rather interested in the general lack of resources necessary for survival, development and the pursuit of goals. We are further concerned with the specific social relations within a society which facilitate the withholding of resources from individual members of the society and the impact that they have on liberty. We now turn our attention to the specific relationship between poverty and liberty and shall demonstrate that:

i. Poverty is a non-arbitrary social construct, unrelated to individual ability, which is upheld and enforced by and embedded in the civil law of modern liberal democratic societies rendering it non-exclusionary and representing a hindrance to liberty;

ii. Poverty represents a violation of nature's law of survival of the fittest by disguising a social construct as a random result/characteristic of nature's role of the die;

iii. Poverty deprives individuals of the ability to act upon the unhindered/ unobstructed path to their goals by denying them access to the resources necessary for their action therefore representing a violation of both positive and negative liberty;

iv. Poverty in its most extreme forms reduces individuals to a condition in which their energy and time must be expended in a struggle for mere survival and minimizes opportunities for individuals to maximize their efforts in pursuit of higher goals.

<u>Access to Resources as an Essential of Liberty</u>

That affluence and poverty are non-arbitrary, social constructs is not a difficult argument to make. The children of wealthy parents are not born poor, except under the most extraordinary of circumstances. This is not a natural or genetic phenomenon, but simply the product of socially constructed arrangements which govern the distribution of property in the modern society for no child born into the state of nature is naturally endowed with a trust fund.

In the state of nature all individual are granted equal access within any given ecological environment to the resources necessary for their survival and development. What determines their achievement of these goals is therefore their individual aptitudes, physical abilities and desire/drive to achieve them. With the transition of societies from the state of nature to modern civilization and in particular with the advent of systems of trade, particularly those based upon the exchange of currency, money itself has become an essential survival tool. For if a poor and starving man picks an apple from the orchard of a wealthy man, he is nonetheless guilty of theft. His physical ability to gather the apple is irrelevant, for he lacks the characteristic (money/wealth), which grants him the right to utilize his ability (taking the apple). He therefore, despite his physical ability to feed himself, is unable to do so without the aid of some benevolent member or agent of society; a condition which, according to Pettit (1997), constitutes a state of unfreedom.

The development of the modern society, has altered the socio-geographical landscape by substituting various economic systems, which regulate the availability of essential resources, for the unbiased laws of genetics and natural selection. In such a state one's ability to eat, find adequate shelter, or learn the necessary skills for success are dependent not primarily upon one's natural ability, but upon the amount of capital one may have accumulated. Therefore, unlike the state of nature, where the unequal distribution of resources is random, and where the acquisition of resources is a measure of natural ability and drive, many economic structures are void of these characteristics.

As argued before, with the implementation of all civil laws, any socially constructed institutions which are intended to regulate human behavior must meet the same qualifying standards discussed earlier, so as to maintain their exempt status as non-hindrances to liberty. However, the substitution of these economic systems has intentionally resulted in unequal access to life's most essential resources. In fact, today we find a condition in the most advanced modern societies where capital is centered in the hands of a small minority.

The role of capital in the modern society poses two fundamental and inter-related problems for liberty. First, the laws which govern the distribution of wealth and therefore access to resources are biased in favor of some, predefined groups of individuals. Whether this fact is right or wrong, just or un-just, is not the question at hand. Here we are simply concerned with the implications of this fact on liberty in the modern society and in particular the implication that economic systems act as hindrances to the natural development of individuals and therefore violate negative liberty. Second, because of the essential role of capital in human life, the systematic depravation of capital resources experienced by the poorest segments of our society denies them of their positive freedom by withholding the means of development and by creating a necessary preoccupation with the most primal instincts on survival. This second condition is of course most meaningful in societies where essential resources have most effectively been converted to commodities. The withholding of capital, the primary means by which individuals in a modern society gain access, is therefore equivalent to the defanging of a tiger expected to hunt for a living.

A significant source of the problem which shades the discourse on liberty is the misclassification of levels of wealth as natural occurrences and not as the direct result of social design. Nature grants that individuals may rise to varying degrees of proficiency in a wide array of activities, some of which are given greater value in some societies. The degree to which an individual rises by nature of his proficiency in his pursuit of his goals is therefore determinant of the status which an individual is given in a society and rightfully so. He who best gathers and protects his acorns is rightfully the best collector and deserves the status that accompanies such. Yet, this variation in abilities and therefore this variation in the degree to which individuals may rise in status does not imply that they are by nature granted varying degrees of freedom. Each individual is endowed by nature with the same right to freedom and the same degree of such. Each savage is equal in his right to collect acorns although not equal in his ability to do so.

Therefore, the natural equality of freedom is not synonymous with equality of achievement or with equality of status. Simultaneously, differences in individual achievement, ability or status should not be equated with differences in levels of liberty. Any social arrangement which denies this fundamental understanding of liberty and which wrongly grants to the weak less freedom than the strong or which rewards achievement with greater or less freedom than nature so decrees is not merely unjust, it is a direct violation of the natural distribution of liberty. More specifically, any arrangement which deprives an individual of the most fundamental right and ability to pursue his goals to the best of his ability renders him unfree.

In the modern civilization however, wealth itself is akin to the individual's natural ability although its origins lie in solely social constructs, (unless of course one subscribes to scientific classism/racism). Whereas, in the state of nature, the individual hunter's ability to hunt, gather or cultivate, alone determines his level of access to available resources necessary for his survival and prosperity, in the modern society his individual ability is of less significance than his social status and wealth. The human being in the modern society is therefore upon birth subject to two "lotteries" which impact upon his ability to survive and to pursue his goals; in a word, his liberty.

One of these lotteries, is essentially based upon the random dissemination of ability and aptitude. This random distribution of individual characteristics produces the inequality which is associated with the process of natural selection. On the other hand, since most essential resources have been converted into commodities in the modern society, access is contingent upon the individual's ability to pay for such resources and this is in turn contingent primarily upon one's birth and parentage. Therefore, unlike the state of nature, only those who have won the birthright lottery have full access to the necessary resources for their survival and "success", however they may define the term.

The poorest segments of some societies, such as children born to homeless mothers, are denied full access to the resources necessary for their survival and pursuit of life goals, therefore, despite their abilities, which may be significant their freedom to choose and pursue a path for themselves is inhibited by their lack of access to essential resources. On the other hand, the children of wealthy parentage, are at liberty to pursue any path they so please within the confines of their natural "God given" ability, even if these abilities may be considerably limited. The question of wealth therefore remains the only area of life in the modern liberal society where it is believed and institutionally supported, that the sins/shortcomings of the parents should be passed on from generation to generation. The latitude granted to the individual by virtue of his access to the most essential resources for his development is contingent upon his lineage and as a result is predetermined, from the point of conception, by civil laws which facilitate and mandate discriminatory access.

Let us return to our hypothetical individual whose tale ushered us into this discussion. Let us suppose for a moment, that he upon his released desired to engage in some private enterprise as a means of sustaining himself. For this he may require, licenses, loans for startup money, various elements of infrastructure, including a location from which to operate. Which of these might he have access to? He lacks the appropriate credentials for the licensing and is incapable of paying the fee. He has no collateral or savings to qualify him for a loan. He is without property and has no means of paying for secure shelter, or supplies. Our hypothetical character is not without options however, for he may sell his labor as a means of securing the necessary capital to embark upon his goal. Putting aside the numerous difficulties he would encounter in finding a position capable of sustaining him, while allowing him to accumulate capital towards his goal, he is steered towards this option by the systematic and institutionalized regulation of his access to resources. Bearing in mind that, as Tully states in his discussion on Locke's interpretation of liberty, "liberty comprises of the will plus the power to do and not to do the action willed: *such that,* freedom is *both* choice and action" (Tully, 1980: 68) he is unfree. It is the right of each man to pursue his goals/desires to the best of his individual ability. A man is unfree to the extent that he is denied the ability to pursue these goals and to the extent that his destiny is determined by others than himself. He is denied, the opportunity to pursue his own goal, because of his social status and his birth rite of poverty which grant him restricted access and therefore diminished power over his possible courses of action. In exchange for his liberty he is offered the opportunity to utilize his labor and skill primarily towards the pursuit of the goals of others than himself.

The problem is not merely that poverty is by definition a lack of resources, or that it denies or impedes access to these resources, but that it systematically chooses those to be denied constituting a violation of liberty by any definition. Furthermore, where this denial of access is most absolute, poverty constitutes a debilitating state where the means to development are withheld and mere survival becomes the primary objective of individuals. The consequence of this diminished access to resources manifests itself in a variety of ways in modern societies ranging from homelessness, malnutrition, poor healthcare and inadequate health care and education to a mere lack of access to networks and other developmental resources. Unlike the state of nature, where such a state of being may occur due to some natural disaster, limiting the general availability of resources, poverty is not the result of a overall shortage of resources, but of specific social arrangements which exclude portions of the population from access to them. As a result, individuals become dependent primarily upon others than himself for their livelihood and in order to gain access to their ration must barter their labor in the realization of goals other than their own. The very economic relations which force them to gather "acorns", to use Locke's analogy, for others than themselves in an attempt to meet basic needs inhibits their ability to gather such acorns onto themselves and to actualize their own goals and objectives. If self-determination and self-actualization are inherent aspects of positive liberty. Poverty denies individuals of these characteristics or at least limits their manifestation in some individuals.

As Berlin recognizes:

> If a man is too poor to afford something on which there is no legal ban...he is as little free to have it as he would be if it were forbidden him by law. If my poverty were a kind of disease, which prevented me from buying bread, (or any other goal), as lameness prevents me from running, this inability would not naturally be described as a lack of freedom...It is only because ... I believe that I am being kept in want by a specific arrangement which I consider unjust or unfair, I speak of economic slavery or oppression. (Berlin: 1969, 35)

The Liberal Society

This of course brings us to the second questions raised at the beginning of this paper. In large part, we have already established that all those members of a society whose lives are defined and directed by their poverty are in fact unfree. However, Berlin's response to this reality is both troubling and flawed:

> If the liberty of myself or my class or nation depends on the misery of a number of other human beings, the system which promotes this is **unjust** and **immoral**. But if I curtail or lose my freedom, in order to lesson the shame of such inequality, and do not thereby materially increase the individual liberty of others, an absolute loss of liberty occurs. (Berlin: 1969, 37-8)

First, it has already been established that in order for individual liberty to flourish in a society of human beings that the extent and the nature of their individual liberty must be curtailed in order to facilitate greater and broader liberty for all members of the society. This inhibition of individual's liberty is required to reduce the area in which the liberty of one individual may inhibit the liberty of others. Second, the notions that the strong should necessarily be allowed to oppress the weak or that weakness or social status entitle one to a reduction of liberty are contrary to the very foundation of every liberal society. And it is precisely notions such as that advanced by Berlin in the excerpt above which defenders of individual liberty wish to protect themselves against.

The liberal society can only be said to exist where its members as a whole are capable of exercising maximum liberty. That is to say, they are free to act within the limits of unbiased prohibitory and punitive law, in pursuit of their goals to the best of their individual abilities. It is furthermore important to understand that liberty is not relative. The liberal society is not defined as that in which some or even most members of its citizenry possess individual liberty. If such were the case then all societies ranging from the most despotic to the most democratic would be in fact liberal. For even in the most dictatorial and despotic societies, there exist members who exercise liberty in their lives at the expense of the liberty of others.

Yet many a "liberal" society has over looked this in their claims to protect individual liberty.

> It is true that to offer political rights, or safe guards against intervention by the state, to men who are half-naked, illiterate, underfed, diseased is to mock their condition; they need medical help or education before they can understand, or make use of, an increase in their freedom... (Berlin, 37)

Berlin is of course correct here, although again narrow sighted in his view of liberty. The needs to which he alludes are not in fact pre-requisites to liberty as he implies, they are rather an intricate part of liberty itself. As he himself argues:

> ... where these glaring injustices lead to the restriction of liberty for some members of the society to the point of enslavement. It is not merely injustice which we are protecting but liberty itself. For "there ought to exist a certain minimum area of personal freedom which must on no account be violated; for if it is overstepped, the individual will find himself in an area too narrow for even that minimum development of his natural faculties which alone makes it possible to pursue, and even

to conceive, the various ends which men hold
good or right or sacred." (Berlin, 1969: 36)

The political aspects of liberty are not to be underestimated. Indeed, freedom of speech, association, movement, and political affiliation are all important and significant. But, in the larger scheme of things, they are only precursors to some deeper, truer meaning of liberty. Although they are ends in themselves they primarily provide protection for and a means to a more fundamental aspect of liberty; the liberty of self-actualization as defined by Miller. This liberty to carve a destiny, actualize one's potential, to excel or not, for freedom must entail the right and ability to go in either direction represent the central pillar of individual liberty. But a man whose future, whose direction, whose limitations are determined, not by the law of nature or by his own abilities and faculties, but by the decisions of another man, directly or indirectly is unfree. He is denied avenues granted him by nature or divine gift. He is not master of his own destiny, but imprisoned in a social condition of non- freedom.

Can such a society be considered a liberal one? Yes, but only if the liberal society is viewed as being in an ongoing process of development towards an ideal. An integral part of this process must involve the reevaluation of social institutions which, although dear to our hearts, undermine the founding principle upon which we base our societies. Otherwise, we must rethink the tenants upon which we claim to base of society.

If poverty threatens the basic tenants of human rights one of which is liberty, through its social, economic and developmental impact on individuals then it must be addressed at the very constitutional core of every society. Even though economic rights are not constitutionally recognized in most nations, many states have intervened to ensure that their citizenry was not left destitute. The problem is as the billionaire, and father of the richest man in the world today, once said in a statement to CNN:

> Most scholars and statesmen accept that human rights are inalienable - that human beings are born with those rights and not merely conferred by legislative bodies... in dealing with human rights, philosophers generally emphasized *universal* civil and political rights and little attention was paid to *universal* economic, social and cultural rights. When national legislatures first took action to have human rights enshrined in their constitutions, the situation was similar. This may be explained by the fact that the nature of economic, social and cultural rights render them non-justiciable in most cases. When it is said that the individual has the right to a fair trial a civil right -it is understood that the state has the duty to protect that right. If the state neglects its duty the aggrieved individual may seek redress... However, in the case of many economic, social and cultural rights it is not always *clear* to whom the duty is imposed. For example the right to work exists in human rights instruments but it is not often obvious who has the duty to provide employment.

A second problem arising from this is the structuring of social institutions which provide a safety net for the poorer members of society. The approach in some societies has been the establishment of "welfare systems" of various sorts which serve to sustain the most needy citizens. Where most have failed is in their focus on physically sustaining individuals as opposed to providing them with meaningful access to the means of development i.e. granting them the positive liberty necessary for their development.

Both dilemmas are brought on by the same core problem, a failure to address the central principles of our socio-economic systems and to address whether or not they are compatible with universal liberty. Since poverty, by its very nature, represents a violation of liberty in the modern society, the question may then be posed can modern socio-economic systems exist without poverty or is the depravation of members of the society essential for their perpetuation. If they are compatible with a state of universal liberty, then the solution to the problem lies in the reformation of these systems at their core to reflect a guarantee of universal access to all essential resources by all citizens. If they are not they are not then what is required in the next stage of development towards a liberal society is the establishment of new socio-economic systems which favor the further development of a truly liberal society. The question begs us to address and prioritize the core tenants of our society? Is liberty truly our foundation and goal?

CHAPTER 7:

Communal Violence in South Asia: Prospects for future comparative study

<u>Theoretical issues in the study of Communal Violence:</u>

In their classic review of the literature on ethnic violence, Brubaker and Laitin (1998) make several observations about the literature on ethnic violence which are pertinent to my current study. As they note, traditional studies of ethnic violence have been derived from "two largely nonintersecting literatures: studies of ethnicity, ethnic conflict and nationalism on the one hand, and studies of collective or political violence on the other." (Brubaker and Laitin, 1998: 425) Within these independent fields, several shortcomings are evident. In the study of ethnicity, accounts of violence have not been sufficiently disaggregated from accounts of conflict. "Violence has generally been conceptualized – if only tacitly - as a degree of conflict rather than as a form of conflict, or indeed as a form of social or political action in its own right." Similarly, they note that in studies of collective violence the significance of ethnicity has often been overlooked. In their words:

> Although the empirical significance of ethnicity was recognized, its theoretical significance was seldom addressed explicitly; it was as if there was nothing analytically distinctive about ethnic (ethnically conditioned or framed) violence. Ethnicity thus remained theoretically exogenous rather than being integrated into key analytical or theoretical concepts. (Brubaker and Laitin, 1998: 426)

In light of these observations, Brubaker and Laitin suggest two important advances which should be made in the study of ethnic violence. First, violence should become a subject of study in its own right. "Violence is not a quantitative degree of conflict but a qualitative form of conflict with its own dynamics."

Second, more careful attention should be paid to the distinctive forms of collective and political violence.

> *That* political violence can be ethnic is well established, indeed too well established; *how* it is ethnic remains obscure. The most fundamental questions – for example, how the adjective "ethnic" modifies the noun "violence" – remain unclear and largely unexamined. Sustained attention needs to be paid to the forms and dynamics of ethnicization, to the many subtle ways in which violence – and conditions, processes, activities, and narratives linked to violence – can take on ethnic hues. (Brubaker and Laitin, 1998: 427)

This paper addresses itself to this challenge. More precisely it transfers these same challenges to the question of communal violence. In this paper, we seek ask what is communal violence? How can it be distinguished from other forms of violence? How does violence become communal? It is presumptuous and premature to imply that I will offer definitive answers to these questions. In fact, this discussion may raise more questions than it answers. I will be content if it sparks in the reader a deeper appreciation of the need to resolve these issues through further investigation.

Additionally, in the following pages I offer some comparative analysis of the developments of communal violence in South Asia and Jamaica. The scope of the comparisons undertaken here is limited by my familiarity with the South Asian case studies. However, I will demonstrate that there exist common elements in the patterns of violence exhibited in Jamaica and those in countries such as India, Sri Lanka and Indonesia. Once again, I hope to lay the foundation for future comparative analysis of the patterns and development of violence in both regions.

Defining Communal Violence:

The term communal violence is most commonly associated with outbursts of large scale civil violence in India and South-East Asia. These episodes of violence have become a common phenomenon in this part of the world and have received significant attention in the literature. Communal violence distinguishes itself from other forms of violence because it pits members of one defined community against other similarly defined communities. The adversarial relationship between the groups is long term and the disputes and clashes may span over several generations. Target selection in cases of communal violence is neither indiscriminate nor finely selective. By this I mean, that victims of communal violence are usually identifiable members of the targeted community and attacks tend to focus exclusively on members of the target group. Within that target group, perpetrators of communal violence tend to be less selective. Men, women and children are all seen as viable targets. Similarly, the economic status or positions of relative power within the community do not increase ones chances of being targeted. Membership in the target group is usually the only essential characteristic.

Some occurrences of violence in Asia take on a communal character in two key ways. On the one hand, violence can be seen as communal when it pits two defined groups against each other. In the Asian case studies, these groups or communities are often defined by their ethnicity and religion. In a society where previous, pre-colonial, caste systems have heavily influenced the development of their modern post-colonial class system, ethnicity weighs heavily on individual identity. Additionally, people of similar ethnic origins, tend to congregate and live in specific and definable geographic locations. Throughout this discussion we shall refer to these forms of communal violence as bilateral conflicts.

Other conflicts take on a communal character through the mobilization of members of a defined community into "combat." In these instances, representatives of particular communities rise up and become engaged in acts of violence against others they view as threatening to their collective interests. These cases shall be described here as unilateral.

The creation of clearly defined communities requires a high degree of solidarity. This solidarity requires the existence of a common defining characteristic shared by members of the groups. This common characteristic must be given a high level of significance by individual members of the group. Community also implies some degree of geographic centralization. By this I mean that members of the group must share a common identifiable geographic space over which they lay claim. Communal groups usually share common interest vis-à-vis the State or other groups. These interests may be social, economic or political. Likewise, these interests may be linked to broader national issues or limited to local concerns or preferences.

Within groups, "solidarity ... increases with their intimacy, cultural homogeneity, and interdependence." (Senechal de la Roche, 2001: 129) In many instances, particularly in the Asian and African contexts, solidarity and community formation are closely and inextricably linked with ethnic and religious identities. As a result, it is common to use the terms "communal" and "ethnic" interchangeably[48]. While there is no doubt that there is significant overlap between the two, the findings of the Jamaican case study show that communal violence can exist without ethnic or religious undertones. This is turn implies that as Brubaker and Laitin suggests there is need for further examination into the true nature of these conflicts and the violence associated with them.

---

[48]	See Ted Gurr and Barbara Harff (1994: 190) as a example by two dominant scholars in the field.

Krishna (1985: 63) states that "the communal problem encompasses social, economic, religious, political, cultural and intellectual spheres – indeed, nothing escapes it because it is concerned with the collective, and through it the individual life of every member of the community." As he further argues, "It is not only that men identify themselves with the community as the bearer of those traditions and culture that define them but see a danger to themselves in the weakening of it. There are therefore no measures they would not employ to defend it..."

An overview of the manifestation of communal violence in Asia may help highlight the issue here. A few cautionary notes must be made here. First, I am not a specialist in Indian or South Asian history or politics. Second, as better informed scholars have warned:

> Although there have been great advances in our knowledge of collective violence, the scale and complexity of the South Asian subcontinent have precluded comprehensive accounts; the local studies necessary for such an undertaking have not yet been done. ... Not much work has been carried out on collective violence for its own sake, there are few studies that trace trends in a given region over a reasonably long period. (Rogers, 1987: 583)

The history of communal violence in India:

India is a richly diverse country in terms of ethnicity, language, religion and social position. Emerging from its own colonial experience, it also combines a complex often contradictory commitment to tradition and western modernity. It was once described as an agglomerative society. Such as society is:

Loosely held together, has a historically evolved shared value framework … and [this] shared culture forms the basis of the minimum necessary cohesion for an ordered collective life. Its social structures change very slowly because it is grounded in an essentially stagnant agrarian political economy. (Karve in Krishna, 1985).

The history of communal violence dates back to the early 18th century. As early as 1714, riots occurred in Ahmedabad. Hindu-Muslim conflicts, which are the most common, first manifested themselves in Kashmir in 1719-20, in Delhi in 1729 and in the Vidarbha region of Maharashtra in 1786. These early disputes were sparked by religious issues such as cow slaughter, or the playing of music in front of Mosques. However, they also had political origins in the "downgrading of the Muslim state functionaries, and the consequent decline of Muslim dominance following the British conquest of the area." (Krishna, 1985: 61)

Conflicts between Hindu and Muslim communities continued in the 19th century. The issue of cow slaughter remained at the center of their conflict. "In 1893 in Mau (Azamgarh), a dispute arose… over the interpretation of the government order prohibiting "all cow sacrifices." The riots that followed spread over a very wide area, encompassing UP, Bihar, Gujarat and Bombay and claimed over 107 lives." (Krishna 1985: 61-62)

Krishna (1985) further notes that the frequency and intensity of these conflict rose in the 1920's. After 1925, religious conversion became a new trigger for outbursts of communal violence. The creation of new militant organizations introduced a new dimension of violence into the equation. Major riots occurred in both Calcutta (1926) and Bombay (1928). In Calcutta 3 riots occurred resulting in 141 deaths and 1,296 reported injuries. In Bombay, 117 people were killed and 791 injured. Further escalation in the violence occurred in the

1930s. "Between 1924 and 1940, the total number of persons killed was 1,175 and the injured 7,615." The partition movement, in the 1940s, which sought to re-establish Muslim political power in Muslim dominated areas also helped to politicize communal violence.

Communal identities are not necessarily natural identities. In many case they are forged over time through the manipulations of political elites. In Jamaica, this was accomplished through the development of housing schemes as a form of long term political patronage. In India, they were forged through the divide and rule tactics of British colonialism. Hasan suggests that after 1857 the British government singled out the Muslim community for "deliberate repression." (Hasan, 1982: 26) By the early 1900s, the British government changed its position and engaged in a practice of appeasement of the Muslim communities, particularly in light of emerging anti-colonial sentiment.

"The introduction of separate electorates was one such favour ... The principle of communal representation inevitably leads to the "creation of political camps organized against each other and teaches men to think as partisans and not citizens." (Hasan, 1982: 26) This move, Hasan argues was driven by the assumption that all Muslims in India shared common economic and political interests and goals. This belief was belied, he notes, by the fact that in 1917 the colonial office received "44 deputations from Muslim bodies each claiming to speak for the community." However, "by approving the principle of communal representation, the Congress was guilty of accepting and perpetuating the misleading and artificial communal categories created by the imperialists." (Hasan, 1982: 26)

The point here is not to suggest that the identities themselves were created by the political environment. Rather "communalism and communal politics took shape and acquired divisive proportions in the colonial period." These communal identities have proven to be self-perpetuating-. In the post-independence era, slow economic development and competition between communities for survival and advancement magnified the divisions between the groups. The self-perception of being "threatened" groups, however defined, strengthened group cohesiveness and the idea that political solutions would best resolve their issues. However, this has served to further marginalize these groups. "Often drawn into the vortex of politics, they have given primacy to the protection of political interests rather than to the alleviation of their economic backwardness." (Hasan, 1982: 30)

In communal politics, all "mobilization took place around individuals, factions and communities," (Hasan, 1982) rather than around issues of development and reform. Furthermore, the development of communal politics in India gave great import to traditional interest groups based on caste, religion, language and region as the organizing principle for articulation of interests and grievances.

After 1964, the frequency and intensity of communal riots again increased drastically. "Incidents over the period 1950 – 1963 was 1,141, giving an average of 81.5 per year, in 1964 it had risen to 2,115 … for the seven years between 1964 and 1970 the average number of incidents per year was 1025 as against 81.5 for the preceding fourteen years." (Krishna, 1985: 65)

The instances of these riots in India are astoundingly numerous. The work of Ali Engineer (1995; 1996; 1998) documents the frequency of these incidents on various scales. Choosing a single incident as representative of the whole is difficult. However, some generalization can be drawn.

The most common form of communal violence in India is what Horowitz describes as the deadly ethnic riot. Horowitz describes these forms of violence as mass civilian intergroup violence in which victims are chosen by their group membership.

> the deadly ethnic riot is marked by highly
> uneven clustering in time and space, relatively

spontaneous character (though not without elements of organization and planning), careful selection of victims by their categorical identity, passionate expression of inter-group antipathies, and seemingly gratuitous mutilation of victims. (Brubaker and Laitin, 1998: 432)

Tambiah (1990: 743) further adds that these riots share several preliminary characteristics. They typically involve urban populations. Those who actually engage in the physical acts of aggressions, as well as those who mobilize and direct the violence are drawn from "certain identifiable segments or categories of the population." They often occur with the complicity or incompetence of law enforcement authorities. In fact, "neutrality on the part of those entrusted with maintaining law and order is rarely witnessed in societies where [this form of violence] is rife." Finally, he argues:

The riots were not simply disconnected occurrences but formed part of a larger incidence of violence that occurred in a wide range of social contexts and political circumstances that can be ordered on a scale of increasing violence, premeditation, and participation.

Scholars (Tambiah, 1996: 230; Chandra, 1993), also note that the violence carried out during these riots often tend to be routinized and ritualistic. Chandra (1993) notes that Communal violence is often converted into a spectacle. "Depending on the degree of communalization within the society, it is valorized by larger or smaller sections of the concerned communities." (Chandra, 1993: 1883)

The arson they indulged in … resembled the community bonfire organized on the occasion of the Holi festival[49]. It bore an even more bizarre resemblance – one with sacrificial 'yajnas' as some of the rioter threw into the flames … live human beings, including children. A display was made of raping Muslim women and girls and there were instances in which the ritual concluded with the killing of the victim… nor were the killings effected by the rioters always simple, quick operations. The victims were made to utter 'Jai Shri Ram' – the war cry of Hindutva – before being hacked to death or burnt alive. (Chandra, 1993: 1883)

Krishna (1985: 62) observes that while these riots are accompanied by acts of individual violence (stabbings, looting and burning of property) they can also take on the form of mass warfare. Accounts of communal mobs of different sizes varying from 100 to 10,000 confronting each other, throwing stones at each other and generally keeping an adversary at bay are common. Common in these riots is the targeted invasion of weakly defended areas of a rival community. "The most endangered lives are those people living in the midst of or close to the adversary community."

While the riots often appear to be spontaneous outbursts of tensions between ethnic communities, there is much evidence to suggest that they are sometimes highly organized and orchestrated. The 1984 Hindu-Sikh riots in Delhi were sparked by news of the assassination of Indira Gandhi by her Sikh bodyguards. The violence which occurred was unilateral,

---

[49]   A Hindu festival in which bonfires are made to re-enact the burning of a corrupted queen who misused the gift of the Gods to serve her own selfish purposes. It represents the triumph of good over evil, righteous over evil.

mostly Hindus attacking Sikhs. The damaged was devastating and targeted.

> The Delhi administration reported to the Misra Commission that a total of 180 *gurudwaras* (Sikh temples) and 11 educational institutions run by members of the Sikh community were affected by arson, looting and burning. That places of worship, store-houses of community goods, and educational institutions and equipment were targeted indicates the purposiveness of the intent to diminish the collective assets of the Sikh community. (Tambiah, 1990: 745)

"The interesting question is ... how crowds that had formed spontaneously after being traumatized by a national tragedy, unleashed riots which by the next morning took the shape of organized purposive violence that systematically committed arson, looting and killing?" (Tambiah, 1990: 744-745) The answer of course lies in the role of community organizers. As has been demonstrated in the Jamaican case, political activists/organizers within the communities often had a hand in directing acts of violence against rival communities. "There is ample evidence that ...residents in the shape of Congress (I) activists and block leaders and the lower echelons of the Congress (I) Party were involved. Local congress offices were frequently the sites for mob assemblies, for burning bodies, and for launching raids... public vehicles were used to transport rioters from place to place ..." (Tambiah,1990: 744-745) Similarly, planning behind the riotous acts in the Calcutta riots of 1946 was evident. The riots undertook a "distinct political dimension for the first time." (Das, 2000: 285) "This was evident from Muslim attacks on the establishments of Congress leaders, pro-congress newspapers and such nationalist Muslims as the former Speaker of the Bengal legislature, Syed Naushar Ali."

Other signs of organization were seen in the use of government resources to aid in the violent attacks and the premeditated stockpiling of weapons prior to the riots. According to Das, "Hindus … purchased as 'a precautionary measure' arms and ammunition from American soldiers which were later used in the riots. Acid bombs were manufactured and stored in Hindu-owned factories long before the outbreak." Even the collection of looted booty was coordinated with goods being loaded onto trucks and transported to a central location. "Shops were carefully marked with signs so that the crowd left untouched the establishments of their coreligionists." (Das, 2000: 285)

Another important feature is the role of criminal elements within the communities. In Jamaica the political parties actively recruited members of the criminal underworld as political organizers and enforcers to support their electoral goals. In India:

> Goondas … - that umbrella term used … to denote a broad spectrum of social groups ranging from various marginalized groups to habitual criminals – emerged as organizers of violence once the riot gained momentum. Links between these goondas – Hindu and Muslim alike – and organized politics were clear. People who would not normally associate themselves with such groups now consorted with them and followed their leadership. (Das, 2000: 286)

As we shall discuss later in this paper, the existence of these groups dramatically affects the dynamics of communal violence.

An important observation about communal violence in India is that it tends to be unilateral. The deadly ethnic riot is a strategy used as a form of social control by dominant groups in various regions to keep minorities in check. As a result, we find that a wide range of communal antagonisms exist. In

Muslim dominated areas, Muslims tend to be the perpetrators of violence against minorities in their midst, where they are in the minority they are targets. The same can be said for most groups in India including Hindus and Sikhs.

Whether the threat to the dominant group is social, cultural, economic or political, communal violence is a mechanism through which the status quo can be maintained. The dominant position of the majority community and its disproportionate access to government resources and sympathy provide an environment in which mobilization is easy and retaliation is unlikely. The cost of engaging in these acts of violence is relatively low. This in part explains the frequency of these riots. The nature of the violence is also reflective of this strategic use of communal violence. Symbolic violence is common in these riots. Banners, verbal insults, degradation of women and other ethno-religious atrocities are all common. Economic, cultural and religious targets are carefully chosen and even when they are not destroyed then are often defaced or otherwise defiled.

Because the issues at hand are related to the overall social status of the community, participation is more widely spread. In these unilateral riots the risk to individual participants is minimized. This is particularly true when law enforcement officials are partisan supporters of the violence. Therefore, as some observers have noted, middle-class citizens are increasingly becoming active participants in these riots.

Sri Lanka: A case of communal violence?

Ignoring the distinctiveness of communal violence is poor analysis. But equally as troubling is the tendency to lump all conflicts which pit one group against another as being communal. The analysis of developments in Sri Lanka seems to fit this description. Sri Lanka has been plagued by many violent disputes between clearly identifiable groups for many years.

Two disputes in particular have gained international attention and have been the subject of some scholarly work. These are the violent dispute between the Tamils and Sinhalese and that between the Buddhists and Muslims.

Buddhist-Muslim conflicts in Sri Lanka follow closely the pattern of communal violence in India. For the most part the conflict between the groups is an example of uses of violence as a form of social control. The upwardly mobile Muslim minority began to assert itself culturally, economically and politically. This included the construction of new mosques near traditional Buddhist ceremonial land. These developments required local Buddhists to modify their traditional ceremonies (alterations in processional routes & limit music playing in front of Mosques, etc.). This "threat" to their communal identity became the banner around which they would mobilize to keep the Muslim outsiders in check.

As Rogers (1987) explains:

> ... the Moors' own religious identity, which had been weak as a political force in the nineteenth century, had become stronger, leading some of them to resist Buddhist processions passing by mosques ... The rioting was also able to draw on the tradition of economic protest because many Moors were shopkeepers who dealt in rice and other necessities and who often extended credit. In some localities their shops were sacked and the produce strewn about, It is important to note, however, that unlike earlier grain riots, these left Sinhalese and Indian merchants untouched. (Rogers, 1987: 592)

Tensions between the Tamil and Sinhalese can be dated back to the 1950s (Kearney, 1984) or as far back as 1915 (Rogers, 1987). As Rogers notes, "At independence ethnic polarization between the Sinhalese and Ceylon Tamils did not appear inevitable. Since 1915 there had been few major riots or other disturbances, and the more serious incidents had been inspired by economic, not ethnic or religious, grievances." (Rogers, 1987: 595) In the 1950s Sinhalese-Buddhist cultural nationalism developed into a mass political force. This nationalist thinking led to the development of policies which discriminated against the Tamils as outsiders. "One of the government's responses … was the virtual end of recruitment of Tamils into many branches of the public service and the establishment of what amounted to ethnic quotas for university admissions." (Rogers, 1987: 597) the 1972 constitution also served to alienate the Tamils further by giving "formal recognition to the dominance of Sinhalese Buddhists." The ethnic polarization was accompanied by "an increase in political violence known as 'thuggery'."

In the 1970s, demands for a separate Tamil state, "Eelam", emerged. The separatist movement was accompanied by "militancy among [the Tamil] unknown to earlier generations." (Rogers, 1987: 597) This movement took on increasingly violent characteristics in the early 1980s with the emergence of the Tamil Tigers as a representative group of the Tamil community committed to the use of violence as a means of protecting and promoting Tamil interests. The Tigers began as a single organization but eventually fractured in multiple splinter groups with varied interpretations of Tamil interest and goals. "Their combined strength has been estimated at anywhere from 500 to 6,000 or more. Among the major groups operating in 1984 were the Liberation Tigers of Eelam and an offshoot, the People's Liberation Organization of Tamil Eelam. Another group, the Eelam People's Revolutionary Front," (Kearney, 1984: 260) also operated during this period.

Violence between the Tamils and Sinhalese people involved riots in 1977, 1981 and 1983. Also, from the 1970s onwards the Tamil Tigers have engaged government forces in combat. During this time, they have used multiple strategies. They carried out violent attacks on Tamil politicians who have collaborated with the government, bomb attacks, kidnappings and other attacks against the established government. In 1983, following government efforts to restrict travel to and from the Jaffna Peninsula, the location of the primary Tamil communities, violence again took on new proportions in Sri Lanka.

> Persons described as "Northern terrorists" massacred 72 Sinhalese men, women and children, settlers in two small farming communities in the northern district of Mullaitivu. The district's population is predominantly Tamil, but many Sinhalese have been moving in the sparsely populated district in recent years. The attacks represented the first deliberate killing of Sinhalese civilians by separatist ... (Kearney, 1984: 262)

Thus, in Sri Lanka, what began as a nationalist and separatist struggle transformed into communal violence. Communal violence in this context seems to be the product of conscious decisions by the Tamils. This transition fits well with the theories of Tarrow (1994) that new forms of violence may be introduced into on-going disputes to heighten or maintain waning movements. Here the emergence of communal violence appears to be a deliberate introduction of new forms of violence to advance the positions of the Tamil separatist in relation to the Sinhalese dominated government. It should however be clear that the violence which preceded this was not essentially communal.

The post 1970 violence between the Tamils and Sinhalese is not defined by the engagement of Sinhalese communities against Tamil communities. Certainly there were earlier examples of unilateral rioting. What we see after 1971 is a violent conflict which pitted one defined group within the state against the state itself. That the state was dominated by Sinhalese people did not lie at the core of this. Similarly, traditional targets of Tamil violence were not geared at Sinhalese communities. The acts of violence tended to be focused on specifically political targets. In some instances, acts of international terrorism were perpetrated. Even then, the targets were not specifically Sinhalese. The most notorious of these was the kidnapping of a group of Americans in an attempt to draw attention to their cause.

The riots which occurred prior to the 1983 massacre laid the foundation for the adoption of communal violence as a strategy in this nationalist struggle. They may even arguable be seen as the first inkling of communal violence. The riots began in the pattern of unilateral violence as seen in India. The dominant Sinhalese residents mobilized against the Tamil minority which they perceived as threatening their security. Here Tamil communities were clearly targeted and the collective group was held liable for the actions of the Tigers in their midst. The riots were clearly instances of unilateral communal violence carried out by the dominant majority against a deviant minority. These riots however also laid the foundation for the emergence of bilateral communal violence which would follow. This bilateral communal violence in Sri Lanka produced a "sustained level of violence throughout 1984, including armed battles between sizable bands of combatants and mounting casualties among the civilian population." (Kearney, 1984: 263)

The Tamil-Sinhalese case in Sri Lanka is best understood as a nationalist movement. This does not dispute the fact that communal violence exists here. Rather, it must be understood that communalism is not a root of the violence. Communal violence in the Sri Lankan context is best seen as one of several strategies being employed in a nationalist struggle. To treat this case as any other form of communal violence denies the true roots and motivations of the violence.

Toward a deeper understanding of communal violence:

Communal violence is not random. It acts as a form of social control. It is as Senechal de la Roche describes it, "a process by which people ... respond to behavior as deviant. ... [this] violence, then, is commonly a moralistic response ... and aptly enough, it is sometimes described as "popular justice." (Senechal de la Roche, 1996: 97-98) Liability is often collectivized in instances of communal violence. The group or members of a group or social category are held accountable for the conduct of an individual(s). "Those held collectively liable might include, for example, a race, religion, ethnic group, nationality, political party, labor organization, family, clan, or tribe." In India, South East Asia and Jamaica this notion of collective liability is popular and deeply rooted. These forms of collective liability are more likely to develop where extreme social polarization exists.

Certain social conditions are conducive to the development of these forms of violence. Collective violence sometimes arises where law is lacking, weak, or openly partisan. Where law is weak or absent, other means of social control tend to arise. (Senechal de la Roche, 1996: 105) All the case studies reviewed in this investigation demonstrated the significance of police involvement. The contributions of law enforcement officials included active participation in the violence, biased protection of one group, refusal to intervene and the partisan arrest and prosecution of rioters and organizers. The following account of police involvement is reflective of the narratives on this issue.

In March of 1990 riots erupted in Nizamuddin, India. The riots were incited by the construction of boundary wall on disputed property. The disputed land lies between an old Muslim burial ground and an expanding Hindu center. According to one report, "a large gathering of Hindus began building the wall without police sanction (but nevertheless with careful police protection)." (Datta, Pati, Sarkar, Sarkar and Sen, 1990: 2487) Observers describe the events which surrounded this as "an invasion. It had not taken placed in a shared space: an organized Hindu crowd coming from other parts of the city, ably supported by the police, had invaded an overwhelmingly Muslim settlement." (Datta, Pati, Sarkar, Sarkar and Sen, 1990: 2487) Although the death toll in this incident was low, it is noteworthy that the only killings were conducted by the police firing on Muslims. Furthermore:

> From the killing of women and children in police firing within an enclosed mosque at Id prayers ... in August 1980 ... down to the Bhagalpur, Gujarat and Nizamuddin in recent months, the overwhelming majority of those killed in communal violence have been Muslims. The offensive almost invariably has come from Hindus, and police and paramilitary forces have been blatantly partial. (Datta, Pati, Sarkar, Sarkar and Sen, 1990: 2489)

Relational distance is also a significant factor in determining the likelihood and severity of collective violence. According to Senechal de la Roche (1996), collective violence varies directly with relational distance. Furthermore, "changes in communities that increase relational distance between groups ... increase the probability of collective violence." (Senechal de la Roche, 1996: 107)

Collective violence:

> Arises historically with the growth of towns and cities where people encounter others across greater distances in relational space. It arises with increasing geographic mobility, as migration and improving transportation circulate strangers with and across nations. It arises with segregation, which reduces or severs ties between co-resident

populations. It arises with in-migration and
desegregation, which suddenly infuse strangers
into communities and neighborhoods. (Senechal
de la Roche, 1996: 108)

The 1983 riots in Sri Lanka exemplify the importance of
this. The Sinhalese rioters who perpetrated acts of violence
against the Tamils, tended to be strangers. Many were "bused
in" from other communities to participate in the conflict.
Local Sinhalese who were relationally closer, participated less
in the violence and tended to either remain neutral or provided
protection to Tamils (Senechal de la Roche, 1996: 108). The
use of outsiders in the perpetuation of violence is common in
mixed communities. Participation by locals is often restricted
to symbolic violence, spectatorship, instigation and fingering.
Nonetheless, communal violence has the effect of making life
uncomfortable and uncertain for targeted residents in mixed
communities. As a result, communities threatened by communal
violence tend to become increasingly homogenous over time.

The establishment of exclusive homogenous communities
contributes directly to further violence. In both the Asian and
Jamaican contexts, conflict between groups led to the purging
of undesirables from communities. The consequence was the
development of definable geographic spaces in which little
interaction occurred between members of the opposed groups.

Cultural distance also facilitates the development of collective
violence. This is particularly evident in the South Asian cases. In
fact, cultural distance appears to be of primary importance in
these cases. The 1984 assassination of Indira Ghandi by her Sikh
body guards, led to extensive rioting and communal violence
and over 3,000 deaths. But more significantly is the extensive
history in India of communal violence triggered by issues such
as cow slaughter, music, or the desecration of religious symbols.

A third condition is the level of interdependence between
the communities. "People are comparatively unlikely to attack

those who are indispensable to their wellbeing, but prefer to kill or maim those they can do without." (Senechal de la Roche, 1996:111)

Communal violence is frequently relatively organized, even formally so, or relatively unorganized. As Senechal de la Roche (1996: 103) states "informal organization also implies relatively open and fluid membership: participation may be possible for nearly everyone in a given community. Even law enforcement officials may join in the violence."

> In the frequent ethnic riots of South Asia in recent times, for example, the "participation during riots of police, army, or other security forces … as vigorous participants favoring the cause of one side or another is a fact of life recorded in country after country[50]." And in the American South of the late 19th and early 20th centuries, whole communities of whites – men, women and children, and police – might attend and celebrate lynching of an alleged black offender. (Senechal de la Roche, 1996: 104)

Communal riots demonstrate distinct signs of orchestration. However, they still involve a degree of genuine spontaneity. The fact that they have been ritualized and routinized means that with each passing cycle, the restraints against active participation are stripped away. As a result, some have noted that over the years the participation of middle class citizens and neighbors has increased.

In Jamaica, communal violence is more formally structured. The political violence of the pre- 1990s provided an established structure through which representatives of each community could be mobilized. Dons, "shottas", and other identifiable

---

[50] This internal quote is credited to (Banerjee, 1990: 55 – 57)

members of the community were given the responsibility for carrying out acts of violence. For most members of the community, participation in communal violence was limited to harboring and protecting these individuals, fingering possible targets and the occasional show of community strength at political rallies or riots. Similar patterns have also presented themselves in Asia.

Some forms of collective violence are unilateral. In these cases, violence tends to be perpetrated by members of the dominant group on the inferior minority. In Asia, many instances of communal conflict are unilateral. Hindu versus Muslim conflict outside of the partitioned states in India is an example. Socio-economic inequality in these cases, make unilateral attacks less risky for the perpetrators. In some instance however, where the opposed communities are of relatively equal socio-economic status the incentives to engage in collective violence are reduced. This occurs because the possibility of retaliation is increased. Where the tensions between the groups are sufficiently strong and where the cost of retaliation is acceptable bilateral communal violence develops.

This bilateral communal violence which takes retaliation as a given, produces a wholly different dynamic. Most communal violence in Asia is enduring, but sporadic. This is in part because many of the conflicts are unilateral conflicts triggered by some deviant behavior. Most instances of communal violence in Asia are also short lived. They tend to consist of riots, looting and occasional military incursions over the course of a few days. Bilateral communal violence presents itself as an on-going extended conflict. The retaliatory nature of the conflict causes the dispute to be extended and often escalated by the renewed perpetuation of acts of violence. Collective liability renews the tensions between the groups. Retaliatory acts against "innocent" members of the community reinforce the sense of animosity. The relative equality in strength of the groups allows the dispute to continue indefinitely with neither group being capable of subduing the other.

An example of this can be seen in the conflict between Protestant and Muslim groups in Sulawesi, Indonesia starting in 1998. As Lorraine V Aragon (2001) observed:

> As conditions worsened, segments of Poso's Muslim and Protestant communities began to respond to any perceived assault with a pattern of multiplied revenge; not tit for tat, not just explosive anger, but the idea that an extra wallop of calculated punishment was required in the vindictive act. "Our cousin was knifed, so we burn your town. You burned our houses, so we ambush hundreds from your community, kill them and cut them into pieces." (Aragon, 2001: 47)

As is the case in Jamaica, the bilateral communal conflict in Poso was closely linked to electoral politics. In the Poso context, redistricting and constitutional reform gave greater political and financial power to local governments. This increased the stakes involved in local elections and thus fueled the pre-existing sense of competition between pre-existing groups. In this new political climate, patron-client relations made religious identity increasingly pertinent.

The tensions between these groups had not produced significant examples of inter-group violence prior to 1998. Previous violence included market fights, nighttime attacks, and religious threats. These was repressed militarily during the 1980s and early 90s. These incidents of "insider – outsider friction over the economic use of land rather than religious strife per se, was the basal line of fracture." (Aragon, 2001: 57). However, population changes and, the new political order established after 1998 increased the significance of these divisions.

> By the late 1990s, the Muslim percentage of the
> Poso city population exceeded fifty percent, and
> Muslim Bugis gained control of much urban
> commerce. Simultaneously ... competition
> increased between Muslim ... and Christian ...
> business people applying to receive development
> contracts through the regent's office. Given
> Indonesian patron-client relations that followed
> communal lines, it became clear that the selection
> of the next Poso Regent would largely determine
> which ethnic or religious groups would have the
> most political and economic support from the
> next regency administration. (Aragon, 2001: 58)

The developments that led to the outbreak of communal violence in Poso bear the closest similarity to the Jamaican case. As such, they present an opportunity for an insightful comparative study. Such an undertaking may deepen our understanding of the manner in which divisions are politicized in competition for scarce resources. Additionally, it may help us better understand how patron-client relations contribute to potentially explosive divisions in societies. While a full comparative study will not be undertaken here, I hope to highlight some common elements.

It is important to note that the 1999 elections were the first free elections held in over three decades. Politics in the Indonesian "New Order" quickly took on a zero-sum quality where individuals linked their economic survival and personal security to the outcomes of the electoral process.

As has been seen in Jamaican case, the violence which engulfed an entire region and brought several communities into heated battle began with small seemingly mundane disputes. Aragon (2001: 60-61) describes the disputes in Poso as developing through four distinct phases. The first phase, which began in December 1998, was sparked by a quarrel between two drunken youth; one Muslim and one Christian. The Muslim was stabbed and fled to nearby mosque. Community leaders and law enforcement authorities agreed that the dispute was alcohol related and resolved that limits on the sale of alcohol should be enforced.

In a less highly charged environment, this incident would have ended here. However, several Muslim youth from the community escalated the violence by carrying out a series of attacks against the property of local Christian residents. These attacks led to rumors that Churches were being attacked and Christian farmers from neighboring communities organized themselves to defend themselves from the Muslim aggressions. "On.. December 27, scores of machete-armed Pamona from the GKST[51] stronghold of Tentena arrived by truck to reinforce the threatened GKST Protestants of Lombogia."

The trajectory of events described here is common. Tambiah (1990) describes it as occurring through two processes, focalization and transvaluation.

> By focalization I mean the process of progressive denudation of local incidents and disputes of their particulars of context and aggregating them, thereby narrowing their concrete richness. Transvaluation refers to the parallel process of assimilating particulars to a larger, collective, more enduring, and therefore less context-bound, cause or interest. (Tambiah, 1990: 750)

These processes have the combined effect of progressive polarization and dichotomization of issues and partisans. In

---

[51] Gereja Kristen Sulawesi Tengah (GKST) translates as Central Sulawesi Christian Church. It is the largest Christian church in Central Sulawesi, Indonesia. It was established in 1893 and became an independent denomination in 1947. It has over 320 congregations throughout Central Sulawesi and is headquartered in Tentena, at the northern end of Lake Poso.

such a climate, acts of violence by groups quickly become "self-fulfilling manifestations, incarnations and re-incarnations, of allegedly irresolvable communal splits between Pathans and Biharis, Sikhs and Hindus, Sinhalese and Tamils … Malays and Chinese [or JLP and PNP]." (Tambiah, 1990: 750)

The involvement of residents from neighboring communities reflects three characteristics which also featured prominently in the Jamaican case. First, the solidarity reflected in their mobilization was based both on their common identity as Christians and on their common political alignment with political parties favorable to their collective interests. The second, important commonality is the role of political elites in organizing, mobilizing and facilitating the violence. As Aragon notes, "these trucks … were led by the DPRD II representative Herman Parimo [and] carried members of the Gerakan Pemuda Sulawesi Tengah (GPST) a resurrected version of the Protestant Pamona militia organization." (2001: 61) Throughout the process of escalation in Poso allegations of direct involvement, support and sponsorship of the violence by political elites were made.

> Many Muslims would blame the initiation of group aggression on Phase one on Parimo's leadership and his anger that Patiro, supported by his Protestant Pamona political faction, was eliminated by Muslim leaders in the early DPRD II nominations for regent. Other[s] … would blame Patiro directly. Christians, by contrast, would defend these two men and deem their protective actions fully justified. (Aragon, 2001: 61)

The third similarity which should be noted here is the pre-existence in these communities of extra-governmental militia, which could be mobilized into action. The existence of these groups affects the dynamics of communal violence. They make the mobilization of communities into violence easier, since there already exists an established network of fighters, and a command structure to control them. Their existence also means that within a community there are identifiable people who are conditioned, trained and willing to carry out acts of violence on behalf of the larger community. In this respect, communal violence, is not always the engagement of regular citizens in battle, but the engagement of militarized segments of communities. This may in some ways account for the level and types of violence involved in these conflicts.

In Poso the mobilization of such groups was bi-lateral. "Muslim reinforcements also arrived from the Muslim Bugis and Kaili area of Parigi to the west." (Aragon, 2001: 61) The battle between these two groups lasted for over a week, drew residents into the rioting and even spilled beyond the borders to neighboring towns.

> During the week of turmoil, nearly two hundred people were injured, mostly Protestants, some tortured ... stabbed, burned, or dragged by ropes from vehicles. Roughly four hundred Protestant and Catholic families saw their houses destroyed. The homes of the Muslim regent, Pateanga, and the two Protestant leaders ... were stormed. The bus terminal along with stores, restaurants, hotels, and vehicles ... were burned down. (Aragon, 2001: 61-62)

The second phase (April 16, 1998 – May 23, 1998) of violence demonstrates the importance of this. Like Phase I, it began with a seemingly insignificant brawl between two residents from each community. Once again local Muslims carried out attacks against their Protestant neighbors and reinforcements from other neighboring communities were brought in. This time, combatants used hand held radios and other communication devices to help coordinate their attacks. Muslim groups also began sweeping campaigns "in which individuals traveling through Muslim neighborhoods were inspected for identity cards … or other indications of their religion. Some Protestants were pulled from vehicles and publicly slashed to death. Muslim groups also began sewing and wearing white headbands to recognize each other." (Aragon, 2001: 65)

The toll for Phase II included the destruction of seven hundred Christian homes, four protestant churches and three Protestant schools. Another consequence of these attacks was the fleeing of Christian residents from "Muslim neighborhoods" into communities were they felt more safe. As mentioned before, this is a common feature of communal violence. "The communal conflicts across Indonesia following the fall of Soeharto produced over 1.3 million internally displaced persons (IDPs). But displacement was often not merely an unintended by-product of conflict. In many cases, it was a deliberate tactic or even – in the form of ethnic cleansing – the objective of the conflict." (Virgoe, 2008: 479) This pattern played a significant role in Jamaica and has also been seen in the Indian case study. Chandra (1993) notes that as incidents of neighbors fingering or targeting each other for attack increased:

> Neighborhoods in the communally more sensitive
> parts of the city are tending to become exclusively
> Muslim or Hindu. The use of paths leading from
> main roads into adjacently situated Muslim and
> Hindu neighborhoods is reported to be acquiring
> a communal character; people belonging to one
> community would rather take a longer detour
> than risk passing through a locality housing the
> other community. (Chandra, 1993: 1884)

This description of Surat, India parallels the developments in Jamaican in the 1970s- 80s. While, it is not clear that homogenization in Poso occurred on the same level as that accomplished in Jamaica and Surat the pattern again bears some similarity. This kind of homogenization further fuels the likelihood and intensity of future communal violence. There is also evidence that this homogenization occurs in cases of both unilateral and bilateral communal violence.

In Poso, the partisan response of local authorities seeking to suppress the violence of Phase I fueled further resentment and division. In the aftermath of the violence eight Protestants were arrested and charged, but no Muslims were implicated. Following the June elections, a new Muslim regent was appointed. However, in the process the representatives from both the local Protestant and Muslim communities were eliminated. While the new Regent was Muslim, he was from a community outside of Poso and held no direct ties to the community. The local Muslim candidate, Ladjalani was demoted from his previous position of Head of the Central Sulawesi Agency for Regional Development to assistant head under the new administration.

Both of these developments may have contributed to the growth of communal violence. For the Christian community, an increased sense of alienation and victimization developed and cemented their solidarity. "Even in the first days of fighting, Poso Protestants sending personal reports claimed that Protestants had long been "stepped on" and for that reason they feared that their community might become vengeful." (Aragon, 2001: 62) In Poso, it is interesting to note that Christians of various denominations and ethnicities were united into a common communal identity. For Muslims their sense of security was threatened by the loss of a direct access to government patronage. This may have further increased their need to re-affirm their common identity as Muslims vis-à-vis other competitors.

From May 23, 2000 – July 2000 communal violence in Poso took on a new form. In this Phase, representatives of Poso's Christian community executed a planned and coordinated strike against the Muslim community of Kayamanya. Their targets included individuals they held liable for the atrocities of Phase II. These attacks were clearly retaliatory and represented an escalation of violence to its highest levels. Within Christian communities emerged attack squads known collectively as "red troops[52]". These red troops were the Christian response to the creation of the Muslim "white troops" in Phase II. These groups engaged in numerous battles and raids on each others communities. Included among these was the May 28 raid on the Muslim community of Sintuwu Lemba, where up to 70 Muslim men were trapped in a boarding school along with women and children. Many of the men were executed and the women and children held hostage for several days. In addition, "dozens of predominantly Muslim villages along the road running west towards Parigi and Palu, as well as the road running east to Ampana, were attacked and burned, effectively closing Poso's major transportation and communication system." (Aragon, 2001: 68-69)

This description of the development in Poso demonstrates that the events in Jamaica are not anomalous. Patron-client relations, democratization and competition over scarce resources produced a perception of politics as being a zero-sum game. In this context political alignments led to further polarization of sub - communities. The relative strength of the two communities allowed for the development of bilateral communal violence. Phase I, in Poso began in the tradition of unilateral communal riots seen elsewhere in Asia. Poso however lacked the vast superiority of numbers and resources need to minimize retaliation.

---

[52] Within this larger category were smaller squads known as "red bats", "black bats" and "masks." They also included a group referred to as the ninjas. This group was among the first and dressed as ninjas to conceal their identities and accommodate their clandestine night-time attacks on Muslims.

Bilateral communal violence in both cases produced common features. Small disputes between individuals were transformed into communal issues with collective liability and sparked disproportionately violent responses. Violence in both cases was perpetuated by militarized, sometimes criminal, elements within the community. These militia/gangs introduced a level of organization and structure to the communal violence which increased the level of violence. Retaliation serves as a motivation for future attacks. This fact accounts for the durability of these disputes. Bilateral violence is proliferated by retaliation. Because of the tensions built up by communal violence in general, communal violence proves itself to be resilient to efforts of reconciliation or negotiation.

Linking communal violence to electoral violence:

An important lesson which has emerged from this investigation is the linkage between political and electoral violence and communal violence. The case for this in the Jamaican case study has been well documented in preceding chapters. However similar developments have presented themselves in the South Asian context also. Tambiah (1990) highlights the following three instances as examples of this connection.

In Bangladesh during the 1988 local elections supporters of the rival candidates engaged each other in heated battles using rocks, guns and homemade bombs. Eighty people were killed and up to two thousand injured in these battles. Voting was suspended at dozens of polling stations, others were ransacked and ballot boxes stolen. In the National elections which followed shortly after, voting was again suspended in over 170 polling places because of instances of ballot rigging.

In India, (1989) violence and corrupt practices obstructed the holding of democratic elections. Acts of electoral fraud, violence and intimidation included the stuffing of ballot boxes, the ransacking of party headquarters, the shooting of party officials and scuffles between supporters of various parties.

> It was reported on the first day of elections, 'armed gangs roamed through the constituency of Prime Minister Rajiv Gandhi, terrorizing voters.' … antigovernment Muslim militants set fire to several polling stations and planted bombs near the homes of party members supporting the coalition between Prime Minister Gandhi's Congress Party and the locally based National Conference of Chief Minister Farooq Abdullah … on the first day of voting, twenty people died and several dozen were wounded in election-related violence throughout the country. (Tambiah, 1990: 753-4)

In Sri Lanka, the election of Jayawardene and the success of a referendum to extend the terms of the sitting parliament, were "secured through … blatant thuggery and electoral infractions." (Tambiah, 1990: 754) The strategies applied included the detention of opposition organizers, the breaking up of election meetings by gangs of government supporters, intimidation of pro-opposition voters at polls, the intimidation of election officials and the forced removal of opposition polling observers from polling stations. As Tambiah points out, the worst instances of communal violence in Sri Lanka occurred since months after this election.

These practices in South Asia parallel those employed in Jamaican politics from the 1960s-80s. The common occurrence of political violence and communal violence in regions as distant as Asian and the Caribbean highlights the relationship between them. A common thread which links them together is the politics of clientelism. As Tambiah suggests, "The politicization of ethnicity [or communalism], ... tied to the politics of elections has much to do with the winning of benefits distributed by the modern state committed to welfare, development, and employment programs." (Tambiah, 1990: 752)

There seems therefore to be a general political root to communal violence. Communal violence is often rooted in burgeoning democracies, where political patron-client relations are linked to the economic survival of underdeveloped communities. The zero-sum politics of these clientelist welfare states contribute to the polarization of communities competing for access to resources and, social and political dominance. Over time political and communal cleavages become cemented into a single divisive element which takes on a character of its own. This divisive character is manipulated by political elites to serve their own electoral goals. In doing so, the practice of political violence becomes normalized and transferred to the resolution of other conflicts. As a result, violence becomes a validated and routinized form of social control used on the communal level to resolve any threats to the collective interest of community.

Conclusion:

This general overview of the manifestations of communal violence in South Asia suggests that there is similarity in causation, developmental processes and outcomes to warrant future comparative study. While, this writing has not and will not attempt such an undertaking, it does lay the groundwork. The challenges presented by Brubaker and Laitin still remain pertinent today. These challenges must also be extended to the analysis of other forms of collective violence.

Cases of communal violence, whether ethnically, religiously, culturally or politically based, share common characteristics. These characteristics are driven by the dynamics of identity formation. The polarization of these divided communities is greatly affected by socio-economic and political developments. In particular, the politics of communalism deserves further attention.

The same must be said of the process of democratization. As we continue to push for the democratization of countries, we must take into account that it can and has produced devastating consequences; one of which is communal violence. Patron-client relations have received little attention recent years. Yet, as revealed in this investigation, these relationships are inextricably linked to communal violence.

WORKS CITED

"12 year-old boy shot dead in barber's chair". (2002, October 20). *Jamaica Observer.*

"A blip in Jamaican stability". (2001, September). *Latin Finance, 130.* p 92.

Albert, Richard Rev. (2005, July 22). "Politicians are responsible." *Jamaica Gleaner:* A9

"A plea for peace" (2002, September 29). *Jamaica Observer.*

Aragon, Lorraine V. (Oct. 2001). "Communal violence in Poso, Central Sulawesi: Where people eat fish and fish eat people." *Indonesia 72* 45 – 79.

Aristotle, Barker, E., & Stalley, R.F. (2009). *The politics.* Oxford: Oxford University Press.

Barak, Oren. (Nov., 2002). "Intra-communal and inter communal dimensions of conflict and peace in Lebanon." *International journal of Middle east studies. 34 (4).* 619 – 644

Beckford, George L. & Witter, Michael. (1982). *Small garden; bitter weed: the political economy of struggle and change in Jamaica 2nd expanded edition.* Morant Bay, Jamaica: Maroon Publishing House.

Benson, Michelle. & Kugler, Jacek. (1998, April). "Power parity, democracy, and the severity of internal violence". *The journal of conflict resolution, 42(2),* 196 – 209.

Berlin, Isiah. (1969) "Two Concepts of Liberty" *Four Essays on Liberty.* Oxford, England: Oxford University Press

Beruff, Jorge Rodriguez & Muniz, Humberto Garcia (Eds.). (1996). <u>Security Problems and Policies in the Post Cold War Caribbean</u> New York, NY: St. Martin's Press "Beyond declarations of peace." (2002, February 04). *Jamaica Observer.*

"Beyond the symbolism." (2002, June 13). *Jamaica Observer.* Editorial

"Blair intervenes in Mountain view dispute". (2002, July 16). *Jamaica Observer.*

"Blair investigating seven cases of political misconduct" (2003, June 18). *Jamaica Observer.*

"Blair orders withdrawal of three political ads". (2002, October 8). *Jamaica Observer.*

Bleiberg, R.M. (1989, January 23). "Down with Manley: Jamaica's future and the Caribbean's is up for grabs next month". *Barron's national business and financial weekly 69,*(Editorial) *11*

"Boisterous JLP supporters mob Assamba's vehicle." (2003, June 27). *Jamaica Observer.*

Bogues, Anthony. (2006, May/June). "Power, violence and the Jamaican "Shotta Don". *NACLA Report on the Americas 39 (6), 21 – 37.*

Boxill, Ian & Unnithan, Prabha N. (1995, March) "Rhetoric and policy realities in developing countries: Community councils in Jamaica, 1972 – 1980." *Journal of behavioral science 31(1),* 65 – 79.

Boyd, Hughlin. (2002, November 18). "Police and politics." *Jamaica Observer.*

Boyd, Hughlin. (2002, October 9). "The politics of crime." *Jamaica Observer.*

Brana-Shute, Rosemary & Brana-Shute, Gary. (1980). *Crime and punishment in the Caribbean.* Florida: Center for Latin American Studies.

Brana-Shute, Rosemary and Brana-Shute, Gary (1982). "The Magnitude and Impact of Remittances in the Eastern Caribbean" In Stinner, William (Ed.) *Return Migration and Remittances; developing a Caribbean Perspective* Washington D.C.: *RIES Occasional Papers 3* Research Institute on Immigration and Ethnic Studies. Smithsonian Institute 1982

Brizan, George. (1984). *Grenada, Island of conflict: from Amerindians to People's Revolution, 1498 -1979.* Totowa, N.J.: Zed Books

Bowman, Larry W. (1991). *Mauritius: Democracy and Development in the Indian Ocean.* San Francisco: Westview Press.

Brown, Geof. (1997, September 13). "War and politics". *Jamaica Gleaner.*

Brubaker, Rogers and Laitin, David D. (1998). "Ethnic and nationalist violence." *Annual review of sociology 24:* 423 – 452.

Buckley, Brown. (2002, June 28). "Builders concerned about political interference in projects." *Jamaica Observer.*

Buckley, Byron. (2002, June 12). "Leaders sign conduct code: Patterson, Seaga pledge to reject violence, intimidation as political strategies." *Jamaica Observer.*

Buddan, Robert. *Topic Four- Voting Behavior.* GT22D – Politics in the Caribbean

"CAFFE Knocks St. Catherine violence and praises Mountain View women" (2002, August 18). *Jamaica Observer*

"Calming Down Jamaica" (1987, November 7). *The Economist, 305,* 50.

Campbell, Dawn. (1997, April 19). "Grants Pen calls for peace". *The Daily Observer.*

Campbell, Olivia. (2002, October 11). "Message of peace from Patterson". *Jamaica Observer.*

Chandra, Sudhir. (Sep. 4. 1993). "Of Communal consciousness and communal violence: Impressions from post-riot Surat." *Economic and political weekly 28(36)* 1883 – 1887.

Chang, Kevin O'Brien. (2000, July 3). "Best of a bad bunch." *Jamaica Observer.*

Chaplin, Ken. (2002, October 15). "Now she knows". *Jamaica Observer*

Chaplin, Ken. (1999, September 14). "Combating election fraud." *Jamaica Observer.*

Charles, Christopher A.D. (2004). "Political identity and criminal violence in Jamaica: The garrison community of August Town and the 2002 election". *Social and economic studies, 53(2), 31 – 74.*

Charles, Christopher A.D. (2002) "Garrison communities as counter societies: The case of the 1998 Zeeks' riot in Jamaica. *Ideaz 1,* 29-43.

"Charles, Dalley call for peace after skirmish in Clarendon". (2002, October 15). *Jamaica Observer.*

Chin, William K. (March 1, 2000). "Letter to Edward Seaga" Kingston JA: Seaga Files UWI Mona Library Rare Book Collection.

Chisolm, Clinton Reverend. (2002, October 16). "My political credo." *Jamaica Observer.*

Clarke, Charmaine. (2002, September 4). "Three miss signing of political code in St. James." *Jamaica Observer.*

Clarke, Colin. (2006). "From slum to Ghetto: Social deprivation in Kingston, Jamaica." *International Development Planning Review.* 28(1): 1 -34.

Clarke, Colin & Howard, David (Jun 2006). "Contradictory socio-economic consequences of structural adjustment." *The geographical journal 172(2), 106 - 129*

Clarke, Paul. (2006, June 19). "Murder drops 62% after crime plan introduced in east Kingston." *Jamaica Observer.* p7

Cohen, Youssef. (1994). *Radicals, Reformers and Revolutionaries.* Chicago, Il: University of Chicago Press

"Communal Violence." (Sep 10, 1977) *Economic and political weekly 12 (37) 1603 – 1605*

Constitution of the United States of America (1789). Modified (1992).

"Cops say four gangs responsible for Mo-Bay killings." (2006, April 27) (12) 101.

Crawford, Charmaine. (Spring/Summer 2003). "Sending love in a barrel: the making of transnational Caribbean families in Canada". *Canadian Woman Studies 22 (3/4)* 104-109.

Crime and violence in Jamaica: Causes and solutions. (1988) Mona, JA: University of the West Indies symposium on Crime and violence.

Cummings, Mark. (2002, September 7). "JLP St. James candidates sign code of conduct." *Jamaica Observer.*

Danisman, H.B. (July 1982) *Annual Report for 1981 Development Co-operation to Mauritius* Port Louis, Mauritius: United Nations Development Project

Das, Suranjan (May 2000). "The 1992 Calcutta riot in historical continuum: A relapse into 'Communal; fury?'." *Modern Asian studies 34 (2)* 281 – 306

Datta, Pradip; Biswamoy Pati; Sumit Sarkar; Tanika Sarkar & Sambuddha Sen (Nov 10, 1990) "Understanding Communal violence: Nizamuddin Riots." *Economic and political weekly 25 (45)* 2487 -2489 + 2491 - 2495

"Denied! No bail for 'Zekes'" (2005, June 2). *Jamaica Gleaner* A2

Dick, Devon. (2001, June 12). "JLP and crime statistics." *Jamaica Gleaner.*

Dominguez, Jorge I. (1998). *Democratic politics in Latin America and the Caribbean.* Baltimore, MD: The John Hopkins University Press.

Dominguez, Jorge. (1993). The Caribbean Question: Why has Liberal Democracy Surprising Flourished? In Dominguez, Jorge. Pastor, Robert and Worrell, Delisle (Eds.). (1993). *Democracy in the Caribbean* Baltimore, MD: The John Hopkins University Press.

Dominguez, Jorge. Pastor, Robert and Worrell, Delisle (Eds.). (1993). *Democracy in the Caribbean* Baltimore, MD: The John Hopkins University Press.

"Drawing a line in the sand." (2006, June 19). *Jamaica Observer.* P8

Duffus Commission. (1987). *Report of the Duffus Commission of the Enquiry into the 1986 Local Government Elections.* Kingston: Government Printing Office

Eaton, G. E. (1975). *Alexander Bustamante and modern Jamaica.* Kingston, JA: Kingston publishers.

Edie, Carlene J. (1994). *Democracy in the Caribbean: Myths and realities.* Westport, CT: Praeger.

Edie, Carlene J. (1991). *Democracy by default: dependency and clientelism in Jamaica.* Boulder, CO: L Rienner.

Edie, Carlene J. (1984). *Dual dependence: patron-clientelist relations in Jamaica.* (Doctoral book, University of California, LA, 1984).

Edie, Carlene J. (1984, July). Jamaican political processes: a system in search of a paradigm. *The journal of development studies 20,* 248-70.

Electoral Advisory Committee. (April 24th, 1996). *Interim Report of the Electoral Advisory Committee on electoral reform*. Kingston, JA: Government Printing Office.

Ellis, Hyacinthye. (1991). Identifying crime correlates in a developing society: A study of socio-economic and socio-demographic contributions to crime in Jamaica, 1950-1984. New York: Peter Lang Publishers.

Engineer, Ali. (Jan 29 – Feb 4, 2000). "Communalism and Communal violence." *Economic and Political weekly, 35(5)* 245-247 +249

Engineer, Ali. (Jan. 25 – 31. 1997). "Communal violence in Maharashtra." *Economic and Political weekly 32 (4)* 148 -149.

Engineer, Ali. (Dec. 23, 1995). "Communalism and Communal violence in 1995." *Economic and Political weekly 30 (51)* 3267 -3269.

Engineer, Ali. (Mar. 1, 1986). "Communal violence and police terror." *Economic and Political weekly 21(9)* 382 -383

Engineer, Asghar Ali. (Dec. 26,1998). "Communal violence, 1998: shifting patterns." *Economic and Political weekly, 33 (52)* 3300 - 3303

Engineer, Asghar Ali. (Feb. 15 – 21, 1997) Communalism and Communal violence, 1996." *Economic and Political weekly32 (7)* 323 – 326.

Engineer, Asghar Ali. (Mar. 7 – 14, 1992). "Benaras rocked by communal violence." *Economic and political weekly 27 (10/11)* 509 – 511

Erickson, Daniel P. & Minson, Adam. (2005, October). The Caribbean: Democracy adrift. *Journal of Democracy 16(4)*, 159 – 172.

Erickson, R.S., Mackuen, M.B., & Stimson, J.A. (2002). *The macro polity.* Cambridge, England: Cambridge University Press.

Eyre, Alan L. (1984, January). Political violence and urban geography in Kingston Jamaica. *The geographical review 74(1)*, 24-37

Eyre, Alan L. (). Effects of political violence on the population and urban environments of Kingston, Jamaica. *Geographical Review*

Fearon, James D. & Latin, David D. (Autumn, 2000). "Review: Violence and the social construction of ethnic identity." *International Organization, Vol. 54 (4)* 845 – 877

Fenno, Richard F. Jr. *US House Members in their constituencies.* In Weisberg, Herbert. Eric Heberlig and Lisa Campoli (Eds.).(1999). Classics in congressional politics. New York. Longman.

Ferejohn. John A. Handout. Seminar on Liberty. New York University, Graduate School of Arts and Science, Department of Politics.

Figueroa, Mark. (1994, December 6-7). Garrison communities in Jamaica 1962 -1993: their growth and impact on political culture. *Democracy and Democratization in Jamaica: Fifty years of adult suffrage.* Symposium conducted in celebration of fifty years of independence Kingston, JA.

Figueroa, Mark. (1985, September). An assessment of overvoting in Jamaica. *Social and economic studies 34,* 71-106.

Figueroa, Mark & Sives, Amanda. (2002, March). Homogenous voting, electoral manipulation and the 'garrison' process in post-independence Jamaica. *Commonwealth and Comparative Politics 40(1)*, 81-108.

Figueroa, Mark & Sives, Amanda. (2002, January). Garrison politics and criminality in Jamaica: Does the 1997 election represent a turning point?. Presented to the *International conference on Crime in the Caribbean* Conference held at UWI Mona, Kingston Jamaica.

Figueroa, Mark & Sives, Amanda. In Harriott, Anthony, (2004. Garrison politics and criminality in Jamaica: Does the 1997 election represent a turning point?.

Figueroa, Mark & Sives, Amanda. (2001, February). The growing impact of Jamaican garrison politics: Does the 1997 election signal a break in the trend. *International conference on Crime in the Caribbean* Conference held at UWI Mona, Kingston Jamaica.

Figueroa, Mark, Harriott, Anthony & Satchell, Nicola (2004, December 1-3) The Political economy of Jamaica's Inner City violence: A Special case? Presented to "The Caribbean City. Leiden University, the Netherlands.

Foran, John. (Ed.) (1997). *Theorizing revolutions: New Approaches from across the disciplines.* New York: Routledge

Forbes, John Douglas. (1985). *Jamaica: Managing political and economic change.* Washington: American Enterprise Institute for Public Research.

French, Howard W. (1991, March 6). Jamaica looks past 2 waning political titans. *The New York times (late edition, A9.*

"Funeral fun". (1989. February 18). *The economist* 310. 44+

Gabbidon, Stacyann. (2003, June 18). "political violence breaks out in the west: two major parties tally injuries." *Jamaica Observer.*

Gais, Thomas L., Peterson, Mark A. and Walker Jr., Jack. Interest groups, Iron Triangles and Representative Institutions. In Walker Jr. (Ed.). (1991). Michigan: The University of Michigan Press

Gager, Wyvolyn. (1999, October 17). "Lessons from Craig Town". *Jamaica Gleaner.*

Gandhi, Krishna. (June 9, 1979). "Capitalizing on communal violence." *Economic and political weekly 14(23)* 963 -964.

Geuss, R. & Hollis, M. (1995). "Freedom as an Ideal" *The Aristotelian Society, Supp. 69.*

Girvan, Norman. (2005, April 30). "Reflections on the pursuit of conflict prevention in the greater Caribbean". *Human rights tribune, 11(2)*

Gloudon, Barbara. (2002, October 11). "Political violence: Monster among us." *Jamaica Observer.*

Goldstone, Jack. (Ed). (2003). States, Parties and Social Movements. Cambridge, UK: Cambridge University Press.

Goldstone, Jack. (1995). In Keddie, N. (Ed.) *Debating Revolutions.* New York, NY: New York University Press.

Goldstone, Jack. (2001). "Towards a fourth generation of revolutionary theory". *Annual Review of Political Science 4*: 139-87

Goldstone, Jack. (April 1980). "Review: Theories of revolution: The third generation." *World Politics 32 (3) 425-453.*

Goldstone, Jack (2009). "Rethinking Revolutions: Integrating Origins, Processes, and Outcomes." *Comparative Studies of South Asia, Africa and the Middle East.* 29

Godoy, Julio. (April 18, 2005). "Development: Millions of migrants send home billions of dollars". *Global information network.* New York.

Gonzalez, David. (2001, July 12). "Violence subsides in Jamaica, but wounds still fester." *New York Times.*

Goulbourne, H. (1984, December). On explanations of violence and public order in Jamaica. *Social and economic studies 33,* 151-69.

"GovStrat to host seminar on crime." (2006, June 11). *Jamaica Gleaner.* C7

Goyal, D. R. (Feb. 21, 1970). "National Integration and Communal violence." *Economic and political weekly, 5(8)* 379 – 381

"Graffiti sparks row between PNP, JLP." (2002, July 15). *Jamaica Observer.*

Gray, Obika. (2004). *Demeaned but Empowered: The* social power of the urban poor in Jamaica. Kingston, Jamaica: University of the West Indies Press.

Gray, Obika. (2003, March). "Predation politics and the political impasse in Jamaica." *Small Axe (13).* Pp72-94

Gray, Obika. (1991). *Radicalism and social change in Jamaica, 1960-72.* Knoxville, Tennessee: University of Tennessee Press.

Griffith, Ivelaw L. (Ed.) (1991). *Strategy and Security in the Caribbean*. New York, NY: Praeger

Griffith, Ivelaw L. (2004). *Caribbean security in the age of terror: challenge and change*. Kingston, JA.: Ian Randle publishers.

Griffith, Ivelaw L. (2000). *The political economy of drugs in the Caribbean*. New York, NY. St. Martin's Press.

Griffith, Ivelaw L. (1997). *Drugs and security in the Caribbean: Sovereignty under siege*. University Park, PA: Pennsylvania State University Press

Griffith, Ivelaw L. (1996). *Caribbean security on the eve of the 21st century*. Washington D.C.: Institute for national strategic studies, National Defense University.

Griffith, Ivelaw L. (1993). *The quest for security in the Caribbean: problems and Promises*. Armonk, NY: ME Sharpe.

Griffith, Ivelaw L. & Sedoc-Dahlberg, Betty N.. (Eds.). (1997). *Democracy and human rights in the Caribbean*. Boulder, Colorado: Westview Press.

Griffith, Ivelaw L.. (Ed.). (1991). *Strategy and security in the Caribbean*. New York: Praeger

Gulhati, Ravi and Nallri, Raj (1990). *Successful Stabilization and Recovery in Mauritius*. Port Louis: Economic Development Institute of the World Bank

Gunst, L. (1992, July 13). P.J. can't help we, really. *The nation, 255*, 48-51.

Gurr, Ted & Harff, Barbara. (1994). National minorities and State Borders. Hiroshima, Japan: Institute for peace studies, Hiroshima University.

Heclo, Hugh. "Clinton's Health Reform in Historical Perspective." In Aaron, Henry J (Ed.)(1996). *The problem that won't go away: Reforming US Health Care Financing.* Washington, DC: The Brookings Institute.

Heine, Jorge. Ed. (1990). *A Revolution Aborted: The Lessons of Grenada.* Pittsburgh, PA: University of Pittsburgh Press.

Hetherington, M. J. (2001). Resurgent mass partisanship: The role of elite polarization. *The American Political Science Review 95 (3),* 619-631.

Hart, Richard. (2006). *The end of empire: Transition to independence in Jamaica and other Caribbean region colonies.*

Harriott, Anthony. (2008). *Organized crime and politics in Jamaica: Breaking the nexus.* Kingston, JA: Canoe Press.

Harriott, Anthony. (Ed). (2003). *Understanding crime in Jamaica: new challenges for public policy.* Kingston JA: University of the West Indies Press

Harriott, Anthony. (2000). *Police and crime control in Jamaica: problems of reforming ex- colonial constabularies.* Kingston, Jamaica: University of the West Indies Press

Harriott, Anthony; Braithwaite, Farley & Wortley, Scot. (Eds). *Crime and Criminal justice in the Caribbean* (2004). Kingston, JA : Arawak publications.

Harrison, F.V. (1988, Summer/Fall). The politics of social outlawry. *Urban anthropology and studies of cultural systems and world economic development, 17,* 259-77.

Hartley, Neita. (2005). *Hugh Shearer: A voice for the people.* Kingston, JA: Ian Randle.

Hasan, Zoya Khaliq. (Feb 1982). *Social Scientist 10 (2)* 25 - 39

Hay, Bedford. (2002, February 9). "Jamaica doesn't need a Political Ombudsman." *Jamaica Gleaner.* Editorial Letters

Headley, Bernard. (1994). *The Jamaican crime scene: A perspective.* Washington, D.C.: Howard University Press.

Headley, B.D. (1987, February). Behind a Manley victory in Jamaica. *Monthly Review 38*: 17-30.

Henke, Holger. (2004, January/March). Freedom, democracy, the state and class constellations in Jamaica and Caribbean political culture: A reply to Nina Glick Schiller, Anotonio Lauria Perricelli, and Edward LiPuma and Thomas Koelble. *Identities 11(1),* 113-28.

Henke, Holger. (2000). *Between Self Determination and dependency: Jamaica's foreign relations 1972 - 1989.* The University of the West Indies Press.Kingston, JA.

Herman, Hall. (1997, May 31). A very personal interview with Michael Manley. *Everybody's 21(3),* 31.

Hillel, E. (1984, July 16). Jamaica's perilous course. *Mclean's 97,* 248-70.

Hines, Joseph C. (1994). *The road to independence: Jamaica 1660 - 1962.* Master's Thesis – Lehman College (CUNY). New York

Huntington, Samuel P. (1991). *The third wave: democratization in the late twentieth century.* Norman: University of Oklahoma Press.

"J. C. Hutchinson accuses Gov't of political victimization" (2002, January 7). *Jamaica Gleaner.*

Jackson Miller, Dionne. (2002, October 17). "Politics – Jamaica: Election violence deeply rooted in poverty." New York: *Global information network.* p1

"Jamaica: No new dawn." (1992, March 21). *The economist 322,* 48.

Jamaican Committee appointed to advise the Jamaican government on the performance, accountability, and responsibilities of parliamentarians. (1991). *Report of the Stone Committee appointed to advise the Jamaican Government on the performance, accountability and responsibilities of elected parliamentarians.* Kingston, Jamaica: Bustamante institute of public and international affairs.

"Jamaican minister warns remittances not long-term economic solution". (2004, June 10) *BBC Monitoring Americas* London.

"JLP thugs assault Observer photographer". (2002, October 17). *Jamaica Observer.*

"JLP wants Patterson to discipline MP over coffin incident." (2002, September 8). *Jamaica Observer.*

Jordan, P. (1989, May 5). "After the storm." *Commonwealth 116,* 261-3.

Johnson, Haynes & David S. Broder (1996). The System: the American way of politics at the breaking point. New York: Little, Brown and Company

Johnson, Hume N. (2005). "Incivility: The politics of 'People on the Margins' in Jamaica". *Political Studies (53)*. Pp 579- 597

Johnson, Judith. (October 24, 2002). "Start the healing". *Jamaica Observer.* Editorial

Kannangara, A. P. (Feb. 1984). "The riots of 1915 in Sri Lanka: A study in the roots of communal violence. *Past and present (102)*130 – 165.

Kaufman, Michael. (1985). *Jamaica under Manley.* Zed Books

Kennes, Walter. (2000). *Small Developing Countries and Global Markets.* New York, NY: St Martin's Press

Klien, Axel; Day, Marcus and Harriott, Anthony (Eds.) (2004). *Caribbean drugs.* Kingston, JA. Ian Randle publishers.

Klinken, Gerry van. (2007). *Communal violence and democratization in Indonesia: Small town wars.* New York: Routledge Contemporary Studies

Knight, Franklin W. (1990). *The Caribbean, the genesis of a fragmented nationalism.* London: Oxford University Press.

Knight, Franklin W. (1978). *The Caribbean, the genesis of a fragmented nationalism.* New York: Oxford University Press.

Knight, Franklin W. & Palmer, Colin. (1989). *The modern Caribbean.* Chapel Hill, NC: University of North Carolina Press.

Kannangara, A. P. (Feb. 1984). "The riots of 1915 in Sri Lanka: A study in the roots of communal violence." *Past and present, No 102* pp 130 – 165.

Kearney, Robert N. (Feb., 1985). "Sri Lanka in 1984: The politics of Communal violence." *Asian Survey, 25(2)* 257 – 263.

Kerr, James. (1996, November 26). "Gov'ts come and go but the poor remain poor." *Jamaica Observer.* Policy perspective

Krishna, Gopal. (Jan 12, 1985). "Communal Violence in India: A study of communal disturbance in Delhi." *Economic and political weekly 20 (2)* 61-74

"KSAC councilors condemn political violence." (2002, October 10). *Jamaica Observer.*

Kuper, Adam. (1989, December 1). "New Manley." *New Statesman & Society, 2(78), 38.*

Kuran, T. (1995). *Private Truths Public Lies: The social consequences of preference falsification.* Cambridge, Massachusetts: Harvard University Press.

Kuran, T. (1992). "Why Revolutions are Better Understood than Predicted: The Role of Preference Falsification" [Comment on an article by Nikki Keddie], *Contention,* 3 (Spring 1992): 199-207.

Kurlansky, M. (1986, August 11). "The voter's choice." *Mclean's, 99,* 30-1.

Kurlansky, M. (1988, November 27). *The New York Times Magazine,* 48+.

Lacey, Terry. (1977). *Violence and politics in Jamaica, 1960-70: Internal security in a developing country.* Totowa, NJ: F. Cass.

Lefort, Rene. (1983). *Ethiopia: An Heretical Revolution.* Totowa, NJ: Zed Press

LaGuerre, J. G. (1983, June). "Democracy and clientelism." *Social and economic studies 32,* 141-56.

LaGuerre, John LA. (1991). "The 1990 Violent Disturbance in Trinidad & Tobago: Some Perceptions" *Caribbean Quarterly Vol. 37 (2 & 3):* P 53-62

Laham, Nicholas (1996) A lost Cause: Bill Clinton's Campaign for National Health Insurance. Westport: Praeger

Le Franc, Elsie (Ed) (1994). *Consequences of structural adjustment: A review of the Jamaican experience.* Kingston, Jamaica. Canoe Press.

Lemard, G. & Hemenway, D. (2006). "Violence in Jamaica: an analysis of homicides 1998-2002". *Injury Prevention (12) pp 15-18.*

Lande, Carl H. (1983). "Political clientelism in political studies: Retrospect and prospects." *International political science review (4) 4, pp 435-454.*

Langton, Kenneth P. (1966, December). "Political partisanship and political socialization in Jamaica." *The British journal of sociology (17) 4.* pp 419-429.

Leifer, Michael. (Oct. 1964). "Communal violence in Singapore." *Asian survey 4(10)* 1115 – 1121

"Let nothing stop us from exercising the right to vote – Philips" (2002, October 15). *Jamaica Observer.*

"Let us reject those who fuel violence." (2002, October 6). *Jamaica Observer.* Editorial

Levitt, Kari. (2005). *Reclaiming development: independent thought and Caribbean community.* Kingston, JA: Ian Randle Publishers.

Levy, Horace. (unpublished). *Inner City reprisal homicides: A Case Study.*

Levy, Horace. (2008, unpublished). *Garrisons: their governance Differences.* Paper presented at the Garrisons community conference at UWI (Mona) February 26, 2008.

Levy, Horace. (2005). UN.ORG/esa/socdev/egm/paper/Horace%20levy.pdf

Lewis, Patsy. (Ed.). (1994). *Jamaica: preparing for the twenty-first century.* Kingston, JA: Planning Institute of Jamaica & Ian Randle Publishers.

Lindo, Locksley Ivanhoe. (2002). *Jamaica betrayed: institutional failure in a Caribbean setting.* Kingston, JA: Arawak Publications.

Lindsay, Louis. (1975). *The myth of independence: middle class politics and non-mobilization in Jamaica.* Mona, Jamaica: Institute of Social and Economic Research, University of the West Indies.

Linton, Neville. (1993). In Dominguez, Jorge. Pastor, Robert and Worrell, Delisle (Eds). *Democracy in the Caribbean.* p238-254. Baltimore, MD: The John Hopkins University Press.

Lipset, Seymore Martin. (1959). *Social mobility in industrial society.* London: Heinemann.

Liu, Yong-chang. (1993). *Patterns and results of the third democratization wave*. Maryland: University Press of America, Inc.

Lloyd, Peter. (1971). *Classes, Crises and Coups*. London England: McGibbon & Kee

Maccullum, Gerald C. Jr. (Jul., 1967). "Negative and Positive Freedom". *The Philosophical Review 76 (3): 312-334*

"Manhunt launched for nine most wanted." (2006, June 16). *Jamaica Gleaner.*

Manley, Michael. (1975). *The politics of change.* Washington. D.C.: Howard University Press.

Mars, Perry. (1995, November). "Foreign influence, political conflicts and conflict resolution in the Caribbean." *Journal of Peace Research, 32(4),* 437 -451.

Martin, Arlene. (2002, November 24). "Pre-dawn terror; senior citizen among four executed in August Town." *Jamaica Observer.*

Martin, Tony. Ed. (1985). *In Nobody's Backyard: The Grenada Revolution in its own words Volume I: The Revolution at Home.* Dover Mass: The Majority Press.

Mayaram, Shail. (Nov. 13 – 20, 1993). "Communal violence in Jaipur." *Social and Economic Weekly, 28 (46/47)* 2524 – 2541

McAdams, Doug; Tarrow, Sidney G and Tilly, Charles. (2001). *Dynamics of contention.* New York, NY: Cambridge University Press.

Meeks, Brian. (2006, May). "The Jamaica moment: New paths for the Caribbean." *NACLA report on the Americas, 39(6)*: 11-15, 37

Meeks, Brian & Lindahl, Folke. (2001). *New Caribbean thought: a reader.* Jamaica: University of the West Indies Press.

Meeks, Brian. (2000). *Narratives of resistance: Jamaica, Trinidad, the Caribbean.* Kingston, JA: University of the West Indies Press.

Meeks, Brian. (1996). *Radical Caribbean: from black power to Abu Bakr.* Barbados: The Press University of the West Indies.

Mehta, Bhavna and Trupti Shah (Nov. 21. 1992) "Gender and communal riots." *Economic and political weekly. 27(47)* 2522 – 2524

"Memories of Wareika Hills, 1980... and how we feel about politics now". (1997, December 12). *Jamaica Gleaner.*

Miller, Al. (2002, December 17). "Anarchy or order ahead, choose!" *Jamaica Gleaner.*

Miller, David. (1991). *Liberty.* Oxford, England: Oxford University Press

Miller, Errol. (2001). *Jamaica in the twenty-first century: contending choices.* Grace Kennedy Foundation.

Miller, Warren and Donald Stokes. *Constituency Influence in Congress* In Weisberg, Herbert. Eric Heberlig and Lisa Campoli (Eds.).(1999). Classics in congressional politics. New York. Longman.

Morgan, Henley. (2005, November 24). "Mr. Patterson, tear down the garrisons." *Jamaica Gleaner* P8

Morrow, William. (1969) Congressional committees. New York. Charles Scribners Press.

Moser, Caroline O & Holland, Jeremy. (1997). "Urban poverty and violence in Jamaica." *World Bank Latin American and Caribbean studies series*. Washington, D.C.: World Bank

"Most Jamaicans feel safe, says poll." (2006, March 15). *Jamaica Gleaner*. A5

Munroe, Trevor. (1999). *Renewing democracy into the millennium: the Jamaica experience in perspective*. Kingston, JA: Press University of the West Indies

Munroe, Trevor. (1990). *Jamaican politics: A Marxist perspective in transition*. Kingston, JA: Heinemann Publishers.

Munroe, Trevor and Robotham, Don. (1977). *Struggles of the Jamaica people*. Kingston, JA: Workers Liberation League.

Munroe, Trevor. (1972). *The Politics of Constitutional Decolonization Jamaica 1944-62*. Jamaica, WI: Institute of Social and Economic Research, University of the West Indies.

Navarro, Vincente. (1993) Dangerous to your health: Capitalism in health care. New York: Monthly Review Press.

"No peace accord: PNP candidate sole signatory to agreement for Central St. Catherine" (1997, December 10). *Jamaica Observer.*

Observer Reporter. (2002, June 1). "Election machinery gets thumbs up from Carter Center." *Jamaica Observer.*

O'Donnell, Guillermo A & Schmitter, Philippe C. (Ed.) *Transitions from authoritarian rule: Prospects for democracy.* Baltimore, MD: John Hopkins University Press.

Orfield, Gary. (1975). *Congressional power: Congress and social change.* New York. Harcourt Brace Jovanich

Palmer, Colin & Knight, Franklin W. (1989). *The Modern Caribbean.* Charlotte, NC: University of North Caroline Press.

Panton, David. (1993). *Jamaica's Michael Manley: The great transformation (1972-92).* Kingston, JA: Kingston Publishers Limited.

"Patterson expresses concern about violence". (2002, October 12). *Jamaica Observer.*

Patterson, P.J. (2004). *The challenges of change: P.J. Patterson budget presentations 1992 – 2002.* Miami Fl: Ian Randle Publishers.

"Patterson, Seaga to review crime report." (2002, January 5). *Jamaica Gleaner.*

Paulin, David. (2002, October 15). "Carter urges peaceful vote: former US president deplores garrison politics" *Jamaica Observer*

Paulin, David. (2002, October 5). "Munroe calls for rival candidates to do more to stop violence." *Jamaica Observer.*

Paulin, David. (2002, September 12). "PNP cries foul over ad: Ombudsman rules against political flags." *Jamaica Observer.*

Paulin, David. (2002, September 07). "PNP apologizes to Seaga: Coffin incident insensitive and indecent, says Henry-Wilson." *Jamaica Observer.*

Paulin, David & Whyte, T.K. (2002, October 9). "Campaign ban on: police accept recommendation for halt to electioneering in six constituencies." *Jamaica Observer*

Payne, Anthony J. (1988). *Politics in Jamaica*. New York, NY: St. Martin's Press.

Payne, Anthony. (1988). *Politics in Jamaica*. New York: St. Martin's Press.

Payne, Anthony John. (1987). *Multi-party politics in Jamaica*. Miami, Fl: Latin American and Caribbean Center.

Payne, Anthony & Clarke, Colin. (Eds.). (1987). *Politics, security and development in small states*. Boston: Allen & Unwin.

Payne, Anthony and Sutton, Paul. (Eds.). (1993). *Modern Caribbean politics*. Baltimore, MD: John Hopkins University Press. 28 - 53

Payne, Anthony and Sutton, Paul. (Eds.). (1993). *Modern Caribbean Politics*. Baltimore, MD.: The John Hopkins University Press.

Payne, Anthony & Sutton, Paul. (Eds.). (1980). *Dependency under challenge: The political economy of the Commonwealth Caribbean*. New Hampshire: Manchester University Press.

Pearnel, Charles. (1989). *The politics of power*. Kingston, JA: Kingston Publishers.

People's National Party. (1989). *PNP, we put people first: a programme for taking Jamaica into the 21st century*. Kingston, JA: People's National Party.

People's National Party. (1979). *Principles and objectives, people's national party*. Kingston, JA: People's National Party.

Pettit, Philip. (1997). *Republicanism: A Theory of Freedom and Government*. Oxford, England: Oxford University Press

Phillips, Dion E. (1986). In Young, Alma & Phillip, Dion E.. *Militarization in the Non-Hispanic Caribbean*. Boulder, CO: Lynne Rienner pp 42-64

Platzer, Michael; Mirella, Flavio and Resa Nestares, Carlos in Klien, Axel; Day, Marcus and Harriott, Anthony. (2004) *Caribbean drugs*. Kingston, JA. Ian Randle publishers.

"PM reports progress- Anti crime proposals, new conduct code expected soon." (2002, September 17). *Jamaica Gleaner.*

"PM, Golding united in fight against crime." (2005, May 7). *Jamaica Gleaner.* A1

"PNP candidate Jennifer Edwards slashed" (2002, October 12). *Jamaica Observer.*

"PNP, JLP make peace pledge." (2002, October 11). *Jamaica Observer.*

"Police swarm Seaview after murder of gang leader." (2005, May 12). *Jamaica Observer.* p3

"Political reps say shooting must stop in Mountain view: another meeting set for next week" (2002, October 22). *Jamaica Observer.*

"Political violence must stop now, say Shipping Association". (2002, October 10). *Jamaica Observer.*

Putnam, R.D. (1995). Tuning in, tuning out: The strange disappearance of social capital in America. *Political Science and Politics 28(4)*, 664-683.

Rapley, John. (September/October, 2003). "Jamaica: Negotiating Law and Order with the Dons". *NACLA Report on the Americas 37(2) 25-29.*

Rattray, Garth. (2004, August 24). "It's up to us to stop the murders." *Jamaica Gleaner* A4

Resnick, Robert J. *APA President* Deleon, Patrick H *Editor* (1995) "The future of health care reform: implication of 1994 elections" *Professional Psychology: Research and Practice 26 (1),* p 3-4

Richards, S. (2004, May). "Code for politicians." *Jamaica Gleaner.* A5

Ritch, Dawn. (1998, November 22). "Government shouldn't throw stones." *Jamaica Gleaner.*

Report of the national task force on crime (1993). Kingston, JA: National taskforce on crime.

"Resist political turpitude". (2002, October 3). *Jamaica Observer.*

"Resist provocation, Patterson tells PNP supporters." (2002 October 5). *Jamaica Observer.*

Robinson, Philip. (2002, October 15,). "Methodist church says don't be intimidated". *Jamaica Observer*

Robotham, Don. (2001). "Crime and public policy in Jamaica". *Wadabagei: A Journal of the Caribbean and its Diaspora, 4,* 69 – 122.

Robotham, Don. (1983). *Early sociology in Jamaica.* Mona, Jamaica. University of the West Indies (Mons Jamaica) Faculty of Social Sciences. Anniversary Conference 1983.

Robotham, Don & Monroe, Trevor. (1977). *Struggles of the Jamaican people*. Kingston, Jamaica: Workers Liberation League.

Roche, James. (2001). *Health care reform: Why we need universal health care and why we need it now*. St. Thomas Law Review. V. 13 No. 4 Summer, 2001. Miami: The University. P 1013 -1049

Rogers, John D. (Aug, 1987). "Social mobility, popular ideology, and collective violence in modern Sri Lanka." *The journal of Asian studies 46 (3)*. 583 – 602

Rouquie, A. (1978). "Clientelist control and authoritarian contexts." In Hermit, G, Rose, R. and Rouquie, A. (Eds.). *Elections without choice* (pp. 19-35). London: McMillan.

Roxborough-Wright, Pat. (2002, October 17). "Peace in central Kingston despite early morning gunfire." *Jamaica Observer*.

Rubenstein, Hymie.(1983). "The Impact of Remittances in the Rural English Speaking Caribbean" *Human Organization 42(2)*. pp 295-306

Rushefsky, Mark and Patel, Kant. (1998). *Politics, power & policy making: The case of health care reform in the 1990s*. New York: M.E. Sharpe

Ryan, Selwyn. (1991). "The Trigger Pulled in the Name of Almighty Allah" *Caribbean Quarterly 37 (2 & 3)*. p15-27

Samms-Vaughan. (2005, July 22). "Our children are wired for violence." *Jamaica Gleaner*. A6

Sandford, Gregory. (1985). *The New Jewel Movement: Grenada's Revolution, 1979 - 1983* Washington DC: Center for the Study of Foreign Affairs. US Department of State.

Scott, James C. (1983). "Everyday forms of class struggle between ex-patron and ex-clients: The green revolution in Kedah, Malaysia." *International political science review. (4) 4 pp 537 – 556.*

Scott, James C. (Nov. 1972). "The erosion of Patron-client bonds and social change in Rural Southeast Asia." *The journal of Asian studies (32) 1 pp 5- 37.*

Schmidt, Steffen, Guasti, Lande and Scott. (1977). *Friends, followers and factions: A reader in political clientelism.* Berkeley: University of California Press.

"Seaga's game". (1983, December 10). *The nation, 237,* 588.

"Seaga, Golding urge supporters to avoid violence." (2002, October 7). *Jamaica Observer.*

"Seaga takes all". (1983, December 3). *The economist 289,* 37-8.

"Seaga reckless, says Phillips." (2002, October 20). *Jamaica Observer.* P3

Senechal de la Roche. (Jul., 2001). "Why is collective violence collective?" *Sociological theory. 19 (2)* 126 -144.

Senechal de la Roche. (Mar., 1996). "Collective violence as social control" *Sociological Forum. 11 (1)* 97 - 128.

"Seven injured at Kayon Heights." (2002, October 17). *Jamaica Observer.*

Shah, Ghanshyam. (May 7, 1994). "Communal consciousness and politics." *Economic and political weekly, Vol. 29. No. 19.* pp 1133- 1140.

Shani, Ornit. (2007). *Communalism, Caste and Hindu Nationalism: the violent in Gujarat.* Cambridge University Press. New York.

Shell, Ross. (2006, May 6). "JDF Chief of Staff urges politicians, business leaders to tackle crime." *Jamaica Gleaner.* A4.

Shell, Ross & Campbell Howard. (2005, May 20). "Zekes still in custody." *Jamaica Gleaner.* A3

Shelton, Michael (2000) Talk of Power, Power of Talk. Westport: Praeger

"Should there be penalties against elected officials, like Members of Parliament, who publicly or privately associate with known criminals." (2001, January 28). *The Sunday Gleaner.* A7

Siaroff, Alan. (2003). Two and a half party systems and the comparative role of the half. *Party Politics, 9(3),* 267-290.

Sinclair, Glenroy and Brown, Ingrid. (December1). "The ugly side of elections: Violence taints voting". *Jamaica Gleaner.*

Sinclair, Glenroy & Mills, Claude. (2004, April 20). "Gangster wage war in 'Jungle'." *Jamaica Gleaner.* A1

Sinclair, G. & Turner, R. (2004, January 29). "Terror reigns in Spanish Town – Two more shot dead – gunfire send commuters running." *Daily Gleaner.*

Sives, Amanda (2002, September). Changing Patrons, from politician to drug don. *Latin American perspectives 29(5),* 66 -89

Sives, Amanda. (1998). Politics and violence in Jamaica: An analysis of urban violence in Kingston 1944-1996. Doctoral book, University of Bradford.

Skocpol, Theda. The Rise and resounding Demise of the Clinton Plan. In Aaron, Henry J (Ed.)(1996). *The problem that won't go away: Reforming US Health Care Financing*. Washington, DC: The Brookings Institute.

Skocpol, Theda. (1979) *States and Social Revolutions: A comparative analysis of France, Russia and China*. Cambridge, UK: Cambridge University Press.

Smith, Derrick, Charles, Wentworth & Henry-Wilson, Maxine. (2001, February 18). "Is the current level of crime beyond the Government's ability to contain?" *The Sunday Gleaner.*

Smith, F. (2006, April). Commentary on 'public bodies'. *Journal of Latin American anthropology 11(1)*, 46-50.

Smith, Lloyd B. (2002, Oct 8). "Wagging the dog." *Jamaica Observer.*

"Smith raps govt on murder statistics." (1999, January 26). *Jamaica Observer*

Smith T., Raymond (1995). "'Living in the Gun Mouth': Race, Class and Political Violence in Guyana" <u>New West Indian/ Nieuwe West Indische Gids</u> Vol 69 No's 3 & 4

Stepan, Alfred C. (1996). *Problems of democratic transition and consolidation: Southern Europe, South America and post-communist Europe*. Baltimore, MD: John Hopkins University Press.

Stepan, Alfred. Bajpai, Kathyayini S. (2007). *Democracy diversity: India and the American experience*. New Dehli: Oxford University Press.

Stephen, Vasciannie. (1999, September 30). "The debate on truth and reconciliation" *Caribbean Today 10 (10)*: Miami p8

Stephens, Evelyne H. & Stephens, John D. (1987, January). "The transition to mass parties and ideological politics: the Jamaica experience since 1972." *Comparative political studies, 19,* 443-83.

Stephens, Evelyne .H. & Stephens, John D. (1985). *Jamaica's democratic socialist experience.* Latin American Program: The Woodrow Wilson International Center for Scholars. Washington DC.

Stephens, Evelyne .H. & Stephens, John D. (1984, June). "Democratic socialism as a development path: Lessons from the Manley government of Jamaica. *Working Paper # 3."* Center for the comparative study of development: Brown University. Boston, MA.

Sterling, Yahneake. (2006, June 25). "Political parties should declare financing source says MacMillan." *Jamaica Gleaner.* A4

"Stewart, Issa urge political peace." (2008, October 8). *Jamaica Observer.*

Stinner, William (Ed.) (1982). <u>Return Migration and Remittances; developing a Caribbean Perspective</u> RIES Occasional Papers no. 3 Research Institute on Immigration and Ethnic Studies. Smithsonian Institute Washington D.C.

Stone, Carl. (1994). *The Stone columns: The last year's work: a selection of Carl Stone's Gleaner articles, January 1992 to February 1993.*

Stone, Carl. (1989) "Power, policy and politics in independent Jamaica." In Nettleford, Rex. (Ed.). *Jamaica in independence: Essay on the early years.* Kingston, JA: Heinemann. 19-53.

Stone, Carl. (1989). *Politics Versus economics: The 1989 elections in Jamaica.* Kingston, JA: Heineman Publishers (Caribbean)

Stone, Carl. (1989). *Carl Stone on Jamaican politics, economics & society: columns from the Gleaner, 1987-88.* Kingston, JA: Gleaner Company.

Stone, Carl. (1986). *Class, state and democracy in Jamaica.* New York: Praeger

Stone, Carl. (1985) *A political profile of the Caribbean.* Washington D.C.: Latin American program, Woodrow Wilson international center for scholars.

Stone, Carl. (1984). *Power in the Caribbean Basin: a comparative study of political economy.* Philadelphia: Institute for the study of human issues.

Stone, Carl. (1984, March). "Reflections on political polling in Jamaica." *Social and economic studies, 33,* 117-42.

Stone, Carl (1982). *The political opinions of the Jamaican people (1976 – 81).* Kingston, JA: Blackett Publishers.

Stone, Carl. (1980). *Democracy and clientelism in Jamaica.* New Brunswick, NJ: Transaction Books.

Stone, Carl. (1978, November). "Regional Party voting in Jamaica (1959-1976)." *Journal of Inter-American studies and world affairs 20(4),* 393 – 420

Stone, Carl. (1974). *Electoral behaviour and public opinion in Jamaica.* Kingston, JA: Institute of social and economic research, University of the West Indies, Mona.

Stone, Carl. (1973). *Class, race and political behavior in urban Jamaica.* Kingston, JA: Institute of Social and Economic Research, University of the West Indies, Mona

Stone, Carl. (1972). *Stratification and political change in Trinidad and Jamaica.* Beverly Hills, CA, Sage Publications.

Stone, Carl & Brown, Aggrey. (Ed.). (1977). *Essays on power and change in Jamaica.* Kingston, JA: Jamaica publishing house.

Springer, Bevan. (March 24 – March 30, 2005). "Caribbean connection: Diaspora sending billions home". *New Amsterdam News 96 (13)* 14

Suglam, Rosean. (2001, June 25). "West Kingston violence preceded Michael Manley." *Jamaica Observer.* Editorial

Sutter, Paul & Payne, Anthony (Ed.) *Size and Survival in the Caribbean and the Pacific.* London: Frank Cass & Co. Ltd.

Tambiah, Stanley J. (Nov. 1990) "Reflections on Communal violence in South Asia." *Journal of Asian studies, 49(4)* 741 – 760

"The code of political conduct." (2002, June 12). *Jamaica Observer.*

"The colours of politics." (2002, September 27). *Jamaica Gleaner:* A4 Editorial

"The garrison warning." (2002, September 13). *Jamaica Gleaner.*

"The making of a desperado: guns, gore and gangs in a life of violence." (2003, May 18). *Jamaica Observer.*

The Office of the Contractor General (2008). www.ocg.gov.jm/ocg

The Office of the Political Ombudsman. *Brief description –The Office of the Political Ombudsman.* Kingston, Jamaica: Office of the Political Ombudsman

The Office of the Political Ombudsman. (October, 2007). *Annual report of the political ombudsman of Jamaica: September 2005 – December 2006.* Kingston 5, JA: Office of the Political Ombudsman..

"The politics of bribery" (2006, January 22). *The Sunday Gleaner.* Editorial page

"This madness must stop now!: Patterson, Seaga denounce political violence, warn Supporters" (2002, October 13). *Jamaica Observer.*

Tilly, Charles. (1978). *From Mobilization to Revolution.* Reading Massachusetts: AddisonWesley

Tomasky, Michael. (Spring 1996). "Why Heath care Reform failed" *Dissent 43*

Tully, James (1980). *A Discourse on Property: John Locke and his adversaries.* Cambridge, England: Cambridge University Press

Twemlow, S.W., et al. (1996, Summer). "Peacekeeping and peacemaking: the conceptual foundations of a plan to reduce violence and improve the quality of life in a midsized community in Jamaica." *Psychiatry, 59,* 156-74

United States Agency for International Development. "Community defuses violence and creates safe environment through police partnership: Transforming Inner City communities in Jamaica." Success Story. www.usaid.gov

Van Beek, Martijn. (Nov., 2000). "Beyond identity fetishism: Communal conflict in Ladakh and the limits of autonomy." *Cultural anthropology (15) 4* pp. 525 -569

Verba, S., Schlozman, K. L., & Brady, H. E. (1995). *Voice and equality: Civic voluntarism in American politics.* Cambridge, Mass: Harvard University Press.

"Violence mars election campaign." (2002, October 6). *Jamaica Observer.*

"Violence worries diplomats: British, Canadian and American envoys tell party leaders to rein in supporters." (2002, October 12). *Jamaica Observer.*

Virgoe, John. (2008). "Book review: Conflict, violence, and displacement in Indonesia. Edited by Eva-Lotta E Hedman. Ithaca, New York: Cornell Southeast Asia Program." *Contemporary Southeast Asia 30 (3) 470 – 81*

Vulliamy, Ed. (1999, August 6). "Roots of Violence". *The New Republic 221(7), 13 - 14*

Walker, J. L. (1991). *Mobilizing interest groups in America: Patrons, professions, and social movements.* Ann Arbor: University of Michigan Press.

Walker, Karyl. (2002, October 18). "Blair leads peace team into Denham Town, Rema." *Jamaica Observer.*

Wambold, K. K. (Sept 1984*) Annual Report for 1983 Development Co-operation to Mauritius.* Port Louis, Mauritius: United Nations Development Project

Weide, Ursula (2000). *Health care reform and the changing standard.* New York Law School Journal of International and Comparative Law. V. 20 No 2 p 249-354.

Weisberg, Herbert. Eric Heberlig and Lisa Campoli (Eds.). (1999). *Classics in congressional politics.* New York, NY: Longman.

Weissert, Carol S. and Weissert, William G. (1996). *Governing health: The politics of health policy.* Baltimore, MD: The John Hopkins University Press.

Wolfinger, R.E., & Rosenstone, S.J. (1980). *Who Votes?* Connecticut: Yale University Press.

Weisberg, Herbrig and Camboli (1999).

Wellington, Andre A. O. (2005, June 8). "What garrisons guarantee." *Jamaica Gleaner* A5

Whyte, T.K. (2002, October 17). "Gun attack forces electoral workers to flee Hannah Town station." *Jamaica Observer.*

Whyte, T.K. (2002, October 11). "Central Kingston roadblocks cleared". *Jamaica Observer.*

Wignall, Mark. (2002, October 17). "Rebuild the JLP now." *Jamaica Observer.*

Wignall, Mark. (2002, June 20). "What of that boo?" *Jamaica Observer.*

Wignall, Mark A. (2006, June 1). "Donmanship not cute anymore". *Jamaica Observer.*

Wignall, Mark A.. (2004, January 29). "Spanish Town: A 'duck ants' nest." *Jamaica Observer.*

Wignall, Mark A. (2002) "The death throes of tribal politics." *Jamaican Observer.*

Wilde, M.D. (1984, June). "Jamaica's deceptive tranquility." *The Christian century, 100,* 11113-14.

Williams, Petre. (2002, October). "Teenager among three shot in Black River political clash." *Jamaica Observer.*

Williams, Petre. (2002, March 8). "New Political party ... oops! movement launched." *Jamaica Observer.*

World Bank._*Caribbean Region: Current Economic Situation, Regional Issues and Capital Flows, 1992*

World Bank *Pacific Island Economies: Toward Higher Growth in the 1990's* Washington DC. 1991

World Bank. *Enhancing the Role of Government in the Pacific Island Economies* Washington DC 1998

Yankelovich, Daniel. The debate that wasn't: The public and the Clinton health Care Plan. In Aaron, Henry J (Ed.)(1996). *The problem that won't go away: Reforming US Health Care Financing.* Washington, DC: The Brookings Institute.

Yankelovich, Daniel."The debate that wasn't: The public and the Clinton health Care Plan" Brookings Review (Summer 1995) Vol 13 No 3 p 36 - 41

Younis, Sameer. (1998, June 20). "Bringing about change in the inner-city". *Jamaica Observer.*

Young, Alma & Phillip, Dion E. (1986). *Militarization in the Non-Hispanic Caribbean.* Boulder, CO: Lynne Rienner.

Zaller, John. (1992). *The nature and origins of mass opinion.* New York: Cambridge University Press

"'Zekes' double murder trial begins: Home circuit court under heavy guard." (2006, March 7). *Jamaica Gleaner.*

ABOUT THE BOOK

Violence and Power is a collection of original essays written by Dr. Ken G. Irish-Bramble. The essays were all written while the author was a graduate student at NYU. The essays cover a wide range of topics in the field of political science and Carribean studies. While they are somewhat dated, they each cover timeless topics and provide meaningful insight.